And They Were
Wonderful Teachers

And They Were Wonderful Teachers

Florida's Purge of Gay and Lesbian Teachers

KAREN L. GRAVES

UNIVERSITY OF ILLINOIS PRESS

Urbana and Chicago

© 2009 by the Board of Trustees
of the University of Illinois
All rights reserved
Manufactured in the United States of America
1 2 3 4 5 C P 5 4 3 2 1

∞ This book is printed on acid-free paper.

Library of Congress Cataloging-in-Publication Data
Graves, Karen, 1959–
And they were wonderful teachers : Florida's purge of gay
and lesbian teachers / Karen L. Graves.
p.   cm.
Includes bibliographical references and index.
ISBN 978-0-252-03438-1 (cloth : alk. paper) —
ISBN 978-0-252-07639-8 (pbk. : alk. paper)
1. Gay teachers—Dismissal of—Florida—History.
2. Lesbian teachers—Dismissal of—Florida—History.
3. Discrimination in education—Florida—History.
I. Title.
LB2844.1.G39G73   2009
371.10086'64—dc22   2008049084

Contents

Preface   vii

Acknowledgments   xix

1. Politics of Intimidation in the Sunshine State   1

2. A Stealth Investigation   20

3. Silence Will Not Protect You   50

4. Doing the Public's Business   98

5. A Profession at Risk   120

Conclusion   145

Notes   149

Index   181

Preface

In October 1960 a physical education teacher sat in the office of the Pinellas County superintendent of public instruction. Under oath and without counsel, she faced interrogation by Remus J. Strickland, chief investigator for the Florida Legislative Investigation Committee; Dave Hooper of the St. Petersburg Police Department was also present. The woman had grown up in the Tampa Bay area, graduated from the University of Florida (UF) with a bachelor's degree in physical education and health, and was in her sixth year of teaching at a local junior high school. The teacher owned her home and lived with another woman, a mathematics and science teacher at the same junior high school.

Strickland got the name of a previous roommate of the second teacher before moving to the subject of his investigation. "While attending the University of Florida, did you have any occasion to hear about or to run into any type of homosexuality?"[1] The witness responded "No," but when Strickland made a second attempt, asking about any case that the teacher might ever have heard about regarding anyone, she came up with two references. Both were based on hearsay, and the witness took care to distance herself from any direct knowledge of alleged events. But she did give Strickland the names of women who "had heard of" these particular cases.

The questioning thus far had produced only vague hearsay information, so Strickland then asked about the witness's softball team in St. Petersburg; she had been playing for ten years. Had "this subject matter" come to the witness's attention, maybe due to incidents at tournaments? The teacher responded to the rather broad question with another "no" and attempted to shift the focus: "There is one thing I didn't approve of, is drinking."[2] She went on to articulate a positive image of her team: Members did not drink excessively, the coach was a family man with six children, and "We have always had the reputation of being a fine bunch."[3] Strickland continued with questions about a recent tournament. The manner in which the witness responded varied as the questions became more specific. When asked if she had heard of any incident that occurred during the tournament, the witness simply stated, "No, sir." Her answer to the follow-up question—Did she visit with members of other teams?—was a bit convoluted: "I say no, I did not. I'm trying to think back in August. I can't even think right now who is [sic] in the state tournament. No, sir, I did not."[4] The word choice and emphasis on not remembering suggest that the teacher might have been trying to avoid admitting that she met with other women at the tournament. It is likely Strickland thought so as he pressed her for details.

> Q. Did you go over to the Capri Motel?
> A. No. I did not.
> Q. At any one time?
> A. No.
> Q. While they were here?
> A. I did not.
> Q. Did you go to any place and play the ukelele [sic] for any of them?
> A. No. I did not.
> Q. I believe you play a ukelele [sic] do you not?
> A. A little bit but not much.[5]

At this point the tenor of the interrogation was on the verge of shifting. The teacher provided more information on the Jacksonville team, including the names of a few teachers, but said she had never heard of any homosexual behavior among the athletes. She characterized the Jacksonville team as rough, loud, and vociferous with language, in contrast to her St. Petersburg team. Strickland, however, had finished his line of questioning in regard to the softball teams; for the rest of the interrogation, he focused relentlessly on the private life of the schoolteacher before him.

With the presence of the St. Petersburg Police Department represented in the room in the form of Sergeant Hooper, Strickland clarified that the witness was under oath, that perjury could result in a penitentiary sentence, and asked if any part of the teacher's testimony thus far was incorrect. She said no. Strickland asked if the woman had been approached for sex or involved in any type of homosexual conduct. When she answered "No," he pressed,

"None whatsoever?" The teacher offered that she had danced with another woman, but both she and Strickland dismissed that, not considering dancing an example of homosexual behavior. Then Strickland asked explicitly about actions that defined one as a homosexual, according to his understanding. "Have you ever allowed another subject to caress your body in any fashion?" The teacher said no. This prompted Strickland to fish for a response without exposing his evidence, or lack thereof. "If this Committee has in file a sworn testimony from some other subject, who states that they have had homosexual acts with you, would that be true or false?" The witness tried to get away with an answer as vague as the question but Strickland would not allow it, and the teacher made the admission that would end her career.

> A. If they say it was true, I would certainly like to know. I hope not.
> Q. I said if this Committee has in file a sworn statement from other subject stating that they had had homosexual acts with you, would that be true or false?
> A. It would be true.
> Q. You have then had homosexual acts with other subjects?
> A. Yes.[6]

Strickland then continued with a series of questions to determine how long the teacher had been engaging in sexual behavior and with what frequency. He asked her to explain "how far and into what degree your contact with people of the same sex has been?"[7] He wanted to know what "brings this on," who the woman's partners had been, and what roles each played during sex. By this time the teacher answered with less resistance but two themes permeated her responses. First, she argued her experiences were not "wrong" since her actions were not perverted or dangerous to society. It appears as if the witness and Strickland shared an understanding of homosexuality as it was defined in the dominant ideology—as sin or sickness—yet the teacher knew that her behavior was not sick or immoral. The superintendent's office of Pinellas County, however, was a bad place to be dealing with this dissonance.

The teacher tried desperately to get Strickland to understand that her behavior did not fit what he and others considered the "depraved" nature of homosexuality. For instance, when Strickland demanded details concerning the witness's contact with other women, she told about kissing two women at a New Year's celebration in her own home. When Strickland asked, she gave the names of the women who were also teachers in Pinellas County but added that they "were very respectable, wonderful teachers."[8] The teacher explained that her first relationship began in college and had lasted six years.

She emphasized, "Neither one of us realized that it would grow and did not realize that what we were doing was wrong and many times we discussed it. We prayed about it. We did not want to do something that was wrong."[9]

In the context of questions regarding the teacher's current relationship, Strickland then asked,

> Q. Is there anything that you can recall, in thinking back now, that brings this on?
>
> A. No. I don't. It's not done wrong or dirty or anything. . . . It's not brought about by any desire or anything, it's just a matter of love for each other I guess.[10]

The second theme that the teacher stressed in the latter part of the interrogation was a desire to cooperate with the investigator, perhaps with the hope—however unrealistic in 1960—that she might save her job and career. Additionally, the threat of prison might have caused the teacher to be as clear as possible in stressing the final points of her testimony. When Strickland again asked if the witness wanted to correct any answers from earlier in the record, she suggested that she had misunderstood what Strickland meant by homosexuality. "I didn't realize to what an extent you meant; I have had acts or whatever you might use the word, with two people and it would come on—not any desire, I don't even have that kind of desires at all."[11] As long as the teacher maintained that her definition of homosexuality centered on some sort of pathological desire, and Strickland's definition was based on particular acts, she could argue that she had not perjured herself. Of course, then she still faced the problem of admitting to acts that violated Florida's "crime against nature" law. The teacher noted that she had corrected her testimony on the advice of Sergeant Hooper. Strickland then got the witness to state that she had given the information "freely and voluntarily," surely an "admission" the teacher found particularly insulting.[12]

In the last pages of the transcript, the witness spoke with a sense of urgency. She wanted state officials to know that, in spite of her behavior, she was not the degenerate that dominant ideology claimed all homosexuals to be. "Will you explain what I told you about, that it was not any desire [for] other people, I mean a lot of times homosexuals have a desire for anyone they see, so to speak. Would you explain that? When you talk to them?"[13] Even as the witness was trying to distance herself from the negative image of homosexuals as people of low character who lacked self-control, she made it clear that she was a person who did not intend to violate social norms, and she pleaded for a chance to "correct" her behavior. "I always tried to live and do the right thing. I was certainly brought up the right way. If I have done wrong, I'm willing to do right and I don't feel that I have any urge or wrongness toward anyone, because to me a homosexual—I haven't ever wanted to be called one. You said that I have committed two homosexual acts, which I have, but I hope that won't brand me for life. . . . I certainly hope that if I can right myself, that you would give me the opportunity to do so."[14]

Chief Investigator Strickland and the Investigation Committee, however, were not in the practice of letting homosexual schoolteachers "right themselves." Even teachers who denied engaging in sexual behavior and did not claim a homosexual identity lost their jobs and teaching credentials once their sexuality was questioned. In this instance, Strickland gave the teacher no reason to think he would intervene on her behalf. After she asked for an opportunity to "right herself," Strickland struck back with the most invasive questions of the interrogation.

> Q. Was there any time that this act reached any degree further than caressing? *Was there any oral copulation by anyone, upon the private parts of the body?*
> A. *Yes.*
> Q. *By whom was that conducted?*
> A. *By me.*
> Q. *Was that also with both subjects?*
> A. *Yes. I would say I was very close with both of those.*
> Q. *And that was also on frequent occasions?*
> A. *Yes.*
> Q. *Was that always the case?*
> A. *Yes.*[15]

And here the transcript ends.

The state legislature established the Florida Legislative Investigation Committee in 1956 in the wake of the *Brown v. Board of Education* Supreme Court decisions (1954, 1955) with an initial intent to impede desegregation efforts. At first the committee of representatives and senators investigated members of the NAACP and other civil rights activists who were pressing for admittance to the University of Florida Law School, carrying out a bus boycott in Tallahassee, and demanding school desegregation in Miami. The NAACP successfully slowed the Investigation Committee's attack in 1958 by ensnaring it in a series of court cases. The Investigation Committee's charter expired at each biennial session of the legislature and by 1959 it appeared as if the committee's continuation might be in jeopardy. With little to show for its campaign to preserve segregation, the Investigation Committee presented a new rationale for its existence, arguing that homosexuality was spreading throughout state educational institutions. In its 1959 legislative account, the Investigation Committee charged that administrators were unable or unwilling to "cope actively, aggressively and effectively with the problem."[16] The "problem" was that gay men and lesbians were among the 40,000 schoolteachers in Florida, and the state had thus far not done a good enough job of finding them, firing them, and stripping them of their teaching credentials.[17] The presentation convinced the legislature to extend the Investigation Committee for another two years, setting in motion a period of state surveillance and intimidation that would not subside until 1965.

And They Were Wonderful Teachers is a history of state oppression of gay and lesbian citizens during the Cold War and the dynamic set of responses it ignited involving the teachers and political, educational, and community institutions. Teachers whose sexuality was questioned or exposed were summarily dismissed for most of the twentieth century in the United States, but the intensity and scope of the Florida purge make it historically significant. The study lends new insight to the Cold War persecution of gay men and lesbians by examining a state-level investigation of members of a profession at the center of American culture. It extends David Johnson's argument that the federal persecution of gay men and lesbians was more sweeping than the communist purges that have come to define the period.[18] Analysis of the state action to govern the "homosexual presence" in Florida suggests that teachers may be distinctly positioned to effect a transformation of the dominant ideology regarding sexuality in American society.

The history of the Florida Legislative Investigation Committee is complex. Various aspects enhance our understanding of the Cold War, the civil rights movement, gay and lesbian history, and education history. Historians were limited in their analyses, however, until the State Archives of Florida opened Investigation Committee files to the public in the early 1990s. Early research relied upon news accounts, court cases, and legislative reports. As interest in the Investigation Committee grew, scholars tapped into the rich collection of sources at the University of South Florida (USF), where alert public relations director John Egerton began stockpiling critical documents in 1962. In the past decade, scholars have concentrated on the Investigation Committee's attack on civil rights activists, its investigation into homosexuality at UF, and the more encompassing probe into communism, homosexuality, and teaching practices at USF.[19]

Comprehensive analyses of the Investigation Committee include the attack on gay and lesbian schoolteachers, and most scholarship mentions this aspect of the history to some degree.[20] To make the schoolteacher purge the central object of examination, however, opens the history up to the sorts of questions posed by education historians. How was the Florida experience different from, and similar to, antigay discrimination aimed at teachers in other states or at other times, and in what ways did the teachers' experiences differ from those of civil rights activists or university personnel? What does this tell us about the conditions required to fend off attacks on civil liberties and academic freedom? How did other state agencies absorb the Investigation Committee agenda? Is the Florida purge an aberration in the history of teaching in the United States, or does it represent business as usual regarding the public's surveillance of teachers? How powerful is the dominant ideology in determining the shape of political-economic structures in American education, history, and culture? What role might one expect teachers to play in dismantling homophobic structures in the United States? Working through the questions raised in this volume will enhance gay and lesbian historiography, for the approach here is to study antigay discrimination as it played out in, arguably, the most central social institution—the school system.

Historical scholarship, writ large, has undergone a rapid expansion of research that focuses on the politics of identity and difference, making way for an explosion of studies on the history of sexuality. Yet, although scholars in history and education in general have produced a good deal of work that puts sexuality at the center of analysis, education historians are only beginning to explore this field. The fact that historians have not readily adopted the driving theoretical engine that lies at the core of much queer scholarship in gay and lesbian studies suggests one reason why educational historians lag behind other education scholars in writing queer analyses. But how does one account for the gap within the discipline of history itself? Schools are prime sites for cultural reproduction, contested terrain for those who wish to preserve or challenge the status quo. Could there be a better subject for study for historians who want to know how political-economic changes influence sexual identity?

It is likely that the same problems of discrimination that dissuaded academics from doing research in gay and lesbian history in its early stages would have carried over to colleges of education where many education historians do their work.[21] The claim that discrimination against gay and lesbian teachers has held on longer than prejudice directed against other professionals raises little argument. Nor is it surprising that some residue of this prejudice would cling to the teachers of teachers. In addition, the very subject matter of education history has made it difficult to examine gay and lesbian issues. Evidence relating to teachers' lives, for instance, is hard to come by. Tracing the influence that authoritative prescription had on actual behavior is difficult. The problems gay and lesbian historians encounter regarding evidence that is hidden, private, or unrecorded are intensified for education historians whose subjects were state employees under the watchful eye of the public.[22] Ironically, it is especially difficult to uncover personal information for professionals who lived in glass houses for most of the twentieth century.

In recent years two groundbreaking books in education history have addressed gay and lesbian issues. Karen Harbeck's 1997 volume, *Gay and Lesbian Educators: Personal Freedoms, Public Constraints,* is a comprehensive examination of the legal status of gay and lesbian teachers in the United States. Harbeck approaches the study from three angles. First, she addresses state and local political initiatives to bar gay men and lesbians from teaching in Florida, California, and Oklahoma by examining Anita Bryant's "Save Our Children" campaign, the Briggs Initiative, and a similar threat in Oklahoma that made its way to the U.S. Supreme Court. Second, Harbeck discusses philosophical arguments regarding morality and privacy that lie at the core of employment issues regarding public school teachers. Finally, she analyzes legal cases and policy formation regarding homosexuality and education in historical context, paying substantial attention to the oppressive Cold War period and documenting the courageous stands taken by one teacher after another in the era of gay liberation.[23]

In 2005 Jackie Blount released her comprehensive history of lesbian and gay school workers in the United States. *Fit to Teach: Same-Sex Desire, Gender, and School Work* reinforces in rich detail the fact that those who desire others of the same sex or transgress gender norms have always been among America's educators even though, for reasons that become clear as Blount traces the shifting political-economic context of the twentieth century, these teachers and administrators have maintained a relatively low profile most often.

As the corpus of Blount's writing since 1996 shows, schools have been, and remain, gender-polarized places. At the turn of the twentieth century, an awareness of same-sex desire began to infuse the public consciousness. Some nineteenth-century sexologists conflated same-sex desire with gender nonconformity, and this impression stuck with the general population. As challenges to notions of acceptable gender identity and new considerations regarding sexual orientation emerged, many expected the school to preserve traditional gender ideology. The school—after all, a conservative institution— obliged. Authorities demanded that school workers model normative gender behavior and present themselves as heterosexual beings (but not *too* sexual) in order to regulate the sexuality of the nation.[24] By the mid-twentieth-century, fears of gender and sexual deviance drove the American public into a frenzy, and it responded by purging teachers who crossed the line of expectations. Blount carries the analysis into recent decades, vividly describing the bind school workers found themselves in—to confront discrimination meant losing their jobs, but without confrontation the oppressive system would continue. She charts key events that arose from the gay liberation movement and the backlash that followed, explains how conservative political and religious groups have manipulated their antigay stance as a wedge issue in politics, and offers a compelling reading of the advances that occurred in the 1990s, giving appropriate credit to student activism.

Harbeck's and Blount's works are wide-sweeping accounts of critical importance. Both authors note the Florida purge but, given the scope and purpose of their arguments, do not examine the event in full. *And They Were Wonderful Teachers*, a contextualized case study, provides the necessary sharp definition to buttress the broad overviews in the pioneering work of Harbeck and Blount.

This book is about stealth, silence, control, and resistance. I begin by introducing readers to the history of the Florida Legislative Investigation Committee, giving particular attention to key events regarding the teacher investigation. I place this history in the political-economic context of the Cold War, a repressive period for gay men and lesbians. The trajectory of the argument then unfolds in straightforward fashion, continuing with a description of how teachers were targeted, interrogated, and stripped of their professional credentials. I examine the degree to which teachers resisted this invasion of their personal lives; analyze the actions of various institutions, organizations, and individuals caught up in the tragedy; and set the episode in the context of education history.

I then explain the methods the Investigation Committee used to target and interrogate teachers, and analyze the range of actions teachers took in response to these attacks. In spite of the overwhelming power differential between the committee and the teachers, testimonies reveal a dynamic interchange between subordinate and dominant forces. Although ultimately the teachers were fired from their teaching positions and lost their professional credentials, teachers were able to resist the state's intrusion into their personal lives to some degree. In fact, teachers and their interrogators employed similar tactics in the struggle for power: secrecy, deception, ambiguity, and resistance.

Following an exploration of that struggle, I contrast the experiences of three groups who were called before the Investigation Committee: civil rights activists, University of South Florida personnel, and gay and lesbian schoolteachers. Civil rights activists and university officials found support from a network that included the NAACP, American Association of University Professors,

American Association of University Women, and media. Hearings for these groups generally occurred in the open, allowing recognition of due process and legal protections. In contrast, schoolteachers' testimonies were usually taken in closed sessions without access to legal counsel, and they had no organizational support to sustain them during the investigations. Rather, the state and county superintendents of public instruction and the Florida Education Association (the state affiliate of the National Education Association) collaborated with the Investigation Committee during its purge of lesbian and gay teachers. Early gay rights organizations such as the Mattachine Society could offer little more than carefully worded criticism of the committee's actions regarding schoolteachers. I illustrate how teachers were different from others swept up into the turmoil of the investigation by underlining the importance of public accountability and group solidarity in fighting oppressive forces.

Subsequently, I turn to an analysis of the turf battle played out between the Investigation Committee and the Florida Department of Education (DOE) regarding state containment of homosexuality and the perceived "threat" caused by gay and lesbian teachers. "Doing the Public's Business" plots the actions of different state agencies in the attack on teachers. "Responsibility" for purging "deviant" teachers shifted from the temporary Investigation Committee to the permanently established DOE between 1961 and 1965 when it became apparent that the committee had overstepped the bounds of its legislative mandate. In addition, professional educators claimed they were capable of policing their own ranks. Finally, the logistics required to maintain state surveillance of teachers' sexuality were subsumed into a bureaucratic system. This transfer of authority and the corresponding laws that codified the process of stripping teachers of their professional credentials allowed for the dismissal of gay and lesbian teachers long after the Investigation Committee shut down.

The Florida purge is then explored in the context of teacher history in the United States. I argue that certain aspects of the teaching profession distinguish it from other types of public employment such as government work and military service, leaving teachers especially vulnerable to homophobic persecution. For instance, the expectation that educators act as exemplars for students has led to intense public scrutiny of teachers' personal lives and restricted professional autonomy. The fact that schoolteachers work with children opened the door to homophobic fears—unsubstantiated but persistent— that gay and lesbian teachers would "recruit" students; this fear reinforced demands that teachers act in accordance with a narrow standard of normative behavior. Analyses of the feminization of teaching (women accounted for 60 percent of teachers by 1870 and more than 80 percent by 1920) provide additional explanations for the relatively low status of the profession, low levels of autonomy for its practitioners, and the great latitude the public has taken regarding supervision of teachers' lives in and outside the classroom. Public perceptions of schoolteachers as guardians of the dominant ideology along with restrictive professional structures (such as contracts that forbade specific personal behaviors) engendered conservative behavior among educators. Since many of the teachers who challenged the standards of normative behavior imposed upon them lost their jobs as a result, the workforce was depleted of its most radical members. Historically, teacher organizations have not supported colleagues who transgressed social norms and, thus, teachers have been easy targets for state suppression of gay and lesbian people. The intersection of these factors regarding public scrutiny, low levels of status and autonomy, and work with children locates teaching in a unique position, even among other public professions, in the crosshairs of antigay forces. I conclude that gay and lesbian teachers, among the entire gay and lesbian population, have been extremely vulnerable to antigay attacks.

The fascinating story of the teachers who faced the Investigation Committee informs our understanding of gay and lesbian history in the post–World War II era; at the same time, the story of these gay men and lesbians informs our understanding of the history of teachers in the United States as it unfolded throughout the latter decades of the twentieth century. In spite of efforts to govern the "homosexual" presence in their culture, this history of the Florida Legislative Investigation Committee suggests that teachers are uniquely positioned to effect a transformation of the dominant ideology regarding sexuality in American society. Schools are critical institutions for maintaining or challenging the dominant ideology, and teachers occupy the most critical positions in schools. To control teachers is to control the dominant ideology. Putting the history of discrimination against gay and lesbian teachers in the context of a broader education history, it becomes apparent that human rights for gay and lesbian citizens cannot be gained in full until gay and lesbian teachers are fully accepted. It follows that to free teachers from antigay discrimination is to take a crucial step in dismantling homophobia in our society.

In 2005 I encountered a woman who had been an educator in Hillsborough County during the Florida purge. When I told her about my research, she rolled her eyes, shook her head, and sighed, "Oh, yes." As we talked, she recalled two colleagues in her school who left their jobs unexpectedly during the turmoil. The woman did not want to say more, and we let the matter drop. But after a moment the retired educator added, "They were wonderful teachers."[25]

Acknowledgments

I am grateful for the support that many colleagues and friends have lent to this work. Archivists and librarians at the State Archives of Florida, Special Collections Department, University of South Florida Tampa Library, Department of Special and Area Studies Collections, George A. Smathers Libraries, University of Florida, University of West Florida Special Collections, and the William Howard Doane Library at Denison University lead the list. I am particularly indebted to Miriam Gan-Spalding and Boyd Murphree in Tallahassee, Mil Willis and Florence M. Turcotte in Gainesville, Mark Greenberg and Andy Huse in Tampa, Jim Schnur in St. Petersburg, Dean DeBolt in Pensacola, and Star Andrews, Mary Prophet, and Susan Scott at Denison for their expertise in helping me navigate the sources that form the foundation for this study. The map in chapter 1 owes its existence to Anne Crowley, Sarah Harris, and John Oswald who, unable to make a cartographer out of me, willingly applied their skill to the cause.

Chapter 4 first appeared in *Educational Studies: A Journal of the American Educational Studies Association* 41, no. 1 (February 2007). Portions of chapters 2 and 3 first appeared in Eileen Tamura, ed., *The History of Discrimination in U.S. Education: Marginality, Agency, and Power* (2008), reproduced with permission of Palgrave Macmillan. Other portions of the manuscript appear in an essay published by the *Florida Historical Quarterly*. I thank the editors for their permission to include that work in this volume. I presented key elements composing the argument in this book at History of Education Society, Canadian History of Education Association, Southern History of Education Society, and American Educational Research Association conferences. I appreciate the interest colleagues showed in my work at those venues and value their critiques. In particular, I wish to thank Jackie Blount, Katherine Chaddock, Deirdre Cobb-Roberts, Roland Sintos Coloma, Sherman Dorn, Vincent P. Franklin, Catherine Lugg, Victoria-Maria MacDonald, Jane Martin, Diana Moyer, Linda Perkins, Susan Semel, Eileen Tamura, Sevan Terzian, and Jonathan Zimmerman. Reviewers for the University of Illinois Press provided keen analyses of the manuscript. Their careful attention to detail, along with the helpful guidance of editors Joan Catapano and Breanne Ertmer, have enhanced the final writing stages. I also with to thank Copenhaver Cumpston, Kelly Gray, Dawn McIlvain, and Joseph Peeples for their many contributions in bringing this book to publication.

Denison University provided tremendous institutional support for this project, including a Robert C. Good Fellowship. Former director of alumni affairs Lyn Boone invited me to make a presentation during the early stages of my research to the Denison Alumni College and current director Sandy Ellinger continues the practice of including scholarship on gay and lesbian issues in the annual event. Members of the Denison Gay Lesbian Bisexual Alumni Association, particularly Rick Carson and Kim Cromwell, have been supportive of this work. Students in my "Partnerships and Politics" and "School's Out: Gay and Lesbian Issues in Education" courses at Denison shared questions and insights on parts of the study, holding their own as critical readers of the text.

This research has taken me into new fields of study. I cannot imagine completing the work without the counsel of four scholars who have contributed mightily to my education. Clarence Karier set a standard of scholarly excellence in those widely appreciated Saturday morning tutorials at the University of Illinois that I'm still trying to reach. His insights on the Cold War have only grown more convincing with time. Margaret Fisher has been generous with her patience, knowledge, and experience, answering questions about the Johns Committee for the hundredth time with wit and grace. On more than one occasion she has corrected my misunderstandings, keeping me from—as she so delicately put it—becoming "toast" in the academic world. Jackie Blount and Catherine Lugg cut paths in education history and policy studies for gay and lesbian studies, pioneering conference panels and authoring work that has influenced the field. Their contributions to this study are immeasurable, beginning with enthusiastic encouragement to get the project off the ground and ending with (multiple) readings of drafts. My scholarly debt here is tremendous and gratefully borne.

Finally, a word of thanks for my Denison colleagues and friends who have offered interest and insight regarding my work. Sylvia Brown, Karolyn Burkett, Lisbeth Lipari, Lyn Robertson, Sandy Runzo, and Mary Tuominen read parts of the manuscript and made critical suggestions as the work unfolded. Sharon Flynn, Kathy Fuson Hurt, Carol Phillips Whitt, and George Williamson have cheered the work on, engaging in spirited discussion and serious commentary.

My earliest recollections of Florida date to 1964, the summer my dad attended classes in Gainesville through a grant from the National Defense Education Act. That was the same year the Johns Committee imploded, but events concerning the state investigation of teachers didn't leave an impression on a child fascinated with glass-bottom boats, alligators in the neighbor's yard, and the beach. What did develop over the years was a respect for educators, set in motion by my parents. I dedicate this book to them.

And They Were
Wonderful Teachers

1

Politics of Intimidation in the Sunshine State

They were "very respectable, wonderful teachers."
—Unnamed teacher, Pinellas County, Florida

The Johns Committee

In July 1956 the Florida legislature met in special session to formulate policy in response to the *Brown* desegregation rulings. Governor LeRoy Collins, a moderate politician, hoped the legislature would extend the 1955 student assignment laws that allowed county boards of public instruction to make student assignments to public schools. Under this arrangement the county boards also ruled on parent requests to place their children in specific schools; boards were bound, by law, to deny requests that would place students in particular schools if doing so was deemed to jeopardize students' safety. The language of the law focused on concerns for efficiency, order, and safety—and indeed, did not mention race—yet it proved an effective means of circumventing *Brown*.[1] Many in the state legislature, however, supported a stronger segregationist position and proposed that Florida sign the Interposition Resolution that would be adopted by Virginia, Georgia, Texas, and Arkansas. An unambiguous rejection of *Brown,* the resolution baldly called for the continuation of segregated schools. In the midst of legislative wrangling over the means by which Florida would maintain its system of segregated schools, state Senators Charley Johns, Dewey Johnson, and John Rawls introduced Senate Bill 38 to establish the Florida Legislative Investigation Committee, charging it to investigate "organizations, persons or groups whose activities would constitute violation of Florida laws, violence, or be inimical to well being and orderly pursuit of business and personal activities of a majority of citizens."[2] The legislation did not identify targets explicitly but the Investigation Committee's aim was clear: The press reported that the "NAACP isn't specifically named, but [cosponsor Johnson] . . . said he didn't know of any other organization the definition would fit."[3] It was widely accepted that the Investigation Committee was established to interrogate, harass, and intimidate members of the NAACP and other civil rights activists pushing for desegregation. Historians have documented the emergence of state and local institutions across the South that employed a similar range of tactics against citizens during the postwar Red scare. In *Black Struggle, Red Scare* Jeff Woods writes, "Segregation and anti-Communism acted as the mutually reinforcing components of an extreme southern nationalism."[4] Legislators established commissions and committees as mechanisms for state intimidation in Georgia, Alabama, Mississippi, Louisiana, Arkansas, and Texas as well as Florida.[5]

The Johns-Johnson-Rawls bill passed in the Senate by a vote of 34–1 but did not pass muster in the House Rules Committee, whose members warned of "witch hunts." The bill could move on to the House floor, however, and pass if it garnered a two-thirds approval. On 1 August the bill passed in the House with a vote of 72–15. The next day Governor Collins, in unprecedented action, brought the special session to an end by issuing an adjournment proclamation. The debate over the Interposition Resolution had stalled and the governor's preferred method of preserving school segregation was secured through an extension of the school assignment laws. He did not veto SB 38, however, which allowed the measure to become law on 21 August without his signature. In the heated context of the segregation battle and with the support of his fellow Pork Choppers, Charley Johns was able to establish the investigation committee that would bear his name, something he had not been able to pull off in previous legislative sessions. In 1953 Johns had proposed a committee be established to investigate crime and gambling. That failed because legislators thought it unwise to draw attention to crime in a state economically dependent upon tourism. In 1955 Johns went further, asking for a committee empowered to investigate, presumably, all manner of criminal and political activity. The broad powers that would have been extended to the committee led to its defeat.[6]

Pork Choppers were a voting bloc of legislators from northern, rural counties who controlled the Senate. By all accounts the Pork Choppers, who represented only about 15 percent of Florida's population, dominated state politics from the mid-1940s to 1968, although their influence stretched before and after those two decades. The name captured both the rural character of the group and the fact that these politicians were quite adept at pork-barrel politics. Above all else, Pork Choppers worked to preserve segregation and to oppose reapportionment. The long-established pattern of unbalanced apportionment in Florida reflected Jim Crow politics and was exacerbated by population shifts to urban areas in the twentieth century. It would take a 1967 U.S. Supreme Court decision, *Swann v. Adams,* to force reapportionment of the legislature and thereby disrupt Pork Choppers' control of the state.[7]

Empowered to hold public hearings and subpoena witnesses, the Johns Committee (as the Investigation Committee was and is more commonly known) began to organize itself in September 1956. On 18 October the *Tampa Tribune* reported, "After weeks of sputtering, the special $50,000 anti-NAACP investigative committee of the State Legislature cranked itself up today and said that its first investigation will begin Monday."[8] Early on, committee members decided to hold most meetings in executive session in order to encourage witnesses to talk freely, to control the flow of information to the media and general public, and to preserve the element of surprise in its investigations. Members agreed that only the chair would release information to the public, and only upon completion of an investigation. Johns Committee members were immune from liability and, should any witnesses bring suit against the Investigation Committee, the attorney general would represent it in civil matters.[9]

When Johns Committee legal counsel Mark Hawes reported on the committee's activities in January 1957, he highlighted the importance of organization in the fight for civil rights and stated that the Investigation Committee intended to attack this critical function of the NAACP:

> The Integration movement in the South could not be progressing at the alarmingly rapid rate of speed with which it is without the organized legal machine of the NAACP. . . . Stripped of this legal machine and left to their own individual initiative and financial resources . . . the integration movement could be slowed down. . . . The [African American] litigant today enjoys an advantage over all other litigants . . . to rely upon their individual initiative and financial resources in prosecuting a cause of action. It is believed that placing these people on the same basis with everyone else in this respect would not be discriminatory, and that legislation which effected that end should withstand attack on constitutional grounds.[10]

Hawes was repeating the illogical but worn charge that oppressed groups who pressed for civil equality were demanding special privileges. With the power of state government on its side, the Johns Committee examined bank account records of the NAACP in Florida and tried to seize membership records; it investigated Florida Agricultural and Mechanical University faculty involved in the Tallahassee bus boycott and the activities of the local Inter-Civic Council. The 1957 legislature rejected most of the legislation proposed by the Investigation Committee, but it did pass a bill to require organizations "whose activities tend to create violence" to file membership lists and financial reports with the state, and it granted the Johns Committee a two-year extension with expanded authority to investigate subversive organizations. Having failed to stop the NAACP in its first few months, the Investigation Committee needed a new angle. As Sputnik circled the Earth, Charley Johns and his committee tried to connect the NAACP to communism.[11]

Meanwhile, state Senator Fletcher Morgan was chairing a committee that oversaw an efficiency study of tuberculosis hospitals in Florida. The review revealed that a number of gay men worked at the Southwest Florida Tuberculosis Hospital in Tampa. The Florida Sheriffs Bureau set up a surveillance system, employed informants, and infiltrated social networks to identify "suspected homosexuals." Once people started naming names, teachers were implicated. The Hillsborough County superintendent of public instruction launched an investigation. According to the special investigator, the personnel director for the Hillsborough County School System provided a list of the names of people for whom he had no substantial information regarding misconduct but were "the ones he wanted run out."[12] The investigator ran the names through his network of informers, working the bars at night, and then approached the teachers themselves. Ten women and seventeen men eventually admitted they were homosexuals; another thirty teachers either refused to comment on their sexuality or escaped interrogation because limited resources brought the investigation to a close after two months. The special investigator told the Johns Committee that he estimated there were as many as two hundred homosexual teachers in the county.[13] He added that several of the teachers said they had their first homosexual experience in college, at the University of Florida or Florida State University. The investigator added that he found it relatively easy to get a "confession" from people questioned about their sexuality. He claimed that, in general, people under interrogation would confess to crimes 75 percent of the time and that 95 percent of those questioned about homosexuality would admit to charges. But the investigator noted a gender distinction among those questioned about sexuality; he found women were the hardest "to break. . . . They go right to the bitter end before they finally give up; and they were the roughest that we had."[14]

Tampa had been roiling with violence against homosexuals and vice squad arrests well before the 1957 hospital investigation, according to Dal McIntire's review of news reports published in *One*. In January a gang of five youths were sentenced on charges related to a three-year run of robbery and assault against "perverts" that included at least one murder. To the defense attorney's pleas for leniency, the judge in the case replied, "These men they robbed were no good, but that doesn't give them a license to hunt them."[15] No defendant, however, received more than a three-year prison term. Later that year in the aftermath of the hospital investigation, the city board voted to work out an ordinance "aimed at chasing sex perverts out of Tampa," as the *Tampa Tribune* so delicately put it.[16] News of the undercover investigation of Hillsborough teachers broke in July. Although the precise number of teachers involved remained a "closely guarded secret," Superintendent Crockett Farnell pledged to fire teachers "as of yesterday when I get proof of any misconduct."[17] While Farnell waited for the sheriff's report, the city vice squad fired its "'opening shot' in a war against sex perverts in Tampa."[18] Although the hospital probe targeted men and both men and women were caught up in the schoolteacher investigation, the Tampa police arrested thirteen women in its July raid. Twelve women "dressed in mannish clothing and wearing ducktail-style haircuts" were arrested at Jimmie White's Tavern, and an additional woman was picked up at Fungie's Tavern "solely on her appearance." Officers asked for the cause of the arrest responded, "If you're a woman, you ought to dress like one."[19] The police fingerprinted, photographed, and checked the records of the thirteen women but did not file formal charges. Noting that the women would be released, Captain Howell Ryals added, "We're going to keep after them until we run them out of town."[20]

Police detectives believed that Tampa had become the new Florida "headquarters" for homosexuals following an infamous purge in Miami. In 1954 a gay man was murdered in Dade County in the midst of a fierce battle over municipal consolidation. Publicity covering the crime and subsequent trial resulted in a "law and order" crackdown against gay men and lesbians—even though one of the two defendants convicted of manslaughter in the case admitted that the pair "had been 'robbin' and rollin' perverts' for approximately five months."[21] Charley Johns weighed in on the tragic situation as acting governor. Florida law stipulated that Senate President Johns become acting governor when Governor Dan McCarty died in office in 1953; by 1954 Johns was a lame duck, having lost a special election to LeRoy Collins. Johns's interest in Miami-Dade politics was connected to a drive for a county-unit voting system that would benefit rural constituencies (and the Pork Choppers who represented them) at the expense of urban voters. He named a local attorney to "coordinate Miami's campaign against perverts" and to assist the major's office "in the eradication and control of sex deviates."[22] A writer for *One* warned that the Miami incident was an example of what "corrupt politicians and opportunistic demagogues" could do through "trumped up hysteria" and surmised that homosexuals had become the primary targets for impending witch hunts in America.[23] Three years later the Johns Committee dispatched R. J. Strickland to look into "a matter in the Gainesville area"; in autumn 1958 the committee launched an undercover investigation into homosexuality at UF that led to the dismissal of more than twenty faculty and staff members and the expulsion of more than fifty students.[24]

Senator Morgan's hospital investigation could not have come at a worse time for gay and lesbian teachers in Florida. The homophobic fury it stirred up coincided with the Johns Committee's desperate search for a link between the NAACP and the Communist Party; for cold warriors, it was a small leap from homosexuality to communism. In early 1958 the Johns Committee ran into a formidable defense when it opened its second round of hearings involving civil rights activists in Miami. As Judith Poucher explained, the Investigation Committee implemented a two-pronged strategy against the NAACP. Its first objective was to charge the civil rights organization with barratry, for inciting lawsuits to force desegregation. The second objective was to paint the NAACP as a communist front.[25] To accomplish this, the Johns Committee adopted a tactic that government officials were employing throughout the South. It first tried to seize membership records in 1957 but Florida NAACP officers surprised the committee by refusing to cooperate. When hearings resumed in February 1958, Johns and his committee were ready to play hardball. The subpoenaed witnesses, however, held their ground as one after another was cited with contempt. Investigation Committee members were furious with frustration, watching the civil rights activists defend constitutional rights with a dignity that electrified the proceedings and confounded the committee.[26] The defiance displayed by the NAACP forced the Johns Committee into the courts, a move that restrained the attack of the Investigation Committee as it drained its resources. The NAACP would finally claim victory over the Johns Committee with a 1963 U.S. Supreme Court decision that kept membership records out of the hands of the state. Roy Wilkins considered the case strategically important "to the survival of the civil rights movement in Florida and the entire southeast."[27] In 1958, however, no one could be assured of this result and the possibility of membership lists falling into the hands of obdurate segregationists took its toll. Historians have noted how the Johns Committee attack on the NAACP slowed the growth of the association and diverted its political energy from an offensive to a defensive posture.[28] The impact of the state's unconstitutional action was widely acknowledged in Florida and throughout the South. A Tampa man wrote a letter to the editor of *One* in 1958, noting the arrest of NAACP officers in Little Rock who refused to open its files to the public; he asked the gay rights organization if it could guarantee that its own membership files would not be confiscated by the government. The letter writer argued that a threat of exposure similar to that leveled against the NAACP was keeping interested readers from subscribing to *One*. "Give us absolute foolproof assurance our names can never be confiscated," he wrote, "and I'll bet membership would go up a hundred percent."[29]

By the time the Johns Committee submitted its biennial report to the 1959 legislature, its NAACP investigation was floundering so it highlighted the recent investigation of homosexuals at UF instead. The Florida legislature granted the Johns Committee another two-year extension to stay in the fight against the NAACP and to continue its investigation of "subversive and homosexual teachers."[30] The Investigation Committee began tracking gay and lesbian educators with unrestrained intensity. For strategic purposes, Chief Investigator Strickland decided not to expose teachers or revoke their certificates until investigations in a particular area had been completed. As Stacy Braukman observes, "Despite the likelihood that teachers around the state were buzzing about the Johns Committee, the ramifications of the inquest remained unknown."[31]

Although the Johns Committee carried out its interrogations of teachers in secrecy, avoiding the publicity and accountability that went along with public hearings, it featured the teacher purge as the central element in its report to the 1961 legislature. Little had changed regarding the battle with the NAACP; according to the committee, this was due to "the willful, persistent and continual refusal" of witnesses to testify and the NAACP's "attempts to obstruct and destroy the Committee's investigations, and even the Committee itself, through litigation."[32] Evidently the Johns Committee was counting on its report on "Homosexual Conduct on the Part of State Employees, Particularly in the Field of Education" to garner the votes that would extend the life of the committee. The report emphasized the committee's "great concern over this problem" and the lack of "effective action" taken thus far by school administrators and law enforcement agencies. The Johns Committee had found "the problem to be more serious and extensive" than first reported, and noted, "The number of practicing homosexuals at the instructional level in our public school system as well as our institutions of higher learning is much more substantial than is generally believed."[33] The 1961 legislature responded with another $75,000 for the Johns Committee and expanded its mandate to include investigation of the "infiltration of agencies supported by state funds by practicing homosexuals and the policies of state agencies in dealing therewith."[34] It passed a bill that required all state employees to be fingerprinted and another that called for an "Americanism versus Communism" course in the high school curriculum.[35]

The Investigation Committee reached a high-water mark in 1963 when the legislature voted in favor of yet another two-year extension and a $155,000 budget for the committee. The votes in that session, however, were a bit harder to come by after Johns moved his investigation to Tampa to scrutinize curriculum and teaching practices at the University of South Florida (USF) in spring 1962.[36] The Johns Committee report of its investigation at USF focused primarily on what it described as a communist influence in teaching, obscenity in books and teaching materials, and professors' disrespect of students' religious beliefs; in addition, the committee remained ever vigilant for signs of the "homosexual menace" but found little evidence of it on the Tampa campus. The public, finally, began to voice its concern that the Johns Committee had gone too far. The writer of one letter to the editor of the *Tampa Tribune* urged the Board of Control (BOC) to reassert its authority in educational matters, fearing "the asinine, stone age pronouncements of Charley Johns and his barbarian pork choppers on such matters as philosophy, literature, and good taste, will make a laughing stock of higher education in Florida."[37] In an effort to muscle its way back to a point of command of Florida universities, the BOC released a "Statement of Policy on Academic Freedom and Responsibilities" in December 1962. Reasserting its responsibility as the chief authority within the higher education system in Florida, the BOC clarified its position on religion, teaching materials, citizenship, and conduct at the state's universities. The BOC charged administrators to continue examining the "general character" and "moral conduct" of university employees and students, "to guard against activities subversive to the American democratic process and against immoral behavior, such as sex deviation."[38]

In addition to an increase in public criticism and the jostling for authority now emerging from other state agencies, the Johns Committee met significant defeat in the courts. In October 1962 the Supreme Court of Florida vacated the action of the Florida State Board of Education (BOE) in revoking the credentials of three teachers in *Neal v. Bryant*. The case turned on technicalities; the state had not followed its own rules in revoking the certificates. This court action forced the Investigation Committee to turn all investigations of gay and lesbian teachers over to the DOE, although the committee would assist in processing cases until 1965.[39] In March 1963 the U.S. Supreme Court ruled in favor of the NAACP on the matter of the membership lists. Although the 5–4 decision represented the slimmest of margins, *Gibson v. Florida Legislative Investigation Committee* was consistent with the current leanings of the federal government.[40] By midcentury, Cold War politics pressured government officials to dismantle racism in the law, at least at the national level. Mary Dudziak documented how the international fight against communism compelled presidents and members of the U.S. Supreme Court to address civil rights abuses so that claims regarding American democracy might be more credible. The United States, in fact, filed an amicus curiae brief in the *Brown v. Board of Education* case, stating, "It is in the context of the present world struggle between freedom and tyranny that the problem of race discrimination must be viewed."[41] It is clear that the federal commitment to civil rights was fueled by foreign policy concerns and thereby limited the scope of the government's response to the movement. Derrick Bell articulated an interest-convergence theory to explain this historical pattern: "Black rights are recognized and protected when and only so long as policymakers perceive that such advances will further interests that are their primary concern."[42] Of course, without the years of protest and courageous action by thousands of citizens to claim their rights, the legal victories would not have been won. Nevertheless, it took the anticommunist campaign to provide the lever to move the nation a few inches toward justice. "Blacks are not neutral observers in their subordinate status, but even their most strenuous efforts seldom enable them to break free of a social physics in which even the most blatant discrimination is ignored or rationalized until black petitions find chance harmony with white interests. Racial justice, then, when it comes, arrives on the wings of racial fortuity rather than hard-earned entitlement. Its departure, when conditions change, is preordained."[43] The timing was right in 1963; taking the civil rights battle from Miami schoolyards and Tallahassee streets to the federal courts proved an effective strategy for the NAACP against the Johns Committee.

In accepting the NAACP's argument that membership records were off limits to investigation committees, the Court stripped the Johns Committee of its method for linking the NAACP to communism. As the rationale for its initial establishment slipped from its grasp, the Investigation Committee clung to the one objective for which the public would still lend its support. In spite of reasonable objections—that secret probes were improper, that the DOE was the agency responsible for regulation of the school system, and that the separation of powers prohibited a committee from acting as prosecutor and jury—the simple fact remained that legislators were afraid to "vote against a committee . . . that was making schools safe from sexual deviants."[44] Homophobia handed the Johns Committee its final term in 1963, and, ironically, contributed in no small degree to its demise.

The Johns Committee overextended its reach with the USF investigation in 1962, opening the way for public criticism. Additional blunders cost the committee political capital, and then in 1964 the Investigation Committee released a publication that alienated many among its core supporters. "Homosexuality and Citizenship in Florida" included crude photographs, a glossary of sexual terms defined in raw language, and an unsophisticated analysis of "the homosexual problem." The report offended taxpayers and even prompted state attorney Richard E. Gerstein to threaten legal action against the Johns Committee for producing such "obscene and pornographic" material.[45] An embattled Investigation Committee drafted a slate of proposals for the 1965 legislature designed to emphasize a legislative approach to the issues it had targeted, but the Sexual Behavior Act, Academic Freedom Act, Communist Party Act, Fingerprinting Act, and amendments to the Teacher Certification Revocation Procedure all failed passage. Recently elected Governor Haydon Burns chimed in, stating that the Johns Committee "does not enjoy the support . . . or the respect of the public . . . and is devoid of any usefulness."[46] The Florida Legislative Investigation Committee officially came to an end on 1 July 1965 when its 1963 charter expired.

Charley Johns resigned from the Investigation Committee in September 1964; he lost reelection to the Florida Senate in 1966.[47] The spent venom of his committee, however, spread beyond the notorious nine years of its existence. In the mid-1990s James Sears interviewed a woman who spoke about the impact the Johns Committee had on teachers who had lived through the experience. "All the women I knew who were teachers had been called into the principal's office and questioned for several hours. Sometimes there were other authority figures there. Sometimes they had been yanked right out of their classes and marched down to the principal's office. They were told that they were 'under suspicion' because of their marital status. Now, those women still lived in fear."[48]

The Teacher Purge

Between 1957 and 1963 the state of Florida actively pursued lesbian and gay schoolteachers, subjected them to interrogation, fired them from teaching positions, and revoked their professional credentials. Through the auspices of a special legislative committee, R. J. Strickland and his team of investigators perfected the techniques of intimidation and harassment illustrated in the case of the junior high school teacher from Pinellas County. The teachers— sometimes taken directly from their classrooms—faced their accusers alone. Other witnesses brought before the Investigation Committee over the course of its nine-year existence appeared with legal counsel; schoolteachers rarely, if ever, did so. In county superintendents' offices or Florida Highway Patrol stations, teachers often confronted three forms of state authority: the super- intendent of public instruction, law enforcement officers, and representatives of the Investigation Committee—all men.

Generally, Strickland followed a set pattern of questioning. One of his goals was to collect names of other "suspects." He could accomplish this by asking for general information regarding roommates, colleagues, and friends. If the witness resisted, Strickland would simply repeat his questions. This might lead the witness to offer vague references or hearsay information, no doubt in the hope that such information would satisfy the investigator. It never did, but the teacher had no way of knowing this. From there Strickland would bring up some detail from the witness's life experience, suggesting he already knew a great deal about the person. This was a critical juncture in the inter- rogation, the point at which Strickland would remind the witness that she or he was under oath and discuss the penalty for perjury. Witnesses didn't know how much evidence Strickland already had, if there was any chance of keep- ing their jobs, or whether they would be arrested. Strickland often informed the witness that the penalty for "crimes against nature" was the same as that for perjury convictions: twenty years in the state penitentiary. In point of fact, the Florida sodomy statute did not include a definition of the sort of conduct that would constitute a crime. It merely stated, in rhetoric echoing biblical law, "Whoever commits the abominable and detestable crime against nature, either with mankind or with beast, shall be punished by imprisonment in the state prison not exceeding twenty years."[49] In an article appearing in the 1959 *University of Florida Law Review,* Richard T. Jones explained that in the absence of a legal description of the crime in question, the common-law definition was generally accepted. In Florida this outlawed only anal-genital copulation although the state Supreme Court expanded the interpretation to also forbid oral-genital copulation. Jones went on to argue that private sex between adults be decriminalized in Florida—the same year the Johns Committee was ac- celerating its attack on gay and lesbian teachers, and two years before Illinois would become the first state to eliminate sodomy statutes.[50] Citizens arrested for "crimes against nature" could not predict the severity of punishment imposed by the court, if convicted. In a glaring example of injustice, a Ft. Lauderdale judge sentenced a sixteen-year-old boy to fifteen years in prison for being a "confirmed homosexual," while a Miami man charged with molesting three young girls was ordered to move out of his neighborhood.[51] In this climate, Strickland's tactic of threatening imprisonment to get people to talk was often effective, yet some courageous men and women denied Strickland's accusations throughout the course of the interrogation and provided very little information. Others, who figured cooperation was the better strategy, shifted from denials to maneuvers that focused on clarifying definitions.

At this point Strickland would pose the most personal of his questions, invading the teacher's privacy in crude fashion. There might still be some wrangling over what "counted" as homosexuality but in most cases witnesses simply answered the questions: How long have you had homosexual tendencies? When was the first time you engaged in homosexual acts? How often do you have sex with another woman [or man]? What caused you to become a homosexual? What kinds of sex acts do you practice? Name your partners. Some witnesses tried to defend themselves by emphasizing that they and their partners were respectable teachers, that they were being questioned regarding events that took place in the privacy of their own homes, that they were people of good character. When these arguments went unacknowledged, some witnesses pleaded for a chance to "correct" their behavior and make amends for violating social norms. The teachers, then, might move from denial, to debating definitions, to defending their behavior, to making attempts to help their case, but in the end the result was the same. By April 1963 the Investigation Committee reported that it had revoked seventy-one teachers' certificates and had sixty-three cases pending. In addition, the committee had in its files information on another hundred "suspects."[52]

The schoolteacher interrogations reached a high-water mark in 1960 (see table 1).[53] Investigations converged on the Tampa Bay area with Pinellas and Hillsborough counties accounting for eighteen cases, 58 percent of the 1960 total. Earlier investigations had also concentrated on the Gulf Coast, with 47 percent of these cases in the Tampa Bay region. Another 47 percent of the early investigations occurred in Alachua County and other northern counties not far from the University of Florida. Presumably, Strickland followed leads stemming from the 1957 Hillsborough County investigation and the subsequent UF investigation in the initial cases.

In 1961 the Johns Committee diverted its attention to rooting out a pornography ring, accounting for fewer schoolteacher investigations that year. Only nine schoolteacher testimonies were recorded, scattered from Bay County in the Panhandle region, to Hamilton County in the north, Citrus County

Table 1. Number and Percentage of Schoolteacher Interrogations,
1957 to 1963, by County

Year	Number	Percentage of Total Cases	Counties
1957–59	17	19.5	Alachua (4), Brevard (2), Duval, Gilcrest, Highlands, Hillsborough (2), Manatee, Pinellas (5)
1960	31	35.6	Alachua, Bradford, Citrus, Collier, Columbia, Dade, Hardee, Hillsborough (5), Lake (2), Manatee, Orange, Palm Beach, Pinellas (13), Sarasota
1961	9	10.3	Bay (2), Citrus, Dade, Duval (2), Hamilton, Osceola (2)
1962	25	28.7	Bay, Broward (9), Dade, Escambia (9), Hillsborough, Jackson, Liberty, Okaloosa, Palm Beach
1963	2	2.2	Clay, Jackson
No Date	3	3.4	Dade, Escambia, Hillsborough

Source: Data compiled from information in S1486.

on the Gulf Coast, Dade County in the south, and the eastern counties of
Duval and Osceola. The centers of investigation moved to the Panhandle
(Escambia, Okaloosa, Bay, Jackson, and Liberty counties) and to the south
(Broward, Dade, and Palm Beach counties) in 1962, with one additional case
in Hillsborough County; these twenty-five cases accounted for 28.7 percent
of all investigations.

Overall, counties with major cities (Pensacola, St. Petersburg, Tampa, Miami, Jacksonville, and Gainesville) accounted for just over half of the investigations, 56.3 percent, meaning that there were also a significant number of
investigations in rural areas. However, fewer cases turned up in Pork Chopper
territory than elsewhere. Two-thirds of the teacher interrogations occurred
in south Florida, a region Kevin Klein defines as the area south of a line one
might draw connecting Hernando County on the Gulf of Mexico, to Sumter,
Marion, Putnam, Clay, Baker, and Nassau counties, ending at the Atlantic
Ocean on the northeast edge of the state (see map). Klein adopted the north-
south divide proposed by Sigismond Dietrich in the mid-twentieth century.
The UF professor drew the line to emphasize that Florida had two distinct
geographical regions that maintained significantly different economies, histories, and demographics, which helps explain the counterintuitive placement of
Duval County in "south" Florida. As Klein and many others have noted, the
political distinction between north and south Florida during the twentieth

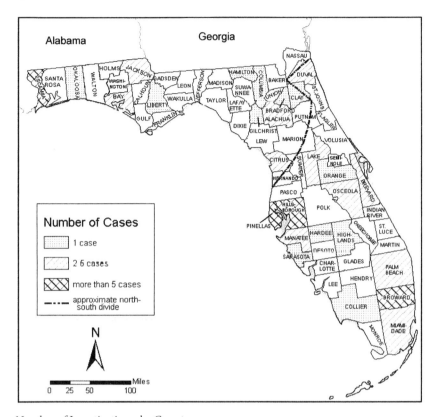

Number of Investigations, by County

century was acute; Pork Choppers hailed from north Florida.[54] The 1939 WPA guide to Florida noted in its opening pages, "Politically and socially, Florida has its own North and South, but its northern area is strictly southern and its southern area definitely northern. . . . At all seasons it is divided into Old and New Florida, separated by the Suwannee River."[55]

Although the BOE could revoke teachers' certificates on the grounds of moral turpitude prior to the Johns Committee's crusade against gay and lesbian teachers, the board did not have investigative power; it could only act when circumstances happened to reveal instances of what the state considered moral transgressions. State Department of Education (DOE) records of certificate revocations between 1954 and 1962 include only twelve cases in the years preceding the establishment of the Investigation Committee. Seven of the twelve cases (58.3 percent) cite causes other than homosexuality as the rationale for revoking the certificates. By contrast, the DOE revoked 111 certificates between 1958 and 1964; only thirteen of these (11.7 percent) cite causes other than moral turpitude—by then, code for homosexuality—as the rationale for revoking the certificates.[56]

The Johns Committee's invasive inquiries regarding schoolteachers' sexuality that triggered the tremendous increase in the number of certificate revocations between 1954 and 1964 remained outside its initial legislative mandate. When the Florida legislature established the committee in 1956, its charge was to investigate organizations that advocated violence or promoted action that violated Florida laws. The legislature expanded the scope of the Johns Committee in 1957 to include investigations of subversive organizations. When the Investigation Committee featured the schoolteacher purge in its 1959 report, homophobic alarm became the central justification to extend committee's operations. Only then, *after* the committee had already begun its investigation of gay men and lesbians in Florida's universities and schools, did the legislature vote to allow it to *continue* this line of investigation.[57]

The Johns Committee had usurped the authority of the DOE regarding surveillance of schoolteachers' morality. In 1959 the legislature gave the BOE investigative and subpoena powers, paving the way for the explosion of certificate revocations that would follow. Immediately the DOE began to work in concert with the Investigation Committee to revoke the credentials of gay and lesbian educators. The high number of investigations that occurred in 1960 reflects the newly established investigative powers of the DOE, the alarm over homosexuality raised in the statehouse to justify the extension of the committee, and, perhaps, so much grist for the legislative mill in 1961—the year the legislature formally granted the committee authority to investigate homosexuals in all state agencies.[58] In spite of the DOE's cooperation, the Johns Committee assailed the entire teaching profession for being indifferent to the "problem" of homosexuality. In response the state superintendent of public instruction assured the public that school administrators were eager to purge homosexuals from the profession, and 1962 brought the second-highest number of teacher investigations on record.

After the state Supreme Court refused to rehear *Neal v. Bryant* in 1963, the Investigation Committee stumbled through one more biennial term even as its direct threat to lesbian and gay teachers was abating. By then, however, the state had installed the bureaucratic mechanism for revoking gay and lesbian teachers' credentials firmly in the DOE.

A Concern of National Interest

The history of the Johns Committee—with its interlocking elements of racism, homophobia, anticommunist sentiment, and attack on the schools— illustrates the American commitment to domestic containment ideology as clearly as any event of the Cold War era. Scholars have explained how efforts to contain Soviet expansion and reassert American hegemony drove foreign policy in the United States after World War II and how the concept of containment found its way into practice in "almost every aspect of postwar American life."[59] As Stephen Preskill notes in his analysis of the role schools played in containing human development during this period, Americans were encouraged to circumscribe any action that might threaten political, economic, or cultural stability. This resulted in the imposition of consensus thinking in the academy, efforts to isolate civil rights protests, and a heightened emphasis on social constraints within the family. Put plainly, the "focus was on limits, boundaries, confinements, and restrictions. Cut-off points beyond which people dare not go were reinforced for behavior, for speech, for politics, and for academic life."[60] Nan Boyd offers a clear explanation of how cultural politics pressed issues of sexuality between the "layers of anxiety" that dominated the mid-twentieth-century American landscape. Boyd argues that postwar concerns over economic and political instability led to a decrease in social and political activism as "the politics of everyday life" became a central focus for many. In this milieu "the meanings of gender and sexuality became contested sites for the expression of domestic policy. McCarthy's quest to rid the country of communism soon developed into a drive against any form of 'internal decay,' and symbolic gestures replaced the actual containment of communist organizations and ideologies. . . . Femininity and homosexuality became potent symbols for weakness and vulnerability . . . and sexual transgressions became tantamount to treason."[61]

As historian John D'Emilio has shown, homosexuality became a major theme in Cold War rhetoric in 1950. In the context of sharp partisan criticism of the Truman administration regarding national security, Senator Joseph McCarthy made the Wheeling, West Virginia, speech in which he charged that the U.S. State Department was riddled with communists. Just a few days later, on 28 February 1950, Undersecretary of State John Peurifoy testified before the Senate Appropriations Committee that most of the ninety-one federal employees recently fired on charges of moral turpitude were dismissed because they were homosexuals. Exploiting public fear, government officials forged the link—logic notwithstanding—between homosexuality and communism. Seizing an opportunity to attack Truman's administration, Republicans made repeated charges that homosexuals had infiltrated the federal government. Finally, in June 1950, the Senate began an investigation into the employment of homosexuals in government. The resulting report released in December was, in effect, the government's imprimatur of the myths, untruths, and fear-ridden rumors that supported the massive public assault against gay men and lesbians in the decade to follow.[62] In *The Lavender Scare: The Cold War Persecution of Gays and Lesbians in the Federal Government,* David Johnson argues that the number of government employees fired on the basis of sexuality far exceeded the number of alleged communists who were dismissed.[63] One aspersion that would come to weigh heavily upon schoolteachers, especially, was the claim that even one "pervert" would have a "corrosive influence" on his or her environment. "These perverts will frequently attempt to entice normal individuals to engage in perverted practices. This is particularly true in the case of young and impressionable people who might come under the influence of a pervert."[64]

The American "preoccupation with the homosexual security question," as evidenced in the 1950 Senate report, even influenced Canadian immigration law. Daniel Robinson and David Kimmel found that officials working on revisions to the Canadian Immigration Act added "homosexuals, lesbians, and persons coming to Canada for any immoral purpose" to their list of prohibited classes of immigrants five days after the release of the U.S. Senate report. The prohibition was adopted into law in 1952, apparently without provoking any comment in debate.[65]

Soon after his inauguration in 1953 President Eisenhower issued Executive Order 10450, barring homosexuals from federal employment. The Department of Defense had already adopted a resolution barring gay men and lesbians from military service in October 1949, formalizing a policy set in place at the conclusion of World War II. Officers issued thousands of dishonorable discharges to gay men and lesbians when their wartime service was no longer needed, depriving them of veteran benefits and civilian job opportunities.[66]

The purge filtered down to state and local levels, and oppression against gay men and lesbians—including surveillance, invasion of privacy, police harassment, physical violence, and public exposure—increased. Private businesses fired men and women suspected of being homosexual; businesses holding a contract with the Department of Defense fell under federal restrictions, and the Federal Bureau of Investigation or local police often pressured other private businesses to fire employees. People who worked in state agencies—hospitals, libraries, and, of course, schools—also lost their jobs. D'Emilio estimates that more than one-fifth of the labor force in the United States underwent loyalty-security investigations in the 1950s.[67]

A repressive backlash whipped through the country in cities, like Miami, that had been relatively tolerant of an emerging gay and lesbian subculture. Following the 1954 Dade County murder that ignited a severe crackdown against gay men and lesbians, Florida lawmakers extended the penalty for "crimes against nature" to twenty years' imprisonment and declared that "sexual psychopaths" were to be confined at the state mental hospital at Chattahoochee.[68] It bears repeating that two heterosexual men committed the crime that set off the fury in south Florida. Local and state officials, however, were keen to preserve the image of a safe, stable society, and as was frequently the case, they blamed crime victims for the demise of law and order. Throughout the 1950s police across the country raided public spaces—bars, beaches, parks—in pursuit of homosexuals. Once arrested, citizens faced the possibility of imprisonment and, in some cases, forced hospitalization. California law, for instance, allowed men arrested twice for public sex to be committed to a maximum security hospital and kept there indefinitely if medically "warranted."[69] It became common practice for local newspapers to print home addresses and photographs of people who had been arrested, a practice that continued into the 1990s in South Carolina.[70] William N. Eskridge Jr. documented the range of antigay repression that surged through the United States in the postwar years in his excellent legal review, "Privacy, Jurisprudence, and the Apartheid of the Closet, 1946–1961."[71]

The hysteria over homosexuality paralleled the rise of another significant cultural concern: deviance and delinquency among youth. In 1950 a popular magazine published what it touted as "a frank and factual discussion of homosexuality" in a piece titled "The New Moral Menace to Our Youth."[72] In 1954 a Senate subcommittee held meetings across the nation—in Boston, Philadelphia, New York City, Denver, El Paso, Los Angeles, San Diego, and San Francisco—seeking information on juvenile delinquency. The San Francisco hearings came on the heels of a bar raid that led to the arrest of twelve high school girls, who critics charged "were being recruited" by homosexuals.[73] Although in the grand jury investigation that followed the San Francisco school superintendent testified that sex perversion was not a major problem in the city's schools, Senate prosecutors persisted in connecting sexual deviance to juvenile delinquency in their televised subcommittee hearings a month later.[74] In 1955 Boise, Idaho, grabbed national attention when arrests led to a story about a homosexual ring that allegedly targeted high school boys. John Gerassi's account of the scandal, *The Boys of Boise*, contrasted sharply with media reports that charged homosexuals with "infecting" youth. What the public read in the media, however, was that "Homosexuals must be sought out before they do more damage to youth."[75] The nation's top cop, FBI director J. Edgar Hoover, published an open letter to American youth in 1957, warning against behaviors that might draw them into sexual corruption.[76]

Throughout the 1950s the American public was bombarded with warnings of the dangers of homosexuality, especially as it pertained to young people. As historian Jackie Blount documents, educators stepped into the fray as "schools became fundamentally important agencies in the nationwide campaign to fight homosexuality."[77] When the Johns Committee took up its crusade against homosexual teachers in 1957, it could rightfully claim that it was addressing a concern of national interest.

2

A Stealth Investigation

We have the power to subpoena you or any other
citizen before this Committee, and to compel the giving
of sworn testimony. We are seeking, however, to
conduct this investigation as quietly as possible, with
as little notoriety as possible; in order to subpoena
people, we have to have a public hearing, with
the attendant publicity and notoriety, naturally. . . .
Are you willing to make a voluntary statement?

—Mark Hawes, chief counsel,
Florida Legislative Investigation Committee

Q. Have you been threatened in any manner?
A. Not unless you'd call warning me
against perjury a threat.

—Chief Investigator R. J. Strickland
and unnamed teacher, Citrus County

These excerpts from testimonies recorded by the Florida Legislative
Investigation Committee illustrate the distinct approach taken by the committee regarding its investigation of teachers' sexuality, the insidious tactics
employed by Chief Investigator Strickland against individual teachers, and
the gritty determination of some witnesses to resist the assault leveled against
them. The Florida legislature had indeed armed the Johns Committee with
subpoena power but, unlike its confrontations with civil rights activists, the
committee interrogated teachers without going to the trouble of issuing subpoenas. As chief counsel Mark Hawes explained, subpoenas brought public
hearings, something the Investigation Committee and most witnesses being
questioned about their sexuality wished to avoid. Reflecting upon its bruis-
ing battles with the NAACP, the Johns Committee determined to conduct
its investigation of teachers' sexuality in secret. This approach preserved the

element of surprise, maintained a sense of isolation among witnesses, and facilitated abuse of witnesses' constitutional rights. Once witnesses "volunteered" to testify, Strickland or other committee agents reminded them that they could be prosecuted for perjury if they did not answer questions truthfully. It was an effective ploy that allowed Strickland to slash through the makeshift defenses put up by reticent witnesses in the absence of legal counsel. Even oppressive state power, however, is never fully controlled, and many educators found a way to leave evidence of their resistance in the Investigation Committee's own files.

In this chapter I sketch a collective profile of eighty-seven educators represented in the extant testimony files of the Florida Legislative Investigation Committee. My purpose is to describe what happened to these primary and secondary school teachers and administrators during interrogations to provide a detailed historical account of state repression during the Cold War. Johns Committee investigators appropriated the technique of the day, brandishing weapons of intimidation under the cover of a stealth operation. But these were not the usual suspects—"subversive" university professors or filmmakers, "disloyal" government workers, "radical" civil rights activists, or "perverted" sexual deviants. In a sense they were, in the eyes of Charley Johns and his committee, all of these things. And their position as schoolteachers put them on the front lines of the domestic battle for containment. That is, the gay and lesbian teachers swept into the Florida purge were caught in an intersection of Cold War currents. An analysis of the Investigation Committee's methods of interrogation and the teachers' responses is necessary to determine whether in this political context the teachers were anything more than sitting ducks.

The Teachers

Although teachers have been dismissed on the grounds of alleged moral transgressions throughout the history of the profession, public officials in the United States did not concern themselves with teachers' sexuality *explicitly* until the mid-twentieth century.[1] Then, as a matter of common practice across the nation, gay and lesbian teachers caught in homosexual raids or otherwise exposed were fired; depending on the circumstances, they were either expelled from the profession or quietly moved on to another position. In point of fact, gay and lesbian citizens remained statutory felons in all states with sodomy laws still on the books until the U.S. Supreme Court overturned such laws in 2003. Up to the point the Court ruled that the laws were unconstitutional, if one were to press the issue, gay and lesbian teachers would lose their teaching credentials in fourteen states under laws that prevented criminals from teaching in public schools. Catherine Lugg noted that even now, in spite of the important step forward in *Lawrence v. Texas,* not one of these states has yet amended its public school code to comport with the decision.[2] For more than half a century, school districts have fired gay and lesbian educators on the basis of their sexual orientation, and state boards of education have revoked their teaching licenses on the grounds of immoral conduct. The Florida purge is unique in all of this history, however, due to the unrelenting focus the state brought to bear on its mission, the resources expended in its hunt for teachers, and the aggression with which it pursued its objective. The existing files of the Investigation Committee are therefore an unparalleled resource for examining the most intense assault aimed at gay and lesbian teachers on record.[3]

Johns Committee records at the State Archives of Florida contain files on eighty-seven educators who worked at primary and secondary schools. Although the Investigation Committee interrogated college students who were planning to become teachers as well as college and university faculty members, those records are not included in this analysis. It is important to note that interrogators did not pose a consistent set of questions in these interviews and some transcripts are incomplete.

Identities of the teachers have been stricken from the official record but language usage and content of the questioning reveal that the Johns Committee took testimony from fifty-three men and twenty-seven women. In seven cases the sex of the teacher was not readily apparent; rather than surmise on this point I have designated the sex of witnesses in these cases "unknown." The cases approach a two-thirds, one-third division regarding sex; 60.9 percent of the teachers were men and 31.0 percent of the teachers were women. During the 1957–58 school year, women accounted for 74 percent of public school teachers in Florida.[4] State agents found it easier to smoke out men in a profession in which most practitioners were women, first, because the Johns Committee began its investigation into homosexuality at the University of Florida. Thus, the male-dominated university rather than the public school system with its large female workforce served as the origin for initial contacts. Second, gender differences in the use of public space brought more men than women to the attention of the Johns Committee. Undercover police officers entrapped men on charges related to public sex in restrooms in the Alachua County Courthouse in Gainesville and the Tallahassee bus station. Investigators made a point of asking men arrested in sting operations if they had

had sexual encounters with teachers, and then they would follow the leads. Occasionally, teachers themselves were arrested. Twelve men (22.6 percent) were arrested or questioned by police before the Investigation Committee caught up with them. Not surprisingly, only two of the women interrogated by the Johns Committee had been questioned first by the police. As Daughter of Bilitis cofounder Phyllis Lyon told Nan Boyd in a 1992 interview regarding the repressive Cold War period, lesbians weren't arrested often for public sex because "basically we didn't do public sex."[5]

Gender differences are evident in many elements of the transcripts. Interrogators would frequently ask men if they were married and had children; they rarely posed such questions to women. Based on the questions asked, 9 men (16.9 percent) were single, 11 (20.7 percent) were married, 7 (13.2 percent) were divorced or separated, and 7 (13.2 percent) had children. Of the women, 1 was married, 2 were divorced or separated, and none had children. The more interesting factor for the women is that 16 (59.2 percent) lived with another woman; only 4 men (7.5 percent) lived with another man. Single women living with other women were likely targets for the Johns Committee. This observation conforms to a pattern traced by historian Jackie Blount. She observes that by the 1950s "unmarried status connoted possible deviance" for women.[6] The men questioned by the Johns Committee were just about as likely to be married as single, divorced, or separated. To be sure, Cold War culture held specific gender expectations for men as well as women. Single status, however, seemed to be taken as more of a "dead-giveaway" regarding women's sexuality, regardless of the accuracy of that perception.

Most of the men who testified before the Johns Committee were secondary school teachers (23, 43.4 percent). Nine (16.9 percent) taught in elementary schools, 7 (13.2 percent) were administrators, 1 taught physical education classes, 8 (15.0 percent) taught music and art classes, 1 taught children with special needs, and in six cases the men's job assignments were not clear. Among the women educators, 8 (29.6 percent) taught at the secondary level and another 8 were physical education teachers. Only 3 (11.1 percent) taught elementary school children, 1 was an administrator, 2 were music teachers, and 1 taught children with special needs. In four cases it was not possible to determine the women's job assignments. While the educators covered a range of assignments, nearly a third of the men (32 percent) taught fine arts classes or in elementary classrooms; 29.6 percent of the women taught physical education—fields susceptible to a homosexual stereotype. Twenty-five (47.1 percent) of the men had served in the armed forces; one woman had been a member of the Air Force Civil Service.

Although the locations of teacher interrogations were not always noted on transcripts, they generally took place in the offices of county superintendents of public instruction or other school administration sites, or in Florida Highway Patrol stations, city police headquarters, or county solicitor's offices. On four occasions testimony was taken at the state capitol in Tallahassee. Twenty-two men (41.5 percent) testified at law enforcement offices and 12 interrogations (22.6 percent) occurred in school administration buildings. Conversely, two-thirds (18) of the women's interrogations were held in school administration buildings and 8 (29.6 percent) were conducted in law enforcement offices.

To some degree the setting probably influenced whether one would claim a homosexual identity or admit having engaged in homosexual acts. Answering questions in a police station and facing arrest might induce more "confessions" than otherwise. About one-third of the men (17, 32.0 percent) denied any connection to homosexuality throughout their interrogations. Twenty-two men (41.5 percent) admitted being homosexual, 3 others (5.6 percent) denied homosexual connections at first but changed their statement (or simply resigned) as the interrogation wore on, and 1 man refused to answer questions, citing the Fifth Amendment. On the other hand, nearly three-fourths of the women (20, 74.0 percent) denied any connection to homosexuality throughout their testimony. Two (7.4 percent) altered their testimony to admit they were homosexual, or resigned, and another 2 claimed a homosexual identity or admitted to engaging in homosexual acts when asked. Recalling that more women faced their accusers in county superintendent's offices than on lawmen's turf might account for some of the difference regarding who claimed a homosexual identity or admitted engaging in sexual acts. The gender gap between interrogator and witness—interrogators were men in just about every instance—may have been at play as well. In any case, these results are consistent with the observations of the special investigator for the 1957 Hillsborough County teacher investigations who found women harder "to break" regarding statements about sexuality.[7]

One can deduce that sixteen of the educators (18.3 percent) were African American based on attendance at historically black colleges or universities, or other clues in the documents. Of these, eight were men, four were women, and in four cases sex could not be determined. In the absence of further documentation regarding ethnicity, I assume that the majority of the teachers were white; most attended predominately white colleges and universities in the South that remained segregated at the time. The teacher purge was driven by homophobia without regard for sex or race but the layered effect of homophobia and racism was apparent. For instance, investigators did not refer to African American men as "Sir" in these transcripts but often kept this custom in place for white men. More troubling were the instances in which investigators probed the intimate details of a person's life; some attacks on African American witnesses were among the most vulgar.[8] There is no apparent pattern in the transcripts, however, suggesting that the Johns Committee targeted African American teachers in their antigay sweep. African Americans constituted nearly one-fourth of public school teachers in Florida according to data compiled by the U.S. Office of Education but only 18.3 percent of the teachers interrogated by the Johns Committee.[9]

Just a decade after Alfred Kinsey published his famous studies on sexuality, Americans had not yet reached a consistent definition or clear understanding of (homo)sexuality, and they were not at all used to talking about the topic. The Florida purge occurred at the historical moment when the homophile movement of the mid-twentieth century was emerging on the West and East coasts to challenge cultural beliefs, practices, and laws that deemed homosexuals deviant and deprived people of their jobs and liberties.[10] Just before the beginning of the twentieth century, medical authorities began to dispute a long-held cultural assumption: sexual behavior that had once been considered a sinful *act* was then put forward as evidence of the pathological *essence* of some individuals. The Johns Committee and those who supported their efforts to bar gay men and lesbians from teaching tapped into both belief systems—that homosexuality was sinful *and* medically pathological. The committee stressed different points of emphasis as its campaign against gay and lesbian teachers advanced. In 1959 when the Investigation Committee first brought the "homosexual peril" to the attention of the Florida legislature, it built its argument around the recruitment myth that had been articulated in the U.S. Senate in 1950. Taking care not to offend University of Florida alumni in the legislative chamber, the Johns Committee argued that, while it was not attacking the "good name of the University," it found the extent of "homosexual practices" in the public school system "absolutely appalling." They believed faculty at the university level were "recruiting" college students into "homosexual practices," many of these students becoming teachers who then "recruited" children and adolescents in Florida's elementary and secondary schools. In a step contradictory to medical opinion describing homosexuality as an inborn condition, the report underscored the particular "danger" posed by professional educators. The Investigation Committee asserted, "Homosexuals are made by training," not born; homosexuality is more prevalent among those with advanced education; and the "problem of homosexuality in educational institutions, while not new, [was definitely] on the increase."[11] The legislators then sanctioned the Johns Committee's probe into the private lives of Florida teachers. Pledging to "weed out known homosexuals" from the state school system, the Investigation Committee sent a memorandum to county superintendents of public instruction requesting the names of all teachers dismissed on moral conduct charges within the past five years.[12] The hunt was on. To purge Florida schools of homosexuals, Strickland began to pry into teachers' sex lives.

As noted in chapter 1, the Florida statute on "crimes against nature" did not describe the behavior it prohibited. In practice, law enforcers defined one as a homosexual based on acts involving anal-genital or oral-genital contact. Strickland's modus operandi with schoolteachers was the same he employed with other homosexual "suspects." Strickland's method of getting witnesses to admit to particular acts was illustrated clearly during a 1959 interrogation. In trying to get a witness to name homosexual teachers, Strickland first wanted to establish that the woman was homosexual. When the witness said she didn't consider herself a homosexual, Strickland immediately asked whether she had ever "practiced homosexual activity." The witness responded "No" and added, "I don't know what you call a homosexual." This launched Strickland into a set of questions about sex roles:

> Q. In making love to the female, what part do you play?
> A. Strictly a woman myself.
> Q. You play the fem or the butch?
> A. I told you—I guess the woman.
> Q. In other words, you play the fem. Have you ever played the butch part?
> A. No, I don't think so.
> Q. Well, either you have or you haven't.
> A. Have you ever heard of any such thing in your life?
> Q. No, frankly, I haven't. Either you have played that part or you haven't. You either play the butch or the fem, one of the two, or both. How long have you been participating in this type of activity?[13]

In this interesting exchange, roles were reversed when the witness began to question Strickland, who apparently thought he knew more about the woman's sexual practices than she herself. Even though Strickland stated he "hasn't heard of any such thing," he wanted the witness to peg her sexual activity according to particular, yet vaguely understood, roles or acts. Later when the woman tried to explain that her "tendencies" were simply a personal expression, Strickland linked the subject to sex.

Q. In practicing this type of activity, when did you first discover that you had these tendencies? Is there some point in your life that . . .
A. You just like to talk to people, that's all.
Q. You don't come to a sexual climax just talking to people, do you?[14]

During the interrogation of a high school teacher at a Florida Highway Patrol station in Miami in 1961, Strickland stated his definition of homosexuality with clarity. It all came down to a physical act. "Do you know that there is more than one phase of homosexual activity, or more than one degree of homosexual activity? . . . Regardless of what the degree of the act itself might be? Whether it's a petting act or a fondling act or goes beyond that degree, you're aware that it has to be an act between two people of the same sex?"[15] By suggesting that almost any intimate physical act with another of the same sex could define a person as homosexual, Strickland stretched the common-law definition, a tactic he relied upon frequently in teacher interrogations.

Teachers who admitted engaging in physical contact with others of the same sex were not necessarily spared further questioning. If Strickland found he had a person who would talk, he showed no compunction in pressing for explicit details. In 1962 a junior high school teacher returned to the solicitor's office in Escambia County to face Strickland for the second time in one day. After she admitted having sex with another woman, Strickland asked for a description of the activity that took place in a private home. The witness explained that the acts involved

A. . . . the mouth, one time the other time it was just with the hand.
Q. It was the injection of the finger into the vagina?
A. Correct.
Q. And the caressing of the breast and kissing?
A. Correct.
Q. And were you the aggressive partner or was she the aggressive partner?
A. Worked both ways.[16]

The teacher named other teachers with whom she had been involved, and then Strickland returned to the most personal of questions, questions that had absolutely no bearing on the case no matter how distorted one's legal perspective.

Q. Did you reach a climax, a sexual climax through these acts?
A. I have never reached a climax.
Q. Through this type of act. Did Miss . . . reach a climax?
A. Yes.
Q. Did you, how do you know she did?
A. Her reactions.
Q. Did she tell you she did?
A. Yes.
Q. You could see the fluid?
A. Yes.
Q. You are confident then, that she did reach an act by your own eyes, is that true?
A. Yes.
Q. Why do you suppose you never reached a [sic] act?
A. I don't know.[17]

Many witnesses found it difficult to articulate a clear definition of homosexuality. Aside from the fact that the culture at large did not discuss the topic openly, these teachers were in a position of gauging every bit of their response to Strickland's questions to avoid arrest and prosecution. In the Tallahassee chief of police office, a junior high school teacher denied he was a homosexual. When asked to give his definition the man explained, "A person of the same sex who, well, in common words, goes after a person of another sex,—of the same sex."[18] In his confused response, the witness allowed the popular notion of homosexual as predator to overshadow the basic element of same-sex desire. In other cases witnesses let investigators fill in the blanks. In 1960 a teacher denied being a homosexual throughout her interrogation at the Citrus County superintendent's office. Finally, Strickland asked,

Q. Just what would you call homosexual?
A. Making out with another girl.
Q. What do you mean, making out?
A. I don't know, kissing somebody I guess. What else can you do?[19]

It was not unusual for witnesses to admit engaging in homosexual acts but deny a homosexual identity. As a teacher who had been arrested for indecent exposure put it, "I have had some homosexual experiences, but I would not say I was a practicing homosexual."[20] A teacher under interrogation at the Kissimmee Police Department acknowledged she had written expressions of love to another woman and that they had exchanged kisses, but flatly denied being homosexual.[21] It is probably true that many teachers could echo the point expressed by a faculty member at Gibbs Junior College in St. Petersburg who told Strickland, "It is the first time in my entire life that I have ever been questioned or told anybody about any of this sort of thing as a homosexual until I talked with you."[22]

Some teachers were able to talk about homosexuality in more sophisticated terms. A former junior high school teacher from Tampa who was currently teaching at St. Petersburg Junior College tried to rebuff Strickland when the investigator asked for names of other homosexual teachers. The witness stated, "I wouldn't know how to go about identifying a homosexual other than the stereotyped pattern that you see characterized in cartoons and that sort of thing." He explained that homosexuals were just as diverse a group as heterosexuals and added, "If this is the way a person is, that's the way they are and I don't particularly take offense at it."[23] A secondary school teacher being questioned in the Pinellas County superintendent's office told Strickland one would have occasion to meet homosexuals "in most any community in existence," suggesting that same-sex desire was quite natural and by no means limited to a few hot spots in Florida.[24] Another teacher under interrogation in the courthouse office of the personnel director of Duval County Schools who denied she was homosexual and refused to name other teachers who might be homosexual declared, "Well, my feeling is, Mr. Strickland, that some of these people that you are speaking of may be living perfectly normal lives in every sense."[25] A junior high school teacher eventually admitted engaging in homosexual acts while being questioned in the Florida Highway Patrol station in Miami, but added, "I still won't admit I'm a homosexual, I, I think that we all have that tendency now and then."[26]

In spite of teachers' efforts to avoid stereotyping and labeling, the Johns Committee juggernaut rolled on, picking up names of teachers to investigate on the basis of someone's claim that they exhibited tell-tale mannerisms or dressed funny. "Have you been dating regularly?" became a critical question. Even one's occupation—men who taught in the fine arts or women who taught physical education—became suspect. A note appended to the June 1962 testimony of a music teacher recorded the interrogator's doubt that the witness knew nothing about homosexuality, given "the field that he's chosen." The investigator took down details regarding the car the witness entered following the encounter, along with a description of the man who had waited there during the one-and-one-half-hour interview.[27] As the Johns Committee gained notoriety, teachers became more vulnerable to student charges based on observations that "[h]e always had flowers on his desk . . . [and] 'minced' around the school building" or "[s]he walks like a man, her voice is very deep and she just has a masculine character."[28]

A number of factors prevent one from making definitive claims about the sexuality of individual teachers interrogated by the Johns Committee. First, as this was a state investigation the teachers knew their jobs were in jeopardy and, perhaps, their liberties. People respond to pressures in different ways, however, and having all that on the line probably pushed some to tell the truth, kept some from telling the truth, and persuaded others to remain silent.

Second, the Investigation Committee based its claims regarding teachers' sexuality on physical acts, a strategy riddled with problems. It is notoriously difficult to gather evidence of sexual behavior, so the committee relied upon hearsay—often from people they did not consider trustworthy, other homosexuals. Many have pointed to the lapse in logic that allowed government officials to purge employees whose sexual orientation supposedly made them unreliable on the word of people whose sexual orientation supposedly made them unreliable.[29]

Finally, even if evidence of sexual acts could be produced, there was no clear, consistent agreement on what constituted homosexual behavior, let alone homosexual identity. This problem was especially acute in the mid-twentieth century in the United States, a critical point in gay and lesbian history when sociopolitical-economic conditions ushered in a transition in focus from homosexual acts to homosexual identities. Historian Estelle Freedman put this moment in clear perspective in her work on Miriam Van Waters. In "'The Burning of Letters Continues': Elusive Identities and the Historical Construction of Sexuality," Freedman cautioned that the social-constructionist perspective, for all its strengths, should not lead one to ignore the individual meaning of sexuality, the fact that "identity formation is . . . as much an individual as a social phenomenon."[30] Freedman explained that the tension between social and individual meanings of sexuality is greatest during periods of transition. Applying her argument to an analysis of the teacher testimonies suggests that the very timing of the Johns Committee purge, occurring during the most significant transition regarding sexuality in the twentieth century, contributed to its complexities. It helps explain how teachers could admit to certain acts but not claim the label or character flaws that dominant society attached to the acts. It helps explain the inarticulate, sometimes contradictory language attributed to witnesses as well as investigators in the surviving documents. And it reminds us that historians, rather like the investigators themselves, should not depend solely on any one factor—labels, hearsay, direct evidence of sexual acts, or even the image one presented to others—to mark these teachers as "gay," "lesbian," "homosexual," or "heterosexual." But the point of this analysis is not to pin a label on someone; the objective here is to study the subjects of gay and lesbian history in as honest and specific a manner as possible.[31]

The Tactics

The Johns Committee confronted the NAACP and witnesses from the University of South Florida (USF) in public hearings. In contrast and by design, the committee wrapped its investigation of gay and lesbian teachers in secrecy. Covert operations allowed the Investigation Committee to violate educators' constitutional rights and evade public accountability.

Still smarting from its battles with the NAACP, the Johns Committee launched its investigation into homosexuality with every intention of keeping its actions hidden from public view; it arranged closed interrogation sessions and controlled the information it released to the media. And when it came to the teacher interrogations, R. J. Strickland—not the representatives and senators who sat on the Johns Committee or their chief counsel—took the lead in gathering information from witnesses. Strickland explained this shift in strategy to committee chair Cliff Herrell in a 1959 letter. Strickland reported that he and chief counsel Mark Hawes had decided that "as long as this investigation [of gay and lesbian teachers] is producing in the manner that it is," Hawes and the committee members should steer clear. Experience had shown that "when a member of the Committee appeared, then these people began to bring in their attorneys and upon advice therefrom, ceased to give information. . . . They don't seem to think it necessary to seek legal counsel as long as the investigation is being processed by others than the Committee members themselves."[32] Strickland also explained that he and officials from the Florida Department of Education had decided not to "expose or revoke the certificates of [teachers] until the investigation is completed . . . as it might have a tendency to completely stop this investigation or to run them underground."[33] Strickland knew that as long as he kept the investigation underground he would maintain a critical advantage.

During public hearings the Johns Committee had no choice but to acknowledge certain rights of those who testified. The committee opened examinations at USF, for instance, reminding witnesses that it was

> . . . strictly a fact finding body. Every witness before this Committee has the right of legal counsel. . . . Your rights here are those fundamentally of any

citizen of any Court of Law in this State and in this country. If we ask you any question that you think invades your rights and you don't want to answer you state so, and the reasons why you feel like you don't want to answer. That is not only permissible, it's your right. And I'm sure you will find we won't insist on any answer that may violate your conscience or invade your rights.[34]

Most interrogations of teachers, however, took place beyond the reach of public accountability in county superintendent or sheriff offices, in the presence of few people other than the witness and the interrogator. In these cases, public hearings emerged as a form of blackmail, the alternative to answering questions to the satisfaction of the interrogator:

You realize this Committee has Subpoena powers but in order to invoke the power to subpoena here, we have to call a public hearing, which of course we can do and if necessary have such people face you that have already given us such testimony as we now have in hand but in order to do that you have all of your news-media press. . . . So I want to warn you that if this Committee should so deem it necessary, after having been presented with the materials and the evidence in your case, decide to call you into such a hearing, then you will be required to be here by subpoena, and to face such witnesses and to put yourself in a position of publicity as it might be necessary. So I'd like for you to think about this for a moment.[35]

Even when interrogators informed witnesses of their rights, the threat of public hearings was powerful enough to get most to talk. In 1959 Strickland told a witness

You do not have to answer these questions—you are within your constitutional rights to refuse to do so, but at the same time, any questions you might answer that we might ask you will be handled in a strict confidential and private way. The other alternative is that if you choose not to answer these questions, we can subpoena you legally and lawfully before this Committee to a public hearing to be held at a place designated by this Committee, where TV, newspaper and radio people will attend. . . . Now, do you want to talk to me and answer such questions as I might ask you?[36]

At a time when the economic, political, and social consequences of coming out were catastrophic, teachers accepted the secret hearings as the lesser of two evils to avoid the broader exposure that public hearings would bring.

Johns Committee investigators were skilled at framing witnesses' alternatives in a good cop–bad cop scenario. Strickland often assured teachers that he was not interested in prosecution; he just wanted to uncover facts concerning homosexuality in the school system. Once testimony was under way, however, Strickland would remind witnesses that they could be prosecuted for perjury if they didn't tell the truth. If witnesses were slow to consent to questioning, interrogators did not hesitate to raise the threat of prosecution in order to force compliance.

> This is a civil investigation. It is not the intention of this Committee to re-lease the testimony that any man gives voluntarily, if he testifies truthfully and fully to the facts in his knowledge, to any prosecuting official. . . . The people who do not cooperate with us, and who we have sufficient evidence to turn over to a prosecutor for his action on it, he runs that risk, if he does not cooperate with us.[37]

True to form for a stealth operation, the Johns Committee targeted its "suspects" through surveillance and entrapment. Strickland and his agents tracked down leads stemming from the 1957 Tampa investigation, the 1958 University of Florida investigation, and arrests made by undercover officers at the Alachua County Courthouse, the Tallahassee bus station, and other locales. Often witnesses would provide names or other information regarding teachers in the course of their own interrogations.

The Investigation Committee staked out gay bars and hired informants to collect information on teachers. A memorandum in the Johns Committee records, for instance, lists nearly forty names and addresses corresponding to the tag numbers of cars parked at Rosalie's Bar, "a well known meeting place for homosexuals," in Jacksonville Beach.[38] Strickland questioned a bartender who worked in St. Petersburg in October 1959, explaining that the purpose of the investigation was to determine "how extensive the homosexual activity exists in the school system." The witness responded, "I don't think a person who is a homosexual should teach smaller children. . . . I'm not running down homosexuals, [he noted he was gay himself] but I don't think they should be teaching children."[39] The man told Strickland that quite a few teachers frequented the bar, but they often used nicknames. Nevertheless, "I can al-most spot school teachers, they seem to stand out." He went on to give the name of a woman in a photograph Strickland presented, describe her social activities, and told of two women who "were really just bragging about how they could live together and tak[e] care of two children."[40] Yet during the Johns Committee purge, few teachers risked being seen at gay bars, as one might expect. One teacher testified, "Well, the witch hunt is on, so therefore they are staying home."[41]

Teachers unable to avoid the Johns Committee faced hours of harassment.

It was common practice to begin interrogations with a series of questions regarding perjury, once again raising the threat of imprisonment for refusing to cooperate with investigators. During testimony taken at a Broward County school administration building, agent James Barker turned to the Florida statute on perjury immediately after swearing in a teacher who had been a Fulbright scholar. Barker informed the teacher that "in this state [perjury] is a felony and it's punishable by a good number of years. So the only reason I bring this out is because you are under oath, it is not in the form of a threat, we don't mean it that way, but we want a person to have every advantage knowing fully what they're doing, see what I mean?"[42] The investigators, of course, did *not* provide witnesses with even the basic protections afforded by law, such as access to an attorney. Teachers were left to navigate their precarious position guided only by whatever legal knowledge they might possess, probably fully aware of the extralegal measures being taken by the state agents confronting them.

The rare instance when a teacher tried to claim his Fifth Amendment right to refuse to answer questions provoked a severe reaction from chief counsel Mark Hawes. During testimony taken in January 1959, the witness asked if he were required to answer questions that might be self-incriminating. Hawes responded that the man was not required to answer such questions but added, "I want you, however, to realize that . . . we didn't just pick your name out of a hat. . . . We have certain testimony concerning you, or we never would have called you over here." Hawes pounded away at the witness, trying to elicit cooperation. He finished, "You may decline to answer any question I ask you, . . . but I want you to realize that you're doing that at your own peril.

> A. And what is that peril, please sir?
> Q. The peril is that this Committee may turn that testimony over . . . to a prosecutor.[43]

The witness refused to answer some questions, answered others in a way that would not give investigators additional leads, and when asked if he had "homosexual contact with more than two University of Florida faculty members," responded rather boldly, "Well, I have not said that I had relations with one yet."[44] Although Hawes applied the intimidating power of the state forcibly in this interview, he wasn't able to crush the witness entirely. The teacher had already raised the issue of Fifth Amendment protection, and when asked if he were homosexual, responded, "Yes. Would you like some sort of proof of that?"[45] The interview continued and then the witness was excused to consider whether he wished to obtain counsel before continuing his testimony. When he was recalled later in the day, the witness seemed to bring Hawes to a point of frustration.

> Q. I've told you that we cannot wait indefinitely for witnesses to make up their minds whether they want to testify or not.
> A. Well, I will make the testimony, but I make it under very strong emotional pressure—I don't know if you want that on this record—
> Q. What sort of emotional pressure are you talking about? You're not going to sit here and give me any testimony, Mr. . . ., prefacing, in the record, with a statement that you are being pressured, that you are being compelled to give any statement here. Do you understand that, sir?
> A. I realize that, Mr. Hawes. You don't have to raise your voice.[46]

As the interview wore on, however, it was quite clear that Hawes held the upper hand. The witness could not control the terms of his cooperation.

> A. Mr. Hawes, it was our understanding that I would not have to name other persons other than those with whom I had had direct homosexual contact.
> Q. Well, I don't know where you got that understanding,—I haven't told you that.[47]

The witness named some teachers, but Hawes did not relent.

> Q. Now, you have given us the names in the Duval County school system up there that you can presently remember. If we call you in a few days, two or three, if you think of others, will you give us those names, or will it be necessary that we ask you to come back down here, or issue a subpoena?
> A. Would you call me at my residence?[48]

Confronted with Hawes's threats and kept off balance by not knowing how the investigation would next unfold, the witness consented. He must have been drained.

> Q. Will you do that, sir?
> A. Yes.
> Q. Will you make an honest effort to recall the names?
> A. Yes.
> Q. Will you do it?
> A. (No answer)

Q. Will you do it, Mr. . . . ?

A. Yes, Mr. Hawes, I will do it.

Q. Now, I'm trying to accommodate you by not calling you back down here—

A. Yes, sir.

Q. —after you've had a chance to refresh your memory. Will you do that?

A. Yes.[49]

One of the reasons investigators were so heavy-handed in the interrogations was that they usually had no proof that the teachers had violated any laws or transgressed the moral code of the community. In one case someone found "paper back books with immoral pictures" in a car left for some work at a service station. The teacher who left the car was summoned to the next school trustees' meeting and questioned about the books. He responded that the car belonged to his roommate, who in turn denied ownership of the books. Although the Orlando Police Department dusted for fingerprints, it could not connect the books to the teachers. Nevertheless, both men resigned. Walton O. Walker, coordinator of secondary schools in Orange County, concluded this was the best that could be accomplished "under the circumstances since definitive proof could not be established."[50] Usually officials had no evidence to support their suspicions regarding teachers' sexuality so, as one county superintendent noted, "We use every bit of influence we can to secure an immediate resignation."[51] L. J. Jenkins, superintendent of public instruction in Lake County, was more direct in a letter to Charley Johns: "As you know, proof is next to impossible to get unless someone testifies or unless the person involved can be bluffed into admission."[52] To be sure, the Johns Committee was well aware of that point.

Johns Committee agents manipulated hearsay and utilized polygraph examinations to pry information from witnesses even though information obtained through such tactics would not be admissible in court. The Investigation Committee had no interest in going to court, however, and it didn't bother with the finer points of the law. If a witness had enough acuity to discern when a line of questioning was relying on hearsay, investigators might respond, "Well that's alright . . . we'll go ahead and make sure it comes out in the record that way. . . . But we're interested in that too, of course, 'cause it helps us know where to look."[53] Other times investigators would emphasize the limitations of hearsay in an effort to get witnesses to talk. Strickland tried to get information from a woman under interrogation at the Florida Highway Patrol station in Tampa through this means: "Realizing of course that it's merely hearsay, that you have no factual proof in regards of such people as were mentioned to you up there, could you tell us what professors were stated to you to be known as a homosexual or having had homosexual activities?"[54]

Investigators pressured some teachers to take a polygraph examination. When one witness refused, Strickland reminded him he was under subpoena (even though this had no bearing on whether or not one submitted to an examination) and then launched into a series of questions regarding the man's medical history. Then came the question again.

Q. Will you take the polygraph examination regarding the questions of your having sex with men, other males?

A. Not this time, I'd like to see my lawyer first.

Q. Who is your lawyer? [The witness answered.] And why did you want to see your lawyer?

A. Because I, I, I don't think you have me. Why do you want me to take the test? I'm not . . .

Q. Haven't I told you that it was to see whether or not the polygraph machine would reflect whether you were lying regarding questions of sex with other males?

A. You said that, but I don't understand why you pick, I mean why I'm being questioned about these kind of things?

Q. Because you have been accused by others of having had and participating in such acts and it's now up to you to refuse or refute or admit such acts and that's the reason I'm asking you these questions at this time. Now do you freely and voluntarily take the test or don't you?

A. No.

Q. You're not going to take it?

A. Not, not at this time. That's not . . . [transcript ends][55]

Although courts considered polygraph examinations too unreliable to admit as evidence in criminal cases, the standard of "proof" was much lower for those seeking to expel homosexual teachers from the profession. In 1963 the Alachua County sheriff sent Strickland a copy of a report initially delivered to a county superintendent. The teacher named in the report had taken a polygraph examination that, according to the sheriff, "verified his guilty knowledge of homosexual activities although he maintains that he is not now or has been a 'Homo.'"[56]

In 1960 Strickland made the mistake of interrogating a teacher from a prominent Florida family. The man's father was a retired county superintendent of public instruction, one relative served in the Florida Senate, and another ran as a gubernatorial candidate. The teacher had been walking home when a Naples police car approached. The officer ordered the teacher to get into the car, handcuffed him, took him to police headquarters, and locked him in an interrogation room. The encounter as detailed in a sworn affidavit fit the pattern Strickland had established in dealing with teachers—except that this time the man contacted an attorney upon his release:

> Affiant later learned and saw a tape recorder in operation concealed and disguised. Affiant was introduced to a man who stated that his name was R. J. Strickland . . . who said he was a lawyer and exhibited a card to show that he was an investigator for the State Board of Education. Affiant was informed by said investigator that it was necessary for affiant to take an oath. . . . Affiant at this time sought to find out from the investigator upon what charge, or for what cause, or by what authority these proceedings were being taken. The said investigator refused to make any charge or to state the reason for such proceedings. Not knowing what to do, affiant requested that he be permitted to call a lawyer, but was refused, and thereupon the said investigator proceeded to propound question after question for a period of 3 1/2 hours concerning affiant's life history, schools attended, association with friends. Several times during the proceedings the investigator stopped and warned the affiant that he was under oath and explained the effect of false answers and finally produced and placed upon the table immediately in front of the investigator a stack of papers which said investigator stated were affidavits showing that affiant had been associated with persons resulting in moral turpitude and that affiant was shown by these documents to be guilty of moral turpitude. . . . The investigator informed the affiant that he would hear from this matter at a later date.[57]

The witness's attorney sent a letter to the state superintendent of public instruction, Thomas D. Bailey, describing the interrogation as "one of the most lawless investigations that has ever come to my attention," a "flagrant violation of law."[58] The attorney clarified that he was not addressing whether or not the teacher was guilty of moral turpitude but the fact that Strickland's interrogation had "completely ignored" the legal procedure for stripping educators of their professional credentials. There were no charges, no hearing, and thus, no chance for the teacher to defend himself.[59] Eventually, the Johns Committee would be called to account on this point but in 1960 the attorney's observations were an accurate description of what happened to teachers who crossed paths with R. J. Strickland, chief investigator for the Florida Legislative Investigation Committee.

Teachers' Reactions

In September 1960 Strickland wrote that he was "leaving the office this morning to make the final sweep of the State in an attempt to gather all information and data possible in re of the 141 teachers whom we have the names and some facts on in our files."[60] Teachers, however, were finding ways to evade Strickland's dragnet. In October 1960 Strickland asked Hawes to stop the Tampa superintendent from allowing teachers to resign without submitting their teaching certificates or making a "truthful confession." In May 1961 Strickland complained to William O'Neill, current chair of the Johns Committee, that teachers simply were disregarding calls to testify about their sexuality unless county superintendents threw their influence behind the investigation.[61] When the Johns Committee proclaimed its antigay mission in the 1959 legislative session, it exposed the clandestine operation, and alert teachers did what they could to avoid confrontations with the committee.

As we have seen, interrogators rained a relentless assault on teachers who did testify, and the statements of educators who cooperated with the Johns Committee must be understood in this context. It's not entirely clear what one should make of a teacher's comment, for instance, "that something could get straightened out and that we could up-rate the profession somehow." When asked if she would assist in a "clean-up campaign" by turning in homosexual teachers, the witness refused, "I like to let people be, you know."[62] It was not unusual for teachers to deny engaging in homosexual acts or knowing gay or lesbian teachers early in an interview, but later change testimony by the end of a grueling period of examination or in a subsequent interrogation. Some teachers refused to give any information; others spoke at length, providing names and descriptions of meeting places and social activities.

Cooperating with the Johns Committee, however, did not protect a person from attack. One witness apparently made a report on another teacher and subsequently found herself in the office of the superintendent of public instruction in Kissimmee being interrogated by Strickland in the presence of three other men. The teacher said she made the initial report because "sometimes you get into a spot where you look out and you see somebody doing something that you don't quite approve of and you feel that they—that maybe you have a certain duty to the majority of people and you wonder what is your duty sometimes and so you go ahead and you stick your neck out."[63] After nine pages of testimony regarding others, Strickland turned on the witness, asking if she had ever been involved with other women. The teacher repeatedly denied engaging in any homosexual acts and was soon asking for a lawyer.

> Q. This Committee does hold in file accusations made against you pertaining to your participation in homosexual activity. I wanted to give you the opportunity to answer questions. . . . You choose to either answer them or not answer them, whichever one you see fit.
> A. I choose to get a lawyer.
> Q. Then you do not want to answer any further questions?
> A. No. . . . I could mix myself up and tell you something that I wouldn't be able to explain . . . and if you wanted to use it you could make me into a beautiful liar . . . so I frankly would like a lawyer.
> Q. I'm not interested in making anyone into a liar, Miss . . ., we're interested in only the facts pertaining to these situations.
> A. I'll answer the questions on my own. You can dig up anything—you can make anybody look guilty at any time. I am not a homosexual. I am not practicing at all. I am not and I don't think there's any need for me to go on.[64]

But Strickland and the witness did go on. When the investigator asked if the teacher had ever spent the night with "any individual girl," she responded, "Sure wasn't a man I was with but I guess I'd better start saying how many men I've been out with, right? I haven't got affidavits on that."[65] Then Strickland attempted to clarify a definition of homosexuality for the record, asking the witness, "Are you also aware that there are several degrees of that, are you not?" The witness was evasive.

> Q. Have you ever caressed the private parts of any girl or adult person?
> A. No.
> Q. Have you ever kissed?
> A. No.
> Q. Any adult female?
> A. No.
> Q. You realize of course certain degrees of that is classified as homosexuality, do you not?
> A. I would say so. Anything that would . . . an interest of the same sex, I would consider that.

Q. Then you deny having ever participated in any of these types of homosexuality whatsoever?
A. Yes. I deny it.[66]

This transcript tells a common tale of resistance in reverse. Rather than
naming homosexual teachers as the result of pressure exerted during the interrogation, this teacher opened her interview poised to cooperate with Strickland but (understandably) moved to a defensive posture once he questioned
her sexuality. By asking for a lawyer and stating that the investigators could
frame anyone, the teacher implicitly tagged the Johns Committee with the
practices of deception and duplicity that characterized its operation. Her resistance intensified as the interrogation wore on, from the defiant "Sure wasn't
a man I was with" to the strong denials of homosexual acts. The ambiguity
produced by the juxtaposition of these seemingly contradictory statements
could itself be interpreted as a form of resistance.

In spite of the fact that the Johns Committee asserted a tremendous abuse
of power, a number of teachers did not fold. Various acts of resistance are
important to note, even if they were not enough to alter the course of the
proceedings. One witness—not a teacher—refused to give information on
social settings where gay or lesbian teachers were likely to be found because
he did not want to jeopardize someone's career. One teacher refused, repeatedly, to provide critical information to Strickland and denied engaging in
homosexual acts throughout the length of her interview. Although she was
forced to resign, the woman did not respond when Strickland asked if the
interview was conducted with her consent. He inquired again of the teacher,
"You consented to the taking of the deposition from you here, did you not?"
She responded, "Well, I had no other choice."[67]

Sometimes resistance was subtle; other teachers were more direct. When
Strickland asked a World War I veteran with twenty years of teaching experience if he realized he was testifying under oath, the teacher replied,
"I realize one thing—I realize that I came in here to give you my information and that you seem to be insisting that any answer I give to you is a lie.
Now I don't like to be—don't like to feel that."[68] A principal who denied
homosexual involvement throughout his interview protested that the Johns
Committee had no grounds to revoke his credentials, as the accusations
against him were not true. A woman with nine years of teaching experience framed her answers "as best" she could recall: "They are accurate to
the best of my knowledge and remembrance. Maybe you can show me a
thousand errors in them. I don't know. Other than that, I have given you

the truth as best I can remember the truth."[69] Strickland pressed on, suggesting that maybe someone had misinterpreted an act or statement the teacher had made.

A. For me to tell you what someone else interprets, I couldn't.
Q. In your opinion, would you or could you have done such a thing or made such a remark?
A. I answer you this way. What is said and what is meant by it is as much by he who hears as he who says it. I do not know.[70]

It is possible that the witness intended to apply the last statement to her current context. Perhaps she was conscious of the fact that Strickland could construct whatever meaning he pleased from her answers to his queries. If that were the case, "I don't know" might prove the safest response.

One transcript exhibited all of these elements that characterized the testimony of witnesses who put up a steadfast resistance to the Johns Committee: refusal to name other teachers, identifying and calling the investigator's tactics into question, and claiming no knowledge of any same-sex activity. Most of the teacher's statements were brief and to the point. The interrogator asked for the name of a woman who played on a softball team with the witness. "Well, I don't think I care to answer that and have somebody else brought into this. This seems to become a vicious circle, doesn't it?" The interrogator tried another approach.

Q. Of course, you realize that we have some knowledge as to who this . . . is or we wouldn't have asked her name to start with.
A. I assume that. I assume that you know who it is. Evidently you know who I run around with, where I go and what I do; where I teach, what I have talked about.[71]

As long as the witness provided only brief responses and claimed little or no knowledge, she deprived the investigator of what he sought most, more information.

Q. During your trips, various trips with the ball club to various tournaments over the area that you have made, have you had the opportunity, or have you run into any homosexuality at all?
A. Not that I know of.
Q. Would you recognize it if you had seen it?
A. I don't know.
Q. I'm beginning to wonder.[72]

But all the investigator could really do, in this case, was wonder; this teacher just wouldn't break.

> Q. So far as you're concerned then, and so far as you know, you do not
>   have any knowledge whatsoever, in regards to any homosexual per-
>   son that is connected with the Public School System of this state?
> A. No.
> Q. And you have had none in the past?
> A. No.[73]

In a few cases witnesses would acknowledge same-sex desire but in one way or another challenge the Johns Committee's understanding of homosexuality. One elementary school teacher expressed no ambiguity about his sexual orientation, telling Strickland, "I know I've had the tendencies for as long as I have memory." The recent Florida State University graduate had "read every book I could find on the subject," which may help account for the unusual degree of confidence evident in the transcript of his testimony.[74] Although this man fit the pattern that the Investigation Committee feared most—the gay college student who became an elementary school teacher—he shattered their theory of environmentalism with a bit of logic. Like 47 percent of the male teachers the Johns Committee interrogated, this witness had served in the military, four years in the navy. When Strickland asked if there was anything about the college environment that would have "caused" his homosexuality, this man, who had been aware of his sexual orientation since childhood, responded, "Seems a pretty far fetched [idea] to think that anything—any type of surroundings could cause it. It's not environmental, in the first place."[75] This perspective, of course, ran counter to the myths of "recruitment" and "homosexual training" that fueled the Johns Committee's crusade against lesbian and gay schoolteachers. Strickland referenced medical experts who supported the environmentalist perspective.

> Q. Well, the reason I asked that question is that we have been told by
>   competent psychiatrists that a lot of this is brought on by environ-
>   ment and association. . . .
> A. Well, if that were environment that were conducive, it would be the
>   barracks type situation I lived in the Navy, and there I abstained.[76]

A considerable challenge to the Johns Committee's ideological framework occurred in a rare interview in which a witness described another woman as a homosexual and yet defended her as "a good person." The two women had established a relationship.

> I can truthfully say I became fond of this girl, almost to the point where I was
> in love with her, or I loved her. . . . I was the happiest I have been in a long time.
> We got along like two sisters. I became terribly fond of her and our relation-
> ship didn't go any farther than being together, being close together.[77]

Perhaps the witness felt confident in defending her homosexual friend as
a good person because she didn't understand the friend to be a "complete"
homosexual. That is, for the witness and the Investigation Committee, the
physical dimension of a relationship was a significant factor in defining "degrees" of homosexuality.

> Q. Was there any bonding of the bodies?
> A. Yes. We slept together several evenings. I had kissed her on several
>   occasions.
> Q. Is that as far as the degree of homosexuality went?
> A. Yes. This girl is mainly mentally homosexual. I don't think she could
>   ever be physically completely homosexual. As far as falling in love
>   with a man, I don't think it's possible for her. I think it would have
>   to be a woman but as far as really being a homosexual is concerned,
>   I don't think she is, although she thinks she is. So I sort of carried
>   on a sort of half-way relationship and satisfied myself with the fact
>   that I was being loved and she told me that she loved me and the
>   fact that I had someone to care for, someone to keep house for; more
>   or less like a husband that I didn't have. And we carried on that
>   relationship.[78]

Although a few women attested to the goodness of a same-sex relationship,
they could not bring themselves to claim—or, perhaps, dare admit to the
committee—a physical relationship. One teacher struggled to reconcile her
intimate feelings in the presence of the superintendent of public instruction
of Citrus County.

> I have been very close to several people but I have not had any sex acts with
> anyone. . . . But I have quite a few girls who are very good friends of mine and
> I have a very closeness with them that I can explain to you but it is not sexu-
> ally. It's just a—I guess it's a need somewhere I'm lacking or something that's
> wrong, that I want to be loved or want to show my love to someone.[79]

Early in the course of the teacher investigations, a witness explained to Strickland that the behaviors he associated with homosexuality could just as easily
be practiced by a heterosexual couple.

A. Well, I tell you, if you look at everyday people—married couples, they do about the same thing.

Q. You mean . . .

A. That's right, like you and your wife and him and his wife.[80]

Although this witness was not a teacher, she seemed intent on teaching Strickland a thing or two about sexuality.

Q. You are telling me that . . . even though a couple may be married, that they carry on at times abnormal sexual relations, is that true?

A. That's right—happens all over the world.

Q. And it does not necessarily mean that just because a couple is married that there is no abnormal relations, does it?

A. That's all a part of love making—just like Kinsey's report on love making, if you read it.[81]

Teachers forged their responses to the Johns Committee drawing from a well-stocked arsenal of strategies: avoidance, denial, ambiguity, cooperation, and argumentation. Once a person was selected for questioning, however, the outcome was predictable. The teacher would resign or be fired and the Florida Department of Education would revoke the person's teaching certificate. In one case a teacher denied all charges throughout the course of her interrogation.

Q. If this Committee holds in file sworn affidavits to the effect that persons have had such acts with you would that be true or false?

A. I'd take it to court.

Q. I'm asking you would it be true or false?

A. It would be false.[82]

When Strickland asked the witness to submit to a polygraph examination, she responded that she would consult her lawyer. The interview continued but the witness did not alter her testimony. After posing many more questions, Strickland tried again.

Q. You still stand by the fact that you will take a polygraph examination after having consulted your attorney?

A. No, I think I want to just go ahead and resign my position and let it go at that.

Q. You refuse then to take the polygraph examination?

A. Well on those grounds, yes I guess so, call it a refusal.[83]

Strickland hadn't been able to shake an admission from the teacher, but he got the resignation anyway. In another case, a teacher did submit to the polygraph examination and then acknowledged he was homosexual. The investigator outlined the process that would follow.

> Q. In view of the different admissions that you have made today, both in this office and in the polygraph room, do you realize that you are in a position now where you are going to have to turn in your resignation . . . and I, in the capacity as an investigator for the Florida Legislative Investigation Committee, will ask you to surrender your certificate. . . . The only alternative we have is to exercise . . . powers of this Committee and bring it out in its entirety, a public hearing in Tallahassee. At this public hearing, we have no control of the news media or anything else, this is our only weapon?
> A. If I don't resign.
> Q. If you do not comply.
> A. I'll resign sir.[84]

As was often the case, the investigator asked the witness to admit, for the record, that he had not been coerced or intimidated during the interrogation.

> Q. Do you feel you've been treated fairly and squarely about this?
> A. I do sir, I do.[85]

That last insult marked the end of another teacher's career.

Conclusion

The Johns Committee's investigation into teachers' sexuality typified the actions of a government chasing after a narrowly conceived sense of security at the expense of civil liberties. Its entire operation rested on tactics of coercion and intimidation; convictions hung on the unstable trio of hearsay, circumstantial evidence, and "guilt" by association. This history illustrates the formidable power of a government granted the veil of secrecy. The Johns Committee exploited the cover of secrecy in two ways. As long as the investigation remained covert, Strickland and the other agents were able to launch a surprise attack, catch teachers off guard, and lessen the possibility of an organized defense. And by keeping individual interrogations out of public view, the Investigation Committee took freer rein in the violation of citizens' rights and evaded accountability for its abuses of power.

The Johns Committee kept witnesses off balance with a barrage of threats peppered with duplicity. Investigators pressured teachers into giving sworn testimony by holding up the specter of a public hearing. In the rare cases where this tactic failed, agents informed teachers that they already had damaging testimony regarding the person and threatened prosecution if they didn't cooperate. Once the interrogations began, witnesses learned that they could go to prison for perjury if they failed to answer questions truthfully. Contradictorily, the investigators reserved for themselves the practice of deception.

Within the space of a few minutes, Strickland and his colleagues would tell witnesses that theirs was a fact-finding mission with no intent to prosecute but then remind teachers that the Investigation Committee had information on the teachers that they could turn over to prosecutors. This was itself misleading, as investigators rarely had any proof of criminal activity that would stand up in court. Interrogators made a practice of appending disclaimers to their obvious threats regarding prosecution, suggesting this was "not a threat, just an effort to inform witnesses of the penalty for perjury." The Johns Committee also issued statements riddled with Orwellian doublespeak. "No one surely wants a witch-hunt," it claimed while announcing efforts to enlarge the scope of the teacher purge throughout the state.[86]

Given the overpowering circumstances that encompassed gay and lesbian teachers in Florida, the range of their responses evident in the Investigation Committee's records is noteworthy. The preferred choice, to be sure, was avoidance. Teachers left the bars, left their schools, and ignored Strickland's summons when they could. But in the eighty-seven documented cases when teachers faced agents of the Investigation Committee, a dynamic quality of exchange surfaced, even in instances when teachers cooperated with the interrogators by telling them what they wanted to hear. Under the pressure of relentless questioning, it was not unusual for a witness to repeatedly deny any knowledge of homosexuality before finally breaking down with an admission about themselves or naming others. In the larger culture, gay men and lesbians were just beginning to define a collective identity based on sexual orientation. Many people didn't yet have what Daughter of Bilitis cofounder Del Martin later identified as "a sense of self-worth to fight for."[87] Martin was explaining why lesbians arrested in bar raids in the 1950s would often plead guilty, but her analysis could also apply to the men and women who supplied information to the Johns Committee. "A lot of it was just fear and not knowing what the law really was. . . . What we were trying to do at that time is survive. What we were trying to do is build a sense of community, among those of us who could, that gave us self-esteem and gave us a sense of our own individual power—and then our power as a group. . . . You have to build a sense of community within your group before you can do anything else."[88] Quite simply, the Florida teachers were trying to survive. Lacking a group sensibility, let alone a powerful political organization, gay and lesbian teachers' sense of individual power vis-à-vis the Johns Committee had to have been minimal. "Those who could," however, resisted the antigay attack in a number of ways.

The teachers who put up the most effective forms of resistance did so by keeping their answers short and providing little additional information to the investigators. Teachers might evade questions by saying they "couldn't remember" or "didn't know," or they could stonewall the Johns Committee with flat-out denials. While this tactic could not protect a teacher from the material loss of power connected to the abrupt ending of one's career, it did afford them the exercise of symbolic power by resisting the committee's questions. Pluckier teachers called the investigators' tactics into question, identifying the vicious circle of naming others as the insidious practice it was, or charging the Investigation Committee with framing witnesses. Others snapped back with sarcasm: "Haven't said I slept with one homosexual yet" or "Sure wasn't a man I was with." Perhaps most significantly, some teachers challenged the Johns Committee's understanding of sexuality by disputing the environmentalist theory at the core of the teacher purge, arguing that homosexuals can be people of good character and reminding the state agents that homosexuals were a diverse lot (unable to peg by specific characteristics) who lived throughout the world.

It is interesting to observe that both the investigators and their targets engaged in secrecy and deception in this Cold War climate that was eroding individual privacy. In Sigmund Diamond's essay on an undercover investigative program at Yale University (1927–52), he notes that the twentieth-century decline in personal privacy paralleled an increase in institutional and government secrecy, intrusiveness, and power. That the loss in individual privacy accompanied "a decline in personal freedom and professional autonomy" is not surprising.[89] Diamond argued that the impact of a government "hunt for heretics" goes beyond the damage done to individual lives. An event such as the Florida teacher purge "freezes the self-confidence people need to express their beliefs and shatters the social connections they need to help translate their beliefs into behavior. Natural history has its ice ages; so does political history."[90]

Diamond's theory provides another way of explaining why some teachers rejected the homosexual label the Johns Committee thrust upon them. Stigmatization and persecution have led to self-censorship throughout history. But as historian Estelle Freedman eloquently argued, rejecting a label is not the same as rejecting a practice. Rejecting a label, however, does put some distance between oneself and others whom society has deemed degenerate.[91] Gay and lesbian teachers, with their middle-class status, civil service position, and professional history, would be particularly susceptible to the urge to distance themselves from social deviants—through denial, apology, or redefinition. The state, looking to schools as central posts in the battle for domestic containment, took no chance on teachers who might be social deviants. Better to purge them all. Clarence Karier aptly described this as a time when Americans, fearing "the enemy without as well as within," learned to look over their shoulders.[92] In effect, this is what the teachers *and* the Johns Committee were doing. The collective impression that emerges from the eighty-seven files that the Investigation Committee kept on teachers is ambiguous, involving distrust, manipulation, and resistance from all quarters.

3

Silence Will Not Protect You

To my sorrow read about the terribly unjust
treatment you have rec'd because you have dared
to stand for the rights of all human beings. . . .
I am sure that in the hearts of thousands
you are holding a deep place.

—Pearl Mitchell to Ruth Perry, 26 May 1959

The Legislative Investigating Committee . . . violated
academic freedom, to the considerable harm of the
universities and colleges of Florida. . . . The Tampa Branch
of the AAUW supports academic freedom and its col-
lateral atmosphere of professional dignity, responsibility,
and scholarly disciplines based on inner worth, as contrasted with a climate of raucous and carnival invasion.

—Tampa American Association of University Women
(AAUW), "Report and Resolution," 1963

First, I want to congratulate your committee on the
fine work it has been doing to stamp out influence of
homosexuals on the lives of the boys and girls attending
the schools of Florida. . . . I am ready and willing to
assist in any way I can to locate and expel such
people from the teaching profession.

—Lewis Bailey, superintendent of public instruction,
Calhoun County, to Charley Johns,
11 November 1961

These statements reflect starkly different responses to the machina-
tions of the Florida Legislative Investigation Committee. While the Johns
Committee rumbled recklessly through an array of investigative interests in
the course of its nine-year existence, it focused primarily on the NAACP,
lesbian and gay educators, and in 1962 the new University of South Florida

(USF). There the intent was to root out communists and homosexuals and purge the university curriculum of what Johns and his committee deemed un-American, antireligious, or otherwise offensive material. Examination of the committee's records, witness testimony, news coverage, legislative reports, and personal papers reveals that, although witnesses employed similar tactics of resistance to the Johns Committee, the experiences of lesbian and gay educators differed markedly from those of civil rights activists and university personnel. Professional organizations and the media supported the latter groups; their hearings generally occurred in the open with some attention to due process and legal protections. In contrast, schoolteachers' testimonies were usually taken in closed sessions without access to legal counsel, and they had no organizational support to sustain them during the investigations. Rather than protecting teachers' civil rights, the state and county superintendents of public instruction and the Florida Education Association collaborated with the Investigation Committee during its purge of lesbian and gay teachers. Fledgling gay rights organizations criticized the Johns Committee's attack on homosexuals but said very little about schoolteachers explicitly.

In this chapter I illustrate how teachers were different from others swept into the turmoil of the Florida investigations by underscoring the importance of public accountability and group solidarity in fighting oppressive forces. I begin with overviews of the Johns Committee's investigations of the NAACP and USF (paralleling the teacher investigation analysis presented in chapters 1 and 2) so the reader may contrast the experiences of the three groups vis-à-vis the investigators. Then I examine the various responses to these investigations, measuring the level of support each group was able to muster in its defense. Those who took the Johns Committee to task for its assault on the NAACP or USF were eloquent and indignant. Supporters of the teachers were virtually silent. My analysis of the public's general acquiescence to the teacher purge reveals some fundamental principles of social movements and contributes to a greater understanding of the early gay rights movement.

In 1964 it was difficult to be anything other than silent in the face of antigay persecution. Reasons had not changed much by the time Audre Lorde encouraged a "transformation of silence into language and action" a few years later: "In the cause of silence, each of us draws the face of her own fear—fear of contempt, of censure, of some judgment, or recognition, of challenge, of annihilation. But most of all, I think, we fear the visibility without which we cannot truly live."[1] And yet the culture of silence did not safeguard gay and lesbian teachers, individually or collectively, nor did it keep them out of the Johns Committee's vise—not that many probably expected it would. To those of another generation who look back on this history, the lesson is clear. "For we have been socialized to respect fear more than our own needs for language and definition, and while we wait in silence for that final luxury of fearlessness, the weight of that silence will choke us."[2]

Civil Rights Activists

In 1957 the Johns Committee opened hearings against civil rights activists in Tallahassee, the state capital. They began by questioning the first African American student to press for admittance to the University of Florida (UF). In 1956 the U.S. Supreme Court upheld this man's right to attend the UF Law School but the Supreme Court of Florida resisted.[3] Battling for the right to attend the state university was a long, arduous process. When the student appeared before the Johns Committee with his attorney, both were adept at stonewalling the committee. An example of the student's ability to stall the proceedings—and consequently evoke bursts of frustration from committee members—occurred when he was recalled for testimony.

> Q. Do you have or desire your counsel here?
> A. Well, I certainly would like to have him, but I think he is, possibly, tired. I hate to put anything more on his shoulders now—hate to do that; but I'll tell you what, I'll just go on without him.
> Q. Do you want him here?
> A. I would like to have him.
> Mr. Hawes: Well, step out there and ask him if he will come in here with you, then.
> THE WITNESS: Well, he might possibly be gone.
> [Another official]: He is just leaving here. I saw him leaving.
> THE WITNESS: All right. Well, it'll be too late.
> Q. Do you want to proceed without him?
> A. Yes. We will have to, sir.[4]

A few days later the Johns Committee interrogated faculty, students, and staff of Florida Agricultural and Mechanical University (FAMU) regarding their participation in the 1956 Tallahassee bus boycott. President George Gore, in the difficult position of shielding his state institution from retaliation by a hostile legislature, employed the tactic of responding briefly to the questions put before him. His concise answers provided little new information to the Investigation Committee. President Gore stated that he had advised faculty and staff not to take an active part in the bus boycott "lest such participation . . . embarrass them and the university."[5] Yet he did not forbid the activism outright and he did not, apparently, take action against those who did participate. He merely reminded university personnel that he wouldn't be able to defend or protect them. For instance, when questioned about the university rule prohibiting coeds from riding in automobiles, Gore admitted that the regulation had not been enforced since the boycott.[6] The field secretary of the Florida NAACP, Robert Saunders, recalls that the Johns Committee made its threats to the university president quite clear; Gore's succinct testimony was no doubt the most effective strategy at his disposal. As protests continued into the 1960s, Florida legislators threatened to dismiss activist faculty members and expel activist students, close FAMU or move it to another location, and bar northern students from enrolling at FAMU and Florida State University (FSU). Nevertheless, President Gore provided support for a 1963 civil rights march in Tallahassee and did not object to student participation, as long as there were no class conflicts.[7]

An art professor at FAMU evaded the Johns Committee for a time by citing illness. When she did testify, she denied involvement in the bus boycott and "couldn't remember" specific events.

Q. You never hauled any colored people from A. and M. over to Princetown and back, in order to keep them from riding the bus during this boycott movement?

A. No, not for that particular purpose. I might have had a friend to take to a doctor, or something. I don't know about that.[8]

Some witnesses combined evasion with an eloquent defense of civil rights and human dignity. In his testimony, the chair of the Political Science Department at FAMU explained that he did not interpret President Gore's speech to faculty as a warning to avoid the bus boycott. This prompted a query into what the professor would do if Dr. Gore or the Board of Control did prohibit such activity.

A. Well, when that happens I will make my decision at that time. . . . You are asking me a question requiring me to speculate.

Q. You do not know whether or not you would respect the wishes of your employer in that regard at this time?

A. I didn't say that.[9]

As the questioning continued the professor, faculty advisor to the student branch of the NAACP at FAMU, refused to allow the course of the interrogation to drift away from the basic issue. "I am a human being in this community and a citizen, and I am teaching students to be citizens and to take part in the activities of their government. After all, I am a political scientist. I tell students to take part in the government, that this is a democracy; then to be told that I can't take part in a movement with which I might identify my interests you see, to me that is a violation of my constitutional rights."[10]

After it wrapped up the hearings in Tallahassee, the Johns Committee moved its operation to Miami to question citizens who were pushing for school desegregation. Again, civil rights activists took command of the public hearings, interrupting the questioning to underscore the inadequacy of segregated facilities and speaking boldly against the principle of segregation.

> Q. That's not a—
> A. I know. I am glad you asked the question because I want everybody present today to know why I went into the school suit. I entered the school suit because I knew that there could never be equality in separation. . . .
> Q. Are [the segregated schools] adequate?
> A. No, sir. I do not think so along with the fact that I wanted my boy to get the very best, and I knew he would never get the best in a separate set-up.
> Q. Are the facilities, as far as teaching and education are concerned—do you feel that they are inadequate and that your boy, in the school that he is now in, cannot receive proper and good education?
> A. I say that we have good facilities but I say, with all the power of emphasis at my command, my boy will never, never get the necessary education that he ought to have as long as he is segregated as he is. There is something that happens to his personality because at the very outset it stamps him as being inferior.[11]

Since this parent would not agree that segregated schools were adequate it appears as if Representative Herrell was trying to get the witness to criticize the quality of teaching in African American schools. The parent did not fall into this trap. Segregation, by its very nature, the witness explained, sustained myths of inferiority and superiority as well as structural inequities. For example, the parent later stated, "Until the citizenry, the [N]egro citizenry raised a howl it was a long time before they got water in the science laboratory. More than that, the high schools, the white high schools here, had much better equipment in their schools than we could ever hope to have in the [N]egro schools."[12]

Ultimately, the Johns Committee's attack on the NAACP resulted in a tête-à-tête confrontation with the Miami branch of the civil rights organization. In her study on the NAACP in Florida, Caroline Emmons notes that Miami had one of the worst reputations in the state for racism well into the twentieth century. The NAACP had no presence at all there until a branch was chartered in 1935.[13] By the 1950s, however, the Miami chapter would be strong enough not only to resist the Johns Committee's assault but to muster a counterforce that ushered in the committee's demise as well.

Soon after the Investigation Committee was chartered in 1956 it embarked on a study of how other states were marshaling forces against the NAACP. The Johns Committee decided on a two-pronged strategy to end the civil rights organization's string of legal victories and to loosen its foothold in building a strong grassroots movement. When it began questioning witnesses in 1957, the Johns Committee's intent was, first, to prove that the NAACP instigated desegregation lawsuits and thereby could be charged with barratry, abuse of the legal system by provoking frivolous suits. The second objective was to link the NAACP to the Communist Party and thus discredit the organization in the eyes of many citizens in the midst of an increasingly heated Cold War. For this, they needed access to membership records. Releasing membership information did more than expose individuals to economic reprisal and other forms of violence; as everyone involved knew, the NAACP found it difficult to maintain stability as an organization during intense periods of personal attack and intimidation.[14]

When the Johns Committee opened its hearings in Miami, it was most interested in the testimony of Father Theodore Gibson, president of the Miami chapter, and Ruth Willis Perry, chapter secretary. Both were active members of the Florida NAACP; their courageous stand against the Johns Committee would play a critical role in civil rights history. Perry, a white woman, was a librarian at the Miami Beach Public Library and had become a prominent news columnist speaking on behalf of the civil rights movement. Shortly after the Johns Committee was chartered, she boldly exposed the real intent of the legislature in a radio broadcast: "We view the setting up of an Interim Committee by the Florida State Legislature, for the ostensible purpose of investigating organizations fostering violence and subversion as, in reality, an attempt to intimidate and embarrass the NAACP. Notwithstanding the unwholesome design of this project, we shall extend to the committee our fullest cooperation and respect as long as it has official legislative sanction. We have nothing to be fearful of, nor anything to hide."[15] The Johns Committee did not, of course, conduct itself according to legal decorum, Perry's and other civil rights activists' "cooperation" with the committee was short-lived, and there was cause enough to produce fear. Days before the Miami hearings began, word leaked of an assassination plot against Perry, Gibson, and two other NAACP officials; luckily, the plan was foiled.[16]

Perry's testimony before the Johns Committee in February 1957 contained the familiar elements of denial, refusing to cooperate, and ceding ground on matters of relatively minor importance. Perry stated she could not produce Miami membership records because she had given them to the chapter's attorney, Grattan Graves, to send to the national NAACP. When pressed to admit that the Dade County desegregation cases were not totally organized by local activists, Perry steadfastly refused—even in the face of Johns Committee chief counsel Mark Hawes's bullying tactics and lies about a previous witness's testimony. When Hawes asked Perry to get the membership records back from the national office, she turned to her attorney and made the request in an exchange that Judith Poucher describes as a charade.[17] Furthermore, Perry had plied the witness's tack of evasion in a preemptive fashion. Suspecting that the Johns Committee would attack the NAACP through its membership, she had prepared no *written* documents for the national NAACP for several months, restricting her communication to verbal reports only. She had announced local meetings through radio broadcasts and newspapers, eliminating a paper trail to members. Perry could evade the Johns Committee's questions because she had eliminated direct connections to NAACP members. When the committee asked why she had kept such loose records, Perry referred to the investigations of the NAACP going on throughout the South and implicated the Johns Committee itself in the unethical behavior.[18]

All things considered, the Johns Committee's first foray into its NAACP investigations had gone badly. Although the committee had little to show for itself, the 1957 legislature extended its charter for a two-year period, increased its budget, expanded its authority to deal "with the activities of people and organizations . . . designed to carry out the purposes of the Communist Party," and passed a law to require certain organizations to file membership lists and financial records with the secretary of state.[19] When the Miami hearings resumed in 1958, both the Investigation Committee and the NAACP were better prepared—the Johns Committee with a list of names, and civil rights activists with the First and Fourteenth Amendments. Charley Johns, now chairing the committee that bore his name, attempted to bar attorneys from being present throughout their clients' testimonies, but they rebuffed this maneuver.[20] Ruth Perry was among the first to testify. With members of the White Citizens Council who had tried to assassinate her in the audience, she read a preliminary statement reserving her right to challenge the proceedings of the committee on the basis of due process violations and First Amendment protections.[21] In short, Perry stated that the NAACP was neither a violent organization nor a communist one. Having stated objections in her prepared comments, Perry refused to answer questions regarding her own activity within the NAACP and she refused to name names. As the interrogation wore on, her repeated refusals incensed the committee, culminating in an explosive attack by Representative Cliff Herrell (legislator for the Miami area). Once the committee allowed Perry to respond, she stated, "I would like to say that I have never been a member of the communist party and am not now and never intend to be. I am an American citizen. I believe in democracy and the Constitution of the United States."[22] The Johns Committee cited Perry for contempt, the audience applauded the action, and the committee adjourned for lunch.

NAACP witnesses and their attorneys hammered out a course of action during the recess. Reverend Gibson took the stand when the proceedings resumed and read the following statement:

> In the light of the action by this Committee at this morning's session following the testimony of Mrs. Ruth Perry which, in effect, endorsed the intemperate remarks by Representative Cliff Herrell reflecting upon the integrity and motivation of witnesses who exercise their constitutional rights before this Committee and in the light of other evidences of the "star-chamber" nature of these proceedings, I believe that this Committee has disqualified itself to sit as an objective fact-finding body and afford to me or any other witness due process of law under the Constitution of the United States and the State of Florida.
>
>   Under these circumstances, I refuse to submit myself further to the jurisdiction of this Committee.[23]

Reverend Gibson then declared he was not a communist and walked out of the courtroom with his attorneys to "thunderous applause." In total, the Johns Committee cited fourteen witnesses for contempt for refusing to answer questions; the witnesses cited the First, Fifth, and Fourteenth Amendments in their defense. The *Miami Times* ran a front-page story on the debacle: "Legislative Communist Investigation Flops." In its coverage, the *Times* noted that the witnesses had been "thoroughly counseled by competent and brilliant legal minds."[24] In point of fact, the 1958 contempt charges ultimately led to the undoing of the Johns Committee vis-à-vis the NAACP. The citations resulted in approximately thirty separate actions in the Circuit Courts of Florida, one case in the District Court of Appeal in Florida, two combined appeals in the Supreme Court of Florida, one case in the District Court of the United States, and one case in the U.S. Supreme Court.[25] The continued court action strained the resources of the Johns Committee and required it to put its NAACP investigations on hold. As a reporter for the *Miami Times* observed, "All Sen. Charley Johns and his legislative investigating committee got out of the 15 subpoenaed witnesses in their alleged probe of communist activities in Florida was a big headache."[26]

University of South Florida

In 1905 Florida consolidated its seminaries into a state university system governed by a single Board of Control (BOC). Twenty years later in *Stetson University v. Hunt* the Florida Supreme Court ruled that schools had the right to "control the general welfare, mental training, and moral discipline" of students, and that the state "could seize this authority by default if school officials failed to maintain harmony on campus."[27] As acting governor in the early 1950s, Charley Johns threatened to dismiss professors who supported the NAACP; more egregious violations of academic freedom occurred in 1962 at the University of South Florida. The newest addition to the state university system had opened on 26 September 1960. Less than two years later a "Strictly Confidential Memorandum" circulated among an "inner group" that included Johns, Hawes, a disaffected instructor at USF, a handful of disgruntled parents of USF students, Dr. Fred Turner (assistant to state superintendent of public instruction Thomas Bailey), and a former chief of public relations at UF—the latter two self-proclaimed enemies of USF president John Allen. The inner group was planning an April 28 meeting with Johns Committee chief investigator R. J. Strickland to gather "evidence" to justify an investigation of communist affiliations, homosexuality, curriculum, and teaching practices at USF.[28] For the past five years Strickland and his investigators had invaded classrooms and campuses across the state, hauling out professors, teachers, and students for questioning regarding their sexual orientation. They brought a larger dragnet to Tampa to catch "commies, pinkos, and queers" and any others whose teaching challenged the Johns Committee's sense of patriotism and morality. By enlarging the range of its targets, however, the Investigation Committee exposed itself to a widening scope of criticism.

The Johns Committee began its secret investigation of USF in April 1962, interrogating witnesses at the Hawaiian Village, a motel on Dale Mabry Avenue in Tampa. The inquiries became public knowledge after instructor Thomas Wenner, apparently something of a loose cannon, spoke with the press; professors, too, began to recognize Strickland's pattern of pulling students from class, and some witnesses later told their professors about the questioning. Once aware of the attack leveled against the university, students, faculty, and USF officials mobilized into action. Forced to conduct its investigation in the light of day, the Johns Committee lost some force of intimidation. President Allen and the USF members of the American Association of University Professors (AAUP) made their cooperation with the committee contingent on a set of parameters: witnesses could only be questioned on matters of legitimate public interest; interrogations were to be held on the USF campus and tape recorded using university equipment; witnesses could receive a written copy of their testimony and have legal counsel; and information would not be released to the public without the consensual agreement of faculty and the university. President Allen informed USF students and faculty of these conditions in a public forum on 21 May, stressing, "If you feel you are being unfairly questioned in any way, you may refuse to answer, and I would appreciate it if you would inform me of any such unfair questioning."[29]

The Johns Committee held formal hearings on the USF campus from 23 May to 7 June 1962. The weekend before the hearings began, students protested with signs around campus: "I AM NOT A COMMUNIST," "I AM NOT A HOMOSEXUAL," "I AM NOT A HETEROSEXUAL," and advertising a "short course in book burning."[30] A number of students volunteered to testify before the Investigation Committee, many reading prepared statements in defense of their university and the principles of academic freedom. One student, the son of a professor, began his testimony by questioning the Johns Committee's claim that it was on campus to clarify issues that had been stirred up by local citizens. Pointing to the furor that the committee had instigated, the student asked, "Would you care to comment on that?" The student went on to remind the legislators that their mandate only allowed for investigations of people suspected of advocating the violent overthrow of the government and suspected homosexuals. This exchange led the committee's spokesman to ask, "Have you come here to interrogate us, or to give us information?"[31]

Another student suggested the Johns Committee was going off on a "half-cocked" mission, stating, "A situation like this can be awfully dangerous. . . . Some of these charges can be—don't have to really be proven for it to damage." When the investigator responded that that was the reason for closed-door interrogations, the student countered with the observation that, if "things be brought out of context, limited testimony and such, [it] could be just a frightful thing for this University, and for freedom in general."[32]

Students from other universities joined the protest against the Johns Committee, at times in quite creative fashion. At the UF homecoming annual lampoon of political figures in autumn 1962, students served up a satire of Charley Johns as the main feature. The *Tampa Tribune* printed a complete transcript of the parody, set to the tune of "I'm in Love with a Wonderful Guy."[33]

The professors and administrators called to testify tried to explain the nature of a university to the Johns Committee. One spoke of the responsibility "to arouse students to the fact there are important sides in the world that an educated person must come to terms with, argue about, and try to reach a decision on in his own mind."[34] But Johns and his fellows had little respect for thinking that challenged their status quo, little regard for critical analysis that embraced multiple perspectives. Two of the most heated controversies that emerged during the USF investigation involved professors whose work fell beyond the pale of conservative ideology. In June President Allen rescinded his nomination to hire Professor D. F. Fleming, a scholar whose work included an analysis on *The Cold War and Its Origins*. Fleming asked the AAUP to investigate the case; upon completion of its inquiry, the organization censured USF for its actions. In August the university hired Dr. Sheldon Grebstein as assistant professor of English. The fall term had barely begun when Charley Johns obtained a copy of one of the articles Grebstein had assigned, "The Know-Nothing Bohemians," by Norman Podhoretz. The article, a critique of beat literature, contained some mild profanity; Johns demanded that the BOC pressure President Allen into firing Grebstein. Allen suspended the English professor, which ignited a statewide revolt. Florida AAUP chapters, the American Association of University Women, the Florida Library Association, and alumni groups from UF and FSU condemned the action. President Gordon Blackwell joined with the FSU faculty senate in protest, and prominent faculty there warned they would leave the state unless academic freedom was protected. The fear that had dominated Florida campuses during the homophobic witch hunts gave way to a sense of anger.[35]

The unbridled assault on academic freedom was, however, not as sharp a deviation from politics as usual as the public outcry suggested. In March

1960 former governor Millard F. Caldwell (1945–49) sent a memo to C. Farris Bryant, who would be elected governor later that year. Caldwell told Bryant that the "racial troubles in Tallahassee" stemmed from three sources: the disinclination of current governor LeRoy Collins to take a position, weakness of the BOC, and "the ultra-left-wing liberalism of Presidents Strozier and Gore."[36] Robert M. Strozier was president of FSU from 1957 until his death in April 1960. Caldwell advised the future governor that he should make it clear that he would "not tolerate the pinks as faculty or students" and suggested that Bryant fire both presidents and reconstitute the BOC. Evidently Caldwell was not pleased with plans regarding USF; he ended the memorandum noting it was "a grave mistake to set up another country club type of school in Tampa."[37]

Perhaps due to a combination of the influence of Governor Bryant and the Johns Committee's attack on universities, the BOC adopted an explicit "Policy on Morals and Influences" on 9 December 1961. The board began by recognizing its long-established practice "to inquire into the cultural, social, moral, and spiritual" backgrounds of faculty and students in Florida schools.[38] The BOC codified its traditional practice by spelling out that state schools shall screen faculty and staff "not only with regard to their professional and academic competency but also with regard to their ideology and their moral conduct." The evaluation of student applicants would rest upon character and behavior as well as academic ability. Specifically, the BOC directed administrators "to be constantly alert to detect any antisocial or immoral behavior, such as Communistic activities or sex deviation." When administrators encountered faculty or student behavior that ran counter to the BOC's directive, they were to "immediately correct or eliminate" it, file a report in the person's "permanent record," inform the BOC of their actions, and—to protect communities from "antisocial and immoral behavior"— cooperate with local and state authorities to stop the deviant behavior.[39] In one stroke the BOC disposed of the right to due process and the right to confront evidence held against a person.

The Johns Committee used this new policy to leverage its attack on USF. In all, the USF investigation yielded charges regarding homosexuality against four men. The university fired an educational resources staff member and a professor who were accused of having sex with students. Another professor questioned about homosexual behavior managed to convince administrators he was not a homosexual and retained his job.

The fourth, caught up in crossfire between the Johns Committee and USF, eventually resigned from the university.[40] The professor's ordeal began on 9

May 1962 during the stealth phase of the USF investigation. The committee obtained testimony from a former student who charged another professor (no longer at the university) with making inappropriate sexual advances. The Johns Committee scrutinized the actions of the professor who served as the former student's faculty advisor and university administrators in dealing with the charge. The advisor had reported the incident to the director of student personnel but considered the student a troublemaker, and so made no further inquiries. The director of student personnel, without information from the student, was limited in her pursuit of the matter. The Johns Committee seized upon this incident to castigate the university for what it saw as a blatant disregard of the BOC policy. It hounded the faculty advisor, charging him with additional counts of misconduct, and pressured President Allen to fire him. Initially, the university did not find enough credibility in the student's claim to warrant further investigation; Allen suspended the advisor in August 1962 while a faculty committee revisited the issue. The committee reviewed the professor's interview with the Johns Committee, conducted its own interviews with the professor and some students, and concluded that the only evidence against the professor was unreliable. Nevertheless, President Allen informed the associate professor that he would not be rehired at the end of his contract. The professor resigned on 21 September 1962, another sacrifice the embattled university offered to the Johns Committee and the BOC.[41]

For the Johns Committee a charge involving homosexuality was enough in and of itself to dismiss faculty—never mind issues of credibility or circumstance. USF administrators called before the committee put up some resistance, emphasizing the importance of due process, legal or ethical limitations, or at last resort, claiming a lack of knowledge about a certain incident or the finer points of a policy. One dean utilized all of these tactics in his encounter with the Johns Committee. He explained that the process of following up on a complaint regarding a homosexual affair depended on circumstances and the credibility of the student. Given the serious nature of the charge, he stated, one should check into the matter before it "flare[d] up . . . [and not] report every little bit of gossip."[42] The witness went on to distinguish between legal action mandated by official policy and ethical responsibility. There was, as far as he knew, no legal duty to file a report on a colleague who transgressed the moral code of the community, although "One would expect him to report it, however, just for his interest in the general image of the University."[43] By this point the dean's answers were in contradiction to the newly minted BOC policy. As the committee hammered away, the dean retreated to the posture of claiming little experience in dealing with such matters to explain his lack of knowledge regarding the policy. When asked whether the BOC required dismissal of a person engaged in homosexual conduct, the dean responded, "This is the first time the allegation has ever been raised with me here and so I can't tell you from experience. . . . I would think it's required, but I don't know for sure. . . . Not to my knowledge. I don't know. I don't know what you're referring to. Do you mean they're requiring—well, if you would spell this out a little more. I don't know."[44] Just as we have seen with other witnesses, ambiguity was the defining element in this testimony.

President Allen's testimony exemplified the battle for authority that was being played out through the USF investigation. Johns and his committee were attempting to solidify authority vested in the state to control the political thought, moral values, and sexual behavior of teachers—and through them, the citizenry. Allen was trying to protect the authority of professional expertise and autonomy claimed by the academy. Toward this end he argued that inflexible directives detailing the process for dealing with charges of homosexuality were unnecessary. After being taken to task for not making sure that deans at USF were knowledgeable about the BOC policy on homosexuality, Allen responded "We shouldn't have to have this in writing. This is just good professional conduct to see that this gets to the proper authorities."[45] The president did not challenge the Johns Committee's stand on homosexuality, stating "we cannot permit a homosexual to stay," but he did reject the notion that a charge of homosexuality automatically meant that a person was "guilty." The president was persistent on this point, testifying, "I don't think that we should discharge a faculty member on the basis of the statement of one student unless we can get this irrefutable evidence."[46] He and Chief Counsel Hawes wrangled over the issue of proof, Hawes noting, "This is the type of thing that juries have to determine every day in our courts of law," and suggesting that if one were just willing to believe the accuser there wouldn't be such turmoil. Hawes pressed on, in the case of one person's word against another's, wasn't it

Q. . . . incumbent on this administration to make a decision on the truthfulness of that charge? . . . Isn't the obligation of the university actually to—

A. Try to find the truth, if we can.

Q. To settle this thing.[47]

Those two statements underscored the clear difference of perspective—Allen holding out for some form of due process, Hawes seeking a swift and pragmatic means to blot out what he conceived as a dangerous type of social deviation. Perhaps the divide was apparent to all; the chair called for a recess so that he could address the committee in executive session immediately after this exchange. When Allen returned for more questioning, Hawes picked up a new line of questioning.

Dr. Margaret Fisher, director of student personnel, employed a variety of tactics in her confrontation with the Johns Committee. The transcript of her testimony suggests an effort on her part to avoid simplistic denunciations of homosexuality; she seemed to understand the complexities of the issues under investigation with more sophistication than others. Fisher's responses to the questions posed by the Investigation Committee were polite, yet she interrupted the interrogator no fewer than seven times to finish her line of thought or clarify a point. In one instance she challenged the assumption of the interrogator directly: "Well, pardon me . . . but I don't believe that we have established that a direct and circumstantial accusation was made."[48]

The Johns Committee grilled Fisher extensively on the role she played in the follow-up to the incident in which a student charged a faculty member with inappropriate sexual conduct. At various points during the questioning, she noted that professional ethics placed certain limitations on her ability to act, that she followed proper channels according to university policy, and, upon occasion when asked about specific details, she deflected the question by framing her response in the context of general procedures. As the interrogation wore on, Fisher adopted the strategy of claiming to have no knowledge of an incident or not enough expertise to answer. When asked whether the university had a duty to determine whether a faculty member might be a "practicing homosexual," she responded, "You're asking about an area of college administration with which I'm not entirely familiar, and I would not be a very good authority on the matter. . . . I don't consider myself completely informed on this information, nor an expert in the matter. In the interest of students, I do not believe that a practicing homosexual should be employed on the staff of the University."[49]

Although Dr. Fisher eventually gave the committee what it wanted to hear—that homosexuals should be barred from university employment—she first distanced herself from having any real authority in the matter and emphasized the importance of evidence based on reasonable "suspicion." In 1960 Fisher and Jeanne Noble had published *College Education as Personal Development*. The analysis of gender and sexuality in this text belies the common assumptions of the Cold War domestic containment ideology of the political context in which it was written, and foreshadowed feminist arguments that would become more prominent in academic scholarship in the next decade. For instance, the authors explained that gender roles are culturally determined and then explored what this meant for a society, such as the United States in 1960, on the cusp of significant change. In challenging the legitimacy of rigid gender roles, Fisher and Noble were able to extend their logic in an even-handed examination of societal expectations that restricted otherwise healthy individual tendencies. "Students whose reactions are 'different' may be teased unmercifully until they are so self-conscious that they can hardly respond comfortably. They may be victims of idle gossip or slander about how effeminate or mannish they are."[50] The authors went on to expose a "lack of maturity and understanding among fellow students" and "stereotyped traditions and standards in the college" as sources of such unnecessary grief. Fisher and Noble wrote explicitly on homosexuality only briefly, citing Kinsey's work to observe that "endless gradations" in sexuality make it difficult to classify one as homosexual or heterosexual, precisely. They explained that social attitudes compounded the issue, given that homosexuality at the time was legally, socially, and religiously disapproved.[51] In another section of the book the authors lamented the fact that same-sex friendships had come to be suspected, disregarded, and undervalued, if not "the occasion for disapproval or slanderous gossip, sanctioned by prevailing student mores."[52] This was the knowledge that Margaret Fisher carried into her encounter with Charley Johns two years later, but the senator could not fathom the depth and complexity of the subject.

Dr. Fisher provoked the ire of Senator Johns when she answered that it wouldn't always be best practice to inform parents of the possibility that their student might be homosexual. She did not retreat from her position and, in the exchange that followed, made sure the senator was aware of the difference between hearsay and factual evidence.

> A [Dr. Fisher]. [There is sometimes] a very hostile and uncooperative attitude on the part of the parents if this sort of question were raised. And also there is—
> SENATOR: Are you sincere in that . . .
> THE WITNESS [Dr. Fisher]: Yes, sir, I am.
> SENATOR: Who's more interested in these here students than anybody in the entire world? Now, who is it?
> THE WITNESS: Well, I believe that the parents have a genuine interest in the students . . .
> SENATOR: And then you sit there and tell us that you don't think they

should be notified if they have a child that's committing a homosexual act, or involved in it?

THE WITNESS: No, sir, I didn't say that. I was trying to point out what some of the consequences might be. . . .

SENATOR: You're wrong.

THE WITNESS: And you see, our evidence in cases of this kind is, as a rule, hearsay.

SENATOR: I'm talking about where you have got concrete facts.

THE WITNESS: Yes, now that's a different matter.

SENATOR: No hearsay.

THE WITNESS: But see, here's the problem. Differentiation between evidence which is concrete, and factual and hearsay, is a problem which . . . in many instances, [is] beyond our competency. Most of the time in these matters, we do act on hearsay, and for this reason, as you know, one must be extremely careful in confronting parents with this kind of hearsay, in which I think the consequences . . . give rise to all sorts of possibilities which are undesirable for everybody. . . . The parents may be much more, much tougher on the student, than really would be the case—parents very often are uninformed about the nature of the problem.

SENATOR: I realize that.[53]

Throughout her testimony Fisher took care to outline the complex nature of sexuality. She noted the elements of fear, shame, and hostility associated with it in 1962 and pointed out that, because of those factors, charges relating to homosexuality were often not rational or objective. She underscored the importance of protecting students and faculty from gossip and accusations. More than once Dr. Fisher reminded the committee that charges of homosexuality were not easily substantiated. "As you are well aware, it's very difficult to evaluate this kind of charge."[54] Therefore, it was imperative that no "guilt" be pronounced without reliable evidence. Finally, Fisher explained to the Investigation Committee that no consistent definition of homosexuality existed.[55] At the end of the day, little of Fisher's perspective seemed to penetrate the thinking of the Johns Committee.

SENATOR: You all have a young University here. You have a very responsible position, and you all, your homosexuality is at a minimum. You practically don't have any at this institution at this time, but let me give you some fatherly advice.

THE WITNESS: Thank you, sir.

SENATOR: You take a hard boiled attitude against it, and keep it out of here, and build an institution that this State will be proud of, but you have got to take a hard boiled attitude. You can't take the attitude you have got.[56]

Dr. Fisher countered the senator yet another time, pointing again to "the limits within which we can be hard boiled," but her argument did not win the day.[57] The Johns Committee met at Joe's Spaghetti House in Tallahassee on 8 August to review the testimony taken at USF. In the release of its findings to the BOC, the Florida State Board of Education, and a Tampa newspaper on 24 August (while President Allen was out of town on vacation), the Johns Committee concluded that "[t]his attitude of administrators wanting what they refer to as irrefutable proof before they act to discharge an educator for homosexual conduct, is one the Committee has been confronted with over and over in its investigations. It is very possible that this attitude is responsible to a large degree for the difficulties in cleaning homosexuality out of our educational institutions. . . . It is simply a matter of the educator being unwilling to face up squarely to his duty and this situation is not unique among our educational institutions at the University of South Florida."[58]

The Importance of Public Accountability

In reading through the transcripts of the testimonies of witnesses called before the Johns Committee, one finds a common battery of tactical responses throughout the decade. Civil rights activists, USF personnel, and lesbian and gay schoolteachers resorted to evasion, denials, and obfuscation in their encounters with the committee. The transcripts reveal another point of commonality among the witnesses, one buttressed by news accounts and personal reflections of those involved in the interrogations: facing the Johns Committee was a most difficult experience. In a news column shortly after her first hearing, Ruth Perry described the event as "a day I will never forget. The initial atmosphere surrounding the hearing could almost be felt physically."[59] Four decades after his confrontation with the Johns Committee, a university professor explained, "It was a fearful time. Every waking moment—fear. . . . At times, I felt like I was in a chapter of a Dostoevsky novel."[60] Even though witnesses often relied on the same types of responses in their individual interrogations and the level of intimidation was intense for all, the absence of public accountability created a significantly different atmosphere for lesbian and gay schoolteachers in comparison to the other groups.

As noted, hearings for civil rights activists and USF personnel were held in the open and the press covered the proceedings; the Johns Committee inter-rogated lesbian and gay teachers behind closed doors and used the exposure of public hearings as a threat to pry information from witnesses. Civil rights activists appeared before the committee with their attorneys, and USF per-sonnel had access to legal counsel; schoolteachers almost always faced the Johns Committee alone. Civil rights activists and USF personnel met with a panel of Investigation Committee members. By the time the committee turned its attention to lesbian and gay teachers, new operating procedures allowed it to meet with a quorum of one. Generally, Chief Investigator Strick-land questioned schoolteachers, sometimes in the presence of Charley Johns, a county superintendent of public instruction, or law enforcement officers. Although the Johns Committee violated the Fifth and Sixth Amendments with abandon, these structural differences—secret interrogations, no access to counsel—allowed for more abuses in the cases of the schoolteachers.

In addition, organizational networks led to a wider range of appeal for civil rights activists and USF witnesses. The NAACP, AAUP, and AAUW played critical roles in the defense of witnesses they supported. The NAACP utilized the courts of law and USF witnesses called upon professional standards in waging counterattacks against the Johns Committee. Lesbian and gay teach-ers had no such means of support; it would be 2003, in fact, before the U.S. Supreme Court struck down consensual sodomy laws as unconstitutional, establishing the legal right to be queer.[61] Consequently, civil rights activists and USF witnesses employed a rhetorical device from time to time that is virtually absent from the schoolteachers' testimonies: an impassioned argu-ment for one's rights and freedoms on the basis of principle.

In the Hearts of Thousands You Hold a Deep Place

The organizational mechanism of the NAACP in Florida geared up to protect its members simultaneously with the establishment of the Johns Committee.[62] By 1957 NAACP attorneys throughout the South were much practiced in the defense of clients who challenged racist actions of oppressive state govern-ments. When Miami activists stood their ground against the Investigation Committee one year later, they drew it into a legal quagmire that would drain resources until a Supreme Court decision brought the matter to a close in 1963. Bogged down with court cases, the Johns Committee had to cancel NAACP hearings in 1958, declaring itself "hamstrung" by the civil rights organization. With the bulk of its operation against the NAACP grinding to a halt, Hawes reported that the investigation into a link between the NAACP and the Communist Party would, nevertheless, continue; he found it "significant that the NAACP should choose to resort to identical tactics used by the Communist Party to fight these hearings. They have but one aim—and that is to kill off the committee."[63] The Johns Committee continued this theme when called to account for its activities before the 1959 legislature—appearing yet again with a sorry record of achievement. "Since February 1958, the Committee has been subjected to numerous sustained legal assaults designed to destroy the Committee or to obstruct and frustrate the Committee's investigations until it expired."[64] Dramatic rhetoric notwithstanding, civil rights activists were simply demanding that their constitutional rights be honored. Reverend Gibson explained, "We cannot afford to let the constitutional right [to freedom of association] that belongs to us become a privilege of Mr. Hawes and his committee."[65]

Repeatedly NAACP witnesses justified their actions by appealing to principle. Clearly, this firm belief sustained many through their difficult ordeal. In her 9 March 1957 column, "Along Freedom's Road," Ruth Perry reflected, "It is not an easy thing to appear in public and defend one's beliefs in an atmosphere of tenseness and strain. Even though I am convinced that my feelings and motives are right and that the cause I am fighting for is a just and right cause, it still was not easy to do."[66] One year later, following Representative Herrell's vicious attack and the contempt citations, Perry wrote, "Those of us who made our stand the way we did, did so on principle. There is nothing wrong with the NAACP, nothing subversive about it, nor do any of us have anything to hide from anyone. . . . There comes a time in each of our lives when we must make a stand for what we believe. If we don't, then what we are fighting for becomes a mockery. All of us who did what we did, acted in this way because of our belief in the principles and guarantees set forth in the Constitution of the United States. If these things are not valid, then the promise of America and the democratic way of life is an empty dream. All of us have faith that our stand will be justified."[67]

A sense of unity also helped to brace civil rights activists during their confrontations with the Investigation Committee. In an early description of what it was like to testify before the Johns Committee, Perry addressed the ordeal of waiting with other witnesses, not knowing how the day would unfold, but wrote of it as "a heart-warming experience to realize the courage and determination of the people sitting in the room, and waiting with you."[68] She explicitly noted that "oneness of purpose" made it possible to manage the stress of the situation, and even described her first round with the Johns

Committee as a "spiritual" experience. "It was obvious that all of us there in the NAACP were bound together by a feeling of brotherhood and human sympathy. For this reason, I am more than ever strongly convinced that the aims and purposes of the NAACP will be attained soon."[69] This perspective did not dim over time or with increasingly hostile attacks. Perry described the infamous 1958 hearings as "the hardest day I ever lived through" and "one of the most wonderful days I ever experienced"—the latter perspective due to Reverend Gibson's courageous act of walking out on the committee and the support of many friends.[70]

A sense of being a part of something bigger than oneself runs through Perry's writings. Among her papers is a Certificate of Appreciation awarded by the Florida NAACP in October 1958 for her efforts to protect constitutional rights.[71] Earlier that year she had reminded readers of the legacy of the NAACP, ending one column by quoting a stanza of James Weldon Johnson's "Lift Every Voice." She exhorted her readers not to yield to despair: "The road to freedom is not soft and easy, and principles and aims of eternal values are not gained by weakness and apathy. The NAACP is an organization . . . made up of men and women determined to fight for their freedom. We will not be deterred."[72]

Civil rights activists who stood up to the Johns Committee shared the knowledge that their cause was just, and they benefited from the organizational structure and legal counsel of the NAACP. They utilized the court system, knowing full well that they would lose in most courts. A law professor from FAMU attending Reverend Gibson's contempt trial in Tallahassee in 1960 noted this point, adding: "It amazes me that we can keep on fighting. . . . But the spirit of freedom burns brightly and strongly now."[73]

Indeed, grassroots pressure was converging with foreign policy interests by the 1960s to compel the federal government into action. Given the well-known abuses of civil rights in the United States at midcentury, it became increasingly difficult to maintain the image of democracy Americans wished to present to the world during the Cold War.[74] If activists could push court cases to the federal level, some civil rights victories might be won if for no other reason than to shore up the reputation of the nation. Legal decrees, of course, have never guaranteed that civil and human rights are honored in practice, but official recognition of rights is not insignificant. For one thing, court decisions provide a toehold for those who challenge injustice whether or not social justice was the original intent of a given action, and whether or not the far-reaching impact of a ruling is ever fully known.

Evidently Henry Fenn, dean of the Florida Law School (1948–58), did not support the stand taken by state officials who tried to ignore the Supreme Court's directive to admit an African American student to the law school; he told UF president Wayne Reitz and the members of the BOC their action was an evasion of law, violated the principles of the Association of American Law Schools, and stated that he would not tolerate it.[75] Fenn's insistence drew President Reitz and members of the BOC into an all-day meeting on 27 May 1958 to seek a compromise that would keep the dean from resigning but according to BOC member James Love, "Dean Fenn never gave an inch on anything. . . . [Fenn argued that] the law must be obeyed and respected whether we approve of it or not."[76] In a confidential memorandum to members of the BOC, Love reviewed the board's position as presented to Dean Fenn: "It was pointed out that this case was of transcending importance, bigger than Florida itself; that there was no question but that the vast majority of the citizens of Florida wanted it resisted to the uttermost in the Courts, that to do less would do U. of F. and higher education in the State great harm."[77] But Fenn would not be moved and at the end of the day members of the BOC met with Governor Collins, who called in Attorney General Richard Irvin. After the attorney general failed to convince the law school dean to cooperate in keeping African American students out of the university, Collins and Irvin decided to let the matter drop. "After reflection, the Governor and the Attorney General figured that the resignation of the Dean and possibly many of the faculty of the Law School would be the worst possible thing that could happen to the State; it would be played up all over the Nation and even to many other parts of the world. They decided that this should not happen and that Fenn must be mollified."[78] Love's memo suggests that Fenn's interest was the rule of law rather than any concern for the African American student who was seeking admission to the law school. Nevertheless the memo, now nearly half a century old, illustrates how court decisions can influence political inner workings, and it underscores the power that university educators could wield in some circumstances when they elected to stand upon principle.[79]

Keeping civil rights battles out of international news was still a matter of policy in 1963 when the Florida NAACP case reached the U.S. Supreme Court. In a 5–4 decision the Court determined that NAACP membership records were off limits to state investigators. Seven years after the Florida legislature granted broad powers of investigation to Charley Johns and his committee, the High Court gutted its raison d'être. In the end, the Johns Committee was no real match for the surging civil rights movement.

Defending Freedom and Dignity in a Climate of Raucous and Carnival Invasion

"What happens to the pursuit of truth and the advancement of learning in such an atmosphere as the heresy hunters and thought controllers have created in parts of the South can only be conjectured."[80] C. Vann Woodward's conclusion regarding "The Unreported Crisis in the Southern Colleges" in 1962 indicates that the Johns Committee's investigation of USF did not occur in a vacuum. In fact, Woodward reported that faculty dismissals and harassments along with student reprisals had reached a new high; AAUP cases involving academic freedom increased from thirty-seven in 1961 to fifty-five in 1962. Woodward attributed much of the activity to the reactionary, anti–civil rights politics of groups such as White Citizen Councils, the John Birch Society, and the Ku Klux Klan. Noting that assaults on academic freedom and due process were by no means limited to the South, Woodward outlined sixteen recent cases in southern schools, adding that extremists' attacks on historically black colleges and universities were particularly intense.[81] Woodward's analysis led him to believe that aroused public opinion was the critical element for ending the attack on academic freedom. In addition, the courts had proved some help and the organizational support of the AAUP was effective in protecting academic freedom to a certain degree.[82]

Woodward's essay probably made the rounds at USF when it was published in *Harper's Magazine* six months after the Johns Committee's investigation and just weeks after the committee released its report on the university. John Egerton, editor of the USF News Bureau, kept a copy of the article in his papers now held in the Special Collections Department, University of South Florida Tampa Library. Woodward's analysis fit the pattern of community reaction that developed in response to the USF investigation as the university, AAUP, AAUW, and media all rose in defense of the principles of academic freedom and due process. Noting that many faculty and students across the nation fought to defend academic principles during the ongoing crisis, Woodward quoted a professor from the University of Alabama who observed, "The place to fight for a principle is where it is a living issue, not where it is an accomplished fact, and still less where it has become a mere object of sanctimonious self-congratulations."[83] In 1962 that fight came to Tampa.

Margaret Fisher recalls that the existence of the Johns Committee was well known among faculty and administrative staff, many of whom had come to USF from other Florida universities when it opened in 1960. "The people I worked with most closely tended to groan, 'Well, here comes one more witch hunt.'" Once university officials became aware that the Johns Committee had begun an investigation of USF, the AAUP advised President Allen to "invite" the committee to campus. "Those who had been through similar trials elsewhere had learned that the best way to cope with ideological attacks is to strip the cloak of darkness away from the sponsors and their proceedings."[84] Fisher likened the university approach to the impending investigation to the efforts that educators make to inform accrediting agencies of the mission and purpose of an institution. That is, if Johns and his committee didn't understand the importance of academic freedom, professional ethics, and due process, USF witnesses would have to teach them.

Attorney Ed Cutler consulted with the AAUP and USF officials. When Fisher was called to testify before the committee, she put off the meeting for one hour and phoned Cutler for advice. She specifically wanted to ask about professional rules of confidentiality. Cutler suggested that Fisher put those questions before the committee—tell them about professional procedures—say you'd rather not discuss particular details concerning individuals in counsel. "And he said for everything else, obfuscate. 'Use your natural talent, obfuscate.'" As Fisher remembered her preparation for the interrogation she added, "I'd thought that Ed Cutler's scenario for the Johns Committee was highly plausible. I thought I could snow 'em."[85]

The USF investigation underscored the necessity for a set of guidelines to assist professors called before the Johns Committee. The response from the academic community regarding the Tampa investigation differed considerably from the weak reaction that had followed the homosexuality investigation four years earlier. According to UF professor William Carleton, "public opposition" to the Johns Committee was "virtually non-existent" concerning the 1958 investigation into homosexuality, although the Gainesville AAUP held a "public meeting at which a senior member of the law faculty advised faculty members of their rights."[86] Once the Johns Committee strayed beyond probes into sexuality, however, the professors circled their wagons. In November 1962 the Florida AAUP organized a committee to study faculty members' legal rights regarding legislative investigations. In July 1963 the resulting Committee on Academic Privileges and Legal Rights released a two-page publication that included six recommendations to faculty regarding individual rights and protections afforded by law.

1. The authorizing statute of the legislative committee enables individuals, if approached, to refrain from answering any questions posed by an agent of the committee.

2. One was entitled under law to decline an invitation to appear before the committee.

3. Legal counsel should be obtained before one responded to a subpoena to appear before the committee. Full judicial procedures provided a method of challenging the validity of the subpoena.

4. Those who appeared before the committee could decline to answer questions. Only under lawful procedure could the committee compel answers to questions.

5. Faculty were encouraged to contact the AAUP Committee on Academic Privileges and Legal Rights immediately at first contact with the investigative committee.

6. Faculty should cooperate with the investigative committee only when all conditions of investigation were in full accord with due process of law.[87]

By the time the AAUP published its recommendations for faculty, the Johns Committee's questioning of university personnel had come to an end, but in response to issues stirred up by the committee the BOC reasserted its authority in higher education. In a September 1962 report, the BOC noted that most of the "problems" the Johns Committee noted at USF were already under scrutiny. Should any doubt remain as to who was in charge of Florida's university system, the BOC clarified that "the Board of Control is the proper body to receive, investigate, and take action upon any and all complaints directed toward or against the institutions under its authority."[88] A special committee recommended that the BOC take aggressive action to disseminate its policy on homosexuality and communist teaching, and see that institutions follow the policy by taking immediate action whenever cases arose. It also suggested that the BOC adopt new policies to require universities to develop plans regarding approval of teaching materials and pedagogy as they relate to religious beliefs.[89]

Although the Johns Committee had ended its investigation of universities, its agenda had been absorbed by the BOC, a permanent state entity. Professors united in protest against the state's extended attack on academic freedom. A statement written by physics faculty at FSU captured the intensity of the affront leveled against institutions of higher learning in Florida: "We condemn the interference of the Legislative Investigating Committee in the academic affairs of the Universities. We are shocked by the submission by the Board of Control to the attacks of the Committee. . . . The responsibility for defense of our freedom finally devolves upon us, the faculty. We declare that we will not collaborate in the destruction of our University."[90]

State newspapers covered the controversy with slants characteristic of their own political leanings. The more liberal *St. Petersburg Times* asked, "Will the Board of Control give the faculties and the university administrations the degree of self-regulation and self-discipline to which great educational institutions are entitled? Even more pertinently, will the State Legislature respect the authority of the Board of Control, and without hindrance permit the universities to police themselves within the guidelines set forth by the Board?"[91] The *Tallahassee Democrat* presented a more conservative "Non-Academic View of Freedom": "Even if we grant that the professional academician has a right to have his judgments tested by men of equal competence, it doesn't follow that he can convert that right into a freedom to shove all sorts of opinions and whims down the throats of immature students for whom zealous teaching can become one-sided indoctrination."[92] The article then suggested sending students into classrooms with tape recorders to intimidate professors who put up a "howl" about academic freedom.[93]

By the end of the year, the BOC and faculty at the state's public universities had agreed upon a compromise "Statement of Policy on Academic Freedom and Responsibilities." Much of the original BOC rhetoric was toned down, especially in regard to curricular and pedagogical concerns that were, in the end, left to the discretion of the individual professor. But the BOC retained the admonition that universities consider "general character" and "moral conduct" in hiring faculty and admitting students. And, in particular, the BOC enjoined university administrators to "continue to guard against activities subversive to the American democratic processes and against immoral behavior, such as sex deviation."[94]

The battle over authority in the academy was being played out in a broader climate of anti-intellectualism. In Hillsborough and Pinellas counties things were particularly hot. Jane Smith, one of the parents of USF students who had enjoined the Johns Committee to investigate the institution, remained in the eye of the stormy controversy. According to notes that John Egerton took at a citizens' meeting in Plant City in December 1962, Mrs. Smith reminded the audience of Governor Bryant's position that academic freedom is not "a license." She claimed that she didn't want to tell people what to think or do, but if they wanted children to remain American and Christian they must do something. Smith suggested that citizens watch, be discerning, and pray.[95] In a thirty-page document to preserve the facts of the USF showdown as she remembered them, Smith revealed the underlying concern that fueled her assault on academic freedom: "We know that as the student goes, so goes the nation; hence, our grave concern over the teachings they receive."[96]

On 10 April 1963 the Women's Republican Club of St. Petersburg adopted a resolution in support of the Johns Committee in light of the upcoming vote in the legislature on extending the life of the committee. Club members urged their legislators to award the committee permanent status. Among the points in their resolution, the women argued that "anguished appeals to 'academic freedom' . . . seem chiefly to serve academic self-interest" and that teachers, "being on the public payroll, deserve 'academic freedom' only to the extent that they use it in the public interest as determined by the public."[97] Obviously, what these citizens meant was that academic freedom should not be maintained at all, even if they were reluctant to say so explicitly. A few days earlier, Wayne Thomas Jr., president of the Plant City Conservative Club, released a document encouraging club members to request copies of the Johns Committee report on its USF investigation. Thomas quoted Charley Johns in the one-page letter: "Our Committee is not against Academic freedom except where they teach our children atheism, softness on communism and request that our children read these obscene books that are not decent for you or me to read."[98]

Johns went on to describe "the hand writing on the wall as to what is going to happen in this country if the brain washing of our children at our colleges and universities is not stopped. . . . Khrushchev's time table is going to become a reality."[99] Thomas, for his part, reinforced the tired themes and echoed Jane Smith's call for action: "When you consider that our children some day may be exposed to some of the atheistic, immoral, gutter trash, presented under the mantle of 'education' and presented by professors who believe in neither God nor a moral code, then *someone* had better take some action."[100]

Constituents who wrote Rep. Terrell Sessums in April and May 1963 argued for and against the continuation of the Johns Committee. Those who supported the committee trampled on the First Amendment and Article VI of the U.S. Constitution (prohibiting religious tests for public service), writing that it could be a "powerful influence for good in the schools, especially in providing teachers who are *not* atheists." They relied on the committee to "protect us from the growing communist peril." One writer quoted Proverbs 17:13 in the header of the letter: "Whoso rewardeth evil for good, evil shall not depart from his house." This writer was concerned that subversive activities would increase since the United States had "emasculated" the sedition laws of the states. Another writer supporting the Johns Committee warned that the United Nations was a "trap for America" and a "[g]reen light for the

Communist & her Sattalits [*sic*]." A slightly more moderate FLIC supporter admitted, "At times perhaps we might question their methods but I *can never doubt* their *motives*."[101] Jane Smith sent Representative Sessums a copy of her report on the USF investigation. In a handwritten note that accompanied the report, she took the gloves off where academic freedom was concerned. "Do I want my sons and daughters *indoctrinated* in the belief that there exists no right or wrong, no morality or immorality, no God, that family life has failed, that pre-marital relations are good, that homo-sexuality is fine? And then told, in the name of academic freedom it's none of your business? If they (AAUP) are to have unlimited freedom, then I say the parents should have unlimited freedom, even if it means seeing the professors—flattened on the floor!"[102]

Sessums sent respectful letters of reply to his Hillsborough County constituents, explaining why he was opposed to the continuation of the Johns Committee, and he was one of fourteen representatives who voted against extension of the committee in 1963. By that point it was a bit easier for lawmakers to oppose the Investigation Committee; the U.S. Supreme Court had just ruled against it and the USF investigation had opened up a hornet's nest of media criticism.

News editors came to the defense of Florida's newest university once the Johns Committee investigation of USF became public knowledge. On 19 May 1962 the *Tampa Tribune* explained that a most basic function of the university was to examine beliefs; this highly revered practice defined the very nature of the academy and would, of course, lead to a clash of ideas. "A university is a place where truth is tested between the hammer and anvil of opposing opinions; by its nature, it generates the sparks of controversy."[103]

From his post at the USF News Bureau, Egerton maintained a running correspondence with many editors as the drama of 1962–63 unfolded. He wrote to Emmett B. Peter Jr., editor of the *Leesburg Commercial* and president of the Florida Society of Editors, that it was "heartening to see newspapers like yours, the *St. Petersburg Times, Daytona Beach Journal,* and the *Tribune* leading the fight to bring a little reason and restraint into play."[104] Peter and Mabel Chesley, associate editor of the *Daytona Beach Evening News,* each ran a series critiquing the Johns Committee. Egerton helped to get copies of Chesley's series to citizens who petitioned their legislators to vote against the committee in 1963. In his series Peter charged that "Florida's Little McCarthy Committee" had proved a "needless waste of tax monies" and "a blot on the good name of Florida because of bungling and the use of highly questionable police methods."[105] In subsequent essays Peter traced the short history of the Johns Committee; offered brief biographical details concerning Charley Johns and investigator R. J. Strickland; exposed the committee's bent toward deception, illegally obtained "confessions," invasion of privacy, entrapment, and defamation of character; and outlined details regarding the Grebstein fiasco.

The national media turned its attention to the USF investigation as well. In July 1962 Edward P. Morgan of the American Broadcasting Company described the USF experience as a "collision with . . . vigilante arrogance" in a commentary on the wave of witch hunting and censorship sweeping the country. "The disturbing fact remains that a handful of self-appointed arbiters of teaching and morals induced a willing committee of peanut politicians to barge into the field of education where it had neither authority nor competence to operate and cause consternation and untold damage."[106] Morgan also alluded to a point that local media were pressing repeatedly: the attack on the academy was sure to drive professors and students from Florida universities. According to media reports, the climate of anti-intellectualism made it increasingly difficult to hire professors who weighed the possibility of persecution, harassment, and intimidation into their job decisions. Following the AAUP censure of USF that stemmed from the Fleming case, Herb Stewart noted, "A lot of us here now never would have come if this had happened before. The difference between a good university & a not so good one is the people you don't get, and we're not getting them. You can't measure that."[107] University officials were even concerned that Florida institutions were at risk of losing accreditation and recognition in other states.[108] As concerns regarding the credibility of higher education in Florida mounted, the media played an important role in alerting citizens to what was at stake if the legislature enabled the Johns Committee to continue its reckless disregard for academic freedom.

One of the most impressive mobilizations against the Johns Committee was organized by the American Association of University Women (AAUW); they investigated the state investigators! Recalling the efforts of Tampa AAUW president Betty Hohnadel, Tampa AAUW chair of higher education Helen Paul, USF counselor Dr. Lucille Foutz, Daytona Beach journalist Mabel Chesley, state representative Beth Johnson, and others, Margaret Fisher concluded, "It was the women who really moved in on the Johns Committee."[109] The Tampa AAUW accepted Fisher into membership at its 5 June 1962 meeting, less than a week after her testimony before the Johns Committee, so there is reason to suspect that Fisher was a motivating factor in launching the AAUW counterassault.[110] The Tampa Higher Education Committee of the AAUW began a series of meetings following the release of the Johns Committee report on USF in autumn 1962. The following February local president Hohnadel reported that the Florida AAUW had formed a committee to investigate the standing of academic freedom at the universities in Florida; Foutz, who had come to USF from Gainesville, served on that committee.[111]

In November 1962 Carol Scott had written USF president John Allen on behalf of the Florida AAUW, asking how the organization could best support the university. She explained, "Through our branches about the state we reach women who would be glad to help our universities gain freedom from meddling by legislative committees."[112] Allen put Scott in contact with John Egerton. In January 1963 Scott reported to Egerton that she had submitted an article to the AAUW bulletin, alerting members statewide to the current crisis regarding academic freedom and the importance of retaining professors of the highest caliber in Florida institutions of higher learning. She encouraged each of the local branches to take up a study of the issue and lobby state legislators—as individuals and collectively, through the branches. Scott informed Egerton that the AAUW State Board had passed a motion calling for a committee to investigate the extent to which the Johns Committee had violated principles of academic freedom, that the committee keep Governor Bryant and all twenty-nine AAUW branches in Florida apprised of its findings, and that it prepare a report for the May 1963 AAUW convention.[113] On 7 February 1963 Mrs. R. George Swift, chair of the AAUW Higher Education Committee, wrote to Egerton requesting copies of Mabel Chesley's *Daytona Beach* series on the Johns Committee. She wrote that the editorials would "provide a point of beginning for a state-wide study of Johns Committee activities" and noted that the AAUW intended to send copies to all twenty-nine branches in Florida.[114] At its 4 April 1963 meeting, the Tampa branch discussed plans for publicizing the newly minted AAUW report on its investigation of the Johns Committee. On 24 April the Academic Freedom Committee of the Florida AAUW formally asked the Florida legislature to abolish the Investigation Committee because of its attack on academic freedom. Upon presentation of the AAUW report at the state convention in May, the Florida division voted to petition the Florida legislature to abolish the Johns Committee. Tampa president Hohnadel sent a copy of this motion to Rep. Terrell Sessums, adding, "Do you realize what the Johns [Committee] has done to Tampa—educationally, and economically? It will be a long time before the damage has been erased."[115]

The women of the AAUW pulled no punches in their "Study of Aspects of Academic Freedom and of Legislative Investigation of Florida Universities." The four-and-one-half-page "Report and Resolution" is a powerful, well-written document. At the outset, authors of the resolution established the legitimacy of their investigation: AAUW policy required that members represent universities that "in no case sacrifice the moral function and individual integrity of its faculty and staff to any economic, political, or doctrinal end."[116] The resolution included a working definition of academic freedom that encompassed the right of students to a dynamic intellectual climate, the right of teachers to select and present course materials in accordance with the ethics and integrity of their disciplines, the right of administrators to maintain the intellectual environment, and the right of executive boards to "*hold in trust for the public community its right to education untrammeled by political expediency, factional censorship, or doctrinal insistence.*"[117] The authors of the resolution then presented in fine detail the results of their investigation of the Johns Committee, comparing the actions of the Investigation Committee to actual authority granted it by the legislature. The AAUW charged that the Johns Committee violated the terms of its charter by suborning witnesses, editing testimony, relying on hearsay evidence, intimidating witnesses, frightening witnesses by the quasi-judicial trappings of the committee, taking secret testimony, acting in the dual capacity of prosecutor and judge, and coercing witnesses. Further, the Johns Committee had judged morals and ethics according to its own definitions, "smeared" individuals relating to charges of homosexuality, assumed the right to search for communists, reported directly to the public press rather than to the legislature, and "created a circus atmosphere inimical to the peace and dignity of the state . . . highly inimical to the dignity of the educational process."[118] The AAUW charged the Johns Committee with claiming authority over the university, making USF vulnerable to national disgrace that would threaten public faith in the institution as well as its Southern Association of Colleges and Schools (SACS) accreditation, and coercing the BOC. The AAUW acted on its findings by calling for the discontinuation of the Johns Committee and asking the legislature for a clear delimitation of the extent to which morality, ethics, and religious beliefs may be controlled by the state; a review of the methods employed by the Johns Committee; an audit of public money expended by the committee; and a consideration of the political and doctrinal motivation for investigative action. Finally, the AAUW underscored the right of an academic community to set its own standards, subject to review of the BOC and SACS.[119]

Margaret Fisher believes that many of the women who challenged the Johns Committee were driven by a well-deserved pride in their new university founded on a shared commitment to liberal arts education based on interdisciplinary principles. They maintained a positive perspective, "trumpeting the fact here that USF was a damn good university that had taken the lead in academic freedom and responsibility."[120] Fisher added that the women of the AAUW had always been "highly skilled in practical judgment and in concerted study and action," and engaged in free, open, responsible, and affirming politics.[121] Quite simply, the women of the Florida AAUW "did not expect universities to have to put up with the Charley Johns-es."[122]

In November 1962 in the wake of the Johns Committee investigation of USF, Egerton reported to his colleague, W. H. Kerns, director of information services at UF, "Uneasy peace and quiet reigns here right now. The end result is a bitter-sweet mixture of relief and demoralization. Don't know what to expect next."[123] In spite of concerted efforts of the media, AAUP, and AAUW in defense of the university, the impact of the 1962 probe was taking a toll. By February 1963 Egerton noted that as USF had identified its mission as providing an "accent on learning," the investigations deflated university morale just the way a fix scandal would at a basketball school. By the end of May it was apparent that the legislature would pass the bill to reauthorize the Johns Committee and Governor Bryant would sign it, in spite of increased public pressure to shut down the Investigation Committee.

As Edward P. Morgan noted, the media had conducted its reporting on the USF investigation ably, arousing public opinion. Even though the Johns Committee got new life, its public image was severely weakened. The newly constituted Investigation Committee acknowledged in September 1963 that it was not engaged in a popularity contest and that it would not pursue its agenda without criticism. The Johns Committee framed its mission as "of vital concern to all who share our desire that Florida be free from the unsavory influences of those 'isms' that would deprive the individual of his rights, and the responsibilities of his citizenship."[124] In a memorandum to fellow members of the 1963 Florida legislature, the Johns Committee tried to counter what it described as "the often unfair picture of the Committee's activities" with an assertion that conversations with governmental agents across the nation reinforced the notion that a definite need for the committee remained. They pledged that, as an investigative arm of the legislature, they would cooperate with law enforcement agencies but not become enforcers themselves.[125]

This, however, contradicted an argument legislators had used in support of the Investigation Committee during the spring debate. At that point the Johns Committee had argued that it was vital to state interests because it was better equipped for "catching" homosexuals in schools and colleges than regular law enforcement agencies. In response, Rep. Robert E. Knowles charged, "This is not a legislative committee any more, it's a police committee."[126] The *Tampa*

Tribune ran an editorial on 27 May 1963 taking the Johns Committee to task on this point, suggesting the committee change its name to "the Legislative Police Bureau on Homosexuality"—to better match its primary function—or, perhaps, "the Legislative Bureau for the Suppression of Sin."[127]

When John Egerton wrote Carol Scott to thank her for the AAUW's "extraordinary efforts in seeking to bring the Legislature to a realization of its responsibilities," he added, "The fact that this effort has failed does not in any sense detract from your hard work or our appreciation of it."[128] Scott responded that she did not feel as bad about the outcome as Egerton. "If the television report was correct the committee has been returned to its original investigative intent: communism and homosexuality. What we in the Academic Freedom subcommittee were working for was just that—keeping it out of literature classes and out of the investigation of religious beliefs of faculty. . . . Surely, no one was so naïve as to think the committee would be dissolved."[129]

Indeed, students' and professors' protests, the organized efforts of the AAUP and AAUW, and the pressure exerted by the media had deflated the draconian policies promoted by the Johns Committee in every area except one. In the face of the systematic purge of lesbian and gay teachers from Florida's elementary and secondary schools, colleges, and universities, the citizenry had not expressed condemnation, outrage, or protest.

Ready and Willing to Expel Teachers from the Profession

By 1959, before the vigorous involvement of the AAUP and AAUW at USF, the legal maneuvers of the NAACP had blocked the Johns Committee's advance. Or, as the committee put it in its report to the 1959 legislature, "being otherwise stayed from pursuing its other investigations" the Investigation Committee directed its attention to rooting homosexuality out of Florida schools. The report went on to describe an ineffectual personnel system that led to few prosecutions and allowed homosexual teachers to resign, maintain their credentials, and quietly move on to another school district.[130] This proclamation and the even more inflammatory 1961 report sent administrators into a tailspin and "professionally minded" educators joined the attack on teachers. Unlike other targets of the Johns Committee, gay and lesbian teachers could not depend on professional or legal organizations for support. While the NAACP orchestrated a legal defense for civil rights activists, the AAUP and AAUW designed a defense for USF professors on the basis of academic freedom, and the media kept the abuses of the Johns Committee in Tallahassee, Miami, and Tampa in the public eye, county superintendents of public instruction and officials in the Florida Department of Education (DOE) and the Florida Education Association (FEA) collaborated with the Johns Committee to purge lesbian and gay teachers from Florida schools.

School administrators throughout the state pledged support for the Johns Committee throughout its tenure. They expressed wholehearted agreement with the aims of the Investigation Committee and appreciated the "interest and concern" that drove its work.[131] Extant committee files contain letters from county superintendents that relay plans for dealing with homosexuality within the teaching ranks of their schools. Many exhibit enthusiastic support of the Johns Committee, and some adopt a more moderate, businesslike tone; none, however, challenged the position of the Investigation Committee on sexual orientation. L. J. Jenkins began his letter to Chairman Johns stating that "We in the school business are also aware of the fact that [homosexuality] is a substantial problem and a growing problem and a problem brought on by an organized and fraternal group of people." He informed the committee that educators in Lake County studied "certain traits and characteristics of these people" and coached principals in applying these newly developed skills during the hiring process to discern which applicants might be homosexual. Superintendent Jenkins noted that he would be "very happy if the Legislative Investigating Committee can furnish the school people some definite aids in getting this thing at least to where it will make it difficult for them to recruit school children into their National organization."[132]

Giving testimony before the Johns Committee, the director of personnel in Broward County wondered if the state could establish some sort of training program to instruct school officials in the finer points of conducting an investigation of teachers, or barring that, perhaps supply "some kind of investigative team" that beleaguered districts could call upon as needed. His office already had adopted the practice of taking "a longer look" at male applicants of "marriageable age" who were single.[133]

Amos Godby attributed Leon County's "fortunate" situation—not one "case" of homosexuality in the past decade—to school officials' vigilance. Principals were ever on the alert for overt evidence, gossip, or rumors; if any signs of homosexuality surfaced, the principal would make a report to the county superintendent, assess the validity of the claims, and prepare a document of pertinent facts. The county superintendent, meanwhile, would inform the school board and the school's attorney. If the charges seemed strong enough to go forward, the principal and superintendent would interview the "suspect" teacher. If the teacher refused to cooperate, the administrators would invite the assistance of the Leon County sheriff in conducting a "quiet" investigation. If substantial "evidence" was found, the case would go to the state superintendent of public instruction and the teacher would be fired, or, if tenured, asked to resign. If the teacher denied the charges or refused to resign, formal charges would be set in motion as provided by the Florida School Code.[134]

State-level education officials aligned the bureaucratic machinery under their command with the Johns Committee's operation. Correspondence from the director of the Division of Teacher Education to Strickland applauded the "excellent cooperation" and "fine relationship which has been established between the committee and the State Department of Education."[135] It appears as if county and state school officials did not hesitate to bend the law in their pursuit of homosexual teachers. A DOE memorandum dated 12 September 1961 discussed the means by which the results of a polygraph test could be transferred from a county superintendent's office to the DOE so that a teacher's certificate could be revoked. The teacher had been found not guilty on homosexual charges in a court of law but then took a polygraph test and supposedly admitted engaging in "homosexual practices." The county superintendent was "most anxious" to send the polygraph results to the DOE but the authority by which he received the test results did not allow for transfer of the information. The personnel director for the county suggested the DOE might issue a subpoena for the test results.[136] By the end of 1962 J. T. Kelley, director of the Division of Teacher Education, estimated that the process for revoking teachers' certificates cost about $400 per case; expecting as many as fifty cases per year, he recommended that state superintendent of public instruction Thomas Bailey ask for an increase of $25,000 in the 1963 budget.[137]

The FEA joined the Johns Committee in the removal of gay and lesbian teachers, rationalizing its action as fulfilling the responsibility to "protect the profession by removing from our ranks those teachers who are adjudged undesirable."[138] In a January 1959 meeting, members of the FEA Personnel Problems Committee (PPC) determined that teachers should be accorded the same responsibilities for identifying undesirable members as other professionals. Months before the Johns Committee drew attention to its homosexual purge in the Florida legislature, the PPC recommended that, although the BOE would retain the right to revoke teaching certificates, the FEA should initiate investigations and propose recommendations regarding disciplinary measures against teachers in ethics and morals cases. To its credit, the FEA called for due process measures, including the right to a public hearing, recourse to the BOE, and the possibility of court review.[139] The FEA lobbied the Florida legislature to pass Senate Bill 237, which would allow the teacher organization to investigate teachers' morality on behalf of the BOE. One county superintendent wrote to Jack Stevens, assistant executive secretary of the FEA, opposing the measure. Superintendent W. T. McFatter emphasized that he was in agreement with the stated objectives of the bill; his objections related only to the procedures outlined in the proposed law. Nevertheless, the superintendent argued that the implications of the bill were "so far reaching as to convince me that proper study was not given to it and that the membership of FEA does not understand its full potential application."[140] In his 6 May reply, Stevens thanked McFatter for his observations and explained that SB 237 was "FEA's proposal to begin in a modest way to police its own ranks."[141] He noted that the FEA had been studying ways to give teachers more control in the profession for the past four years and emphasized that controlling who is admitted and who remains in the ranks is a central marker for what counts as a profession. Stevens added that he thought the majority of FEA members would support action that would "more firmly establish teaching as a profession."[142] When the bill went before the Florida House later that month, it attracted significant opposition. Stevens later praised Representatives Chappell and O'Neill for working with the FEA to ensure the bill's passage.[143]

The Steering Committee of the PPC met with FEA executive secretary Ed Henderson, assistant attorney general Ralph Odum, and DOE administrators J. T. Kelley and Thomas N. Morgan in January 1960 to iron out policy regarding teacher investigations. In accordance with Section 229.08(16) of the Florida statutes (resulting from the passage of SB 237) the committee (and later, the board of directors) adopted the following procedure: After an offense was reported to the BOE or state superintendent, the superintendent could choose to forward the case to the FEA. If a preliminary investigation warranted, a three-person committee would continue the investigation and present its findings to a hearing officer who had been appointed by the BOE. The hearing officer would hold a formal hearing according to law and report to the BOE. At that point the BOE would determine whether to revoke the teacher's certificate or seal the person's file.[144] Revisions to Section 231.28 broadened the authority of the BOE in revoking certificates, both in terms of what it deemed objectionable offenses (the vague phrase "grossly unethical" was covered by the statute) and regarding sufficient evidence for action. The list of acceptable evidence expanded to include police records, one's admission of guilt, and voluntary surrender of a certificate.[145]

FEA officials explained the purpose of the organization's investigative role differently at times. In a 1960 report published in *Florida Education* and read, presumably, by the FEA rank and file, PPC chair Hugh B. Ingram Jr. noted that the primary responsibility of the teacher investigation committee would be to protect the rights of all teachers. At an August board of directors meeting, however, executive secretary Henderson framed the development as part of a process to secure legal status for the profession. He observed that Florida and California were leading the nation in strengthening the legal authority of educators by using teachers as legal experts in dismissal cases against other teachers. Courts recognized members of the California Teachers Association who served on teacher dismissal cases as expert witnesses in that state, something Henderson pushed the Johns Committee to consider for Florida.[146] It appears that educational leaders used gay and lesbian teachers as fodder in their quest for professional respect since California and Florida also led the nation in purging homosexuals from the ranks of teachers.[147]

Apparently the FEA's desire to police its own ranks stirred up some concern among teachers. Minutes from a November 1961 PPC meeting included a report on the "homosexual cases." The committee was concerned that teachers be "fully aware" of the steps the FEA was taking to "protect the rights of teachers" and some time was spent discussing teachers' fears. The notes are cryptic on this point, but the committee passed a motion acknowledging "anxiety on the part of teachers and other instructional personnel is a very definite problem," and it requested that the board of directors take up the issue.[148] It is important to keep these concerns for teachers' welfare in clear perspective; alleviating fears and requiring due process in investigations did not supersede the FEA's commitment to purging gay men and lesbians from the teaching profession. When a member of the FEA Board of Directors replied to the Investigation Committee's request for assistance in removing homosexuals from state agencies, he stated that "every legal and ethical method should be used to seek out such people," adding that the FEA "is interested in doing everything possible to eradicate such undesirable activities in relation to school or other type of work."[149] In Henderson's response to a principal's concern that teachers be protected from unjust accusations, he admitted that there was no way to guarantee such protection; but from Henderson's perspective, "innocent people are seldom involved in scandal or unjust accusations."[150] Evidently, the executive secretary of the FEA was willing to link association with a "known degenerate" to one's own status.

The FEA had established the PPC in 1956, the same year that the Florida legislature voted the Johns Committee into existence. In 1963 the FEA changed the name of the PPC to the Professional Rights and Responsibilities Committee. The shift from a focus on "problems" to "rights and responsibilities" resulted in the use of language similar to that adopted by the BOC when it issued personnel policy statements in the wake of the USF investigation. Although the set of objectives the Professional Rights and Responsibilities Committee identified included the defense of teachers against unjust attacks, the promotion of fair dismissal laws, and a pledge to advance teachers' civil and academic rights, the committee also proclaimed that it would investigate controversies involving teachers "fearlessly" and "expose subversive teaching and teachers whose actions are found to be inimical to the best interests of our state and country."[151]

There was little doubt how the Professional Rights and Responsibilities Committee would deal with gay and lesbian teachers. In a March 1962 letter FEA executive secretary Henderson informed R. J. Strickland that the policy of the association was "to urge the immediate elimination of any individuals found guilty of homosexual tendencies."[152] Prior to 1959 the FEA had no legal standing to investigate teachers' sexuality; at that time, Henderson explained, "Our work had to be done very quietly in extreme confidence in calling occasional cases to the attention of local school boards and supporting them in their investigations."[153] Once the legislature empowered the FEA to investigate teachers, Henderson claimed, certificate revocations proceeded without difficulty. Henderson added a caveat regarding the importance of protecting teachers from false accusations and, as usual, amended a statement that "laws must also provide opportunity for protecting the children from the influence of those who are moral deviates."[154]

When the Johns Committee summoned Henderson to report on the FEA's stance toward homosexuality, he clarified that the organization was eager to participate in the process of "ferret[ing] out these people," and that teachers were cooperating in the investigations of their colleagues. "[Teachers] are as interested as anyone else in cleaning this situation out. We have had no difficulty in having anyone hold back and not want to testify."[155] When asked whether teachers under interrogation ought to be able to take the Fifth Amendment, Henderson stated, "I don't believe in the Fifth Amendment. . . . It seems to me that the individual's refusal to answer a direct question by an authorized agency of the state or the county would in itself seem to carry with it the admission of guilt."[156] When FEA vice president Darden testified, he explained why the committee organized to investigate revocation cases was sailing through its work. The professional autonomy that allowed for the policing of one's ranks did not require the same level of proof normally expected in a legal investigation; the FEA, a professional organization doing grunt work for the DOE, only needed to establish a preponderance of evidence beyond reasonable doubt to send cases forward. From Darden's perspective, addressing the problem of sexual deviants in a "competent" manner would secure the status the profession of teaching deserved.[157] The FEA, in point of fact, was willing to trade information on all teachers in its grab for status. In May Henderson informed Charley Johns that the FEA supported legislation that would require all public employees in Florida to be fingerprinted and he offered to speak in favor of the legislation.[158]

When the FEA reviewed the work of the PPC in 1963, it acknowledged a significant "adjustment in the image of the professional" teacher since the birth of the committee and attributed that development to the vision of its first chair, Leo Cahill. Cahill wanted educators to accrue some of the professional responsibilities afforded attorneys, and he thought the public would view teachers policing the ranks of teachers "as behavior becoming a mature and responsible profession."[159] In April 1964 Robert B. Turner Jr., chair of the Professional Rights and Responsibilities Committee, confirmed that the committee's investigative activity during the past six years had bolstered the image of teachers' professional status. Turner then tied this development to hopes for financial gain. "Never before have Florida educators so visibly and forcefully affirmed their dedication to public service. . . . The public heartily approves of this bargain. In return for the authority to establish, maintain and control the standards of the profession and those who practice, we are offering an unmistakable commitment to public service. As with other professions which have negotiated a similar bargain, the economic status of our profession will also improve."[160] In short, the Johns Committee's heyday coincided with the FEA's pursuit of professional status. In that setting the teacher organization considered gay and lesbian colleagues too much political baggage, or perhaps saw them as dispensable offerings too good to pass up. In any case, the FEA sacrificed the most vulnerable of teachers on the altar of professionalism.

Evidence of school or other government officials, citizens, or organizations who defended gay and lesbian teachers during the homosexual purge is slim. In a few instances a superintendent might have defended a particular teacher as "not guilty," but the dominant homophobic narrative of the Johns Committee went, for the most part, without challenge. In one interview a teacher explained that her superintendent believed her to be "innocent" of sexual deviation but added that, if he found otherwise, "I would be fired within twenty-four hours."[161] In another case a Mississippi official reported to Investigator Strickland that a superintendent in Vicksburg during the tenure of two women "under suspicion" found the two teachers "beyond reproach. . . . He had never heard of either being involved in any immoral activities. . . . If they were, he would have known it."[162] E. D. Manning Jr., superintendent of public instruction in Alachua County, raised the concern that superintendents were expected to "pre-judge" teachers charged with homosexuality and recommend revocation of the certificate "even before guilt has been established"; he urged lawmakers to clarify this cart-before-the-horse procedure. Beyond that, however, Superintendent Manning was "happy to cooperate" with the Johns Committee in dealing with the "problem" of homosexuals.[163]

In October 1960 Strickland investigated five St. Petersburg teachers—four white women and one African American man; eventually the BOE revoked these teachers' certificates on the grounds that the teachers were homosexuals. Three of these teachers took the unusual step of challenging the Johns Committee in court in a case that would have significant ramifications on the teacher purge (discussed in chapter 4). Documents regarding the case suggest some level of local support for these teachers, who appealed to their local Classroom Teachers Association for help. In December, Pinellas County superintendent Floyd Christian urged the DOE to conduct the hearings that had been promised "at an early date" as soon as possible. Superintendent Christian was finding it "difficult to keep down the rumors" and he was concerned about the effect the investigation and its aftermath was having on other teachers "fearful of this Legislative Investigation Committee."[164] One month later Christian wrote to the secretary of the NEA's Commission for the Defense of Democracy through Education, who had apparently inquired into the St. Petersburg investigation. Christian outlined the steps that had been taken, emphasizing his legal responsibility and "a degree of compassion" for those snared in the teacher purge. Yet he made it clear that the suspended teachers would be returned to their classrooms only if they were found "innocent of misconduct"—that is, not homosexual. Superintendent Christian seemed surprised that his actions had drawn criticism.[165]

In a DOE memorandum dated 24 March 1961, J. T. Kelley informed state superintendent of public instruction Thomas Bailey that Christian had taken some heat from friends of the dismissed St. Petersburg teachers and the NEA. In Kelley's opinion the criticism would have dissipated had school officials been allowed to discuss the details of the case publicly, but he counseled that as long as the certificates were revoked the "school and community problem will be settled."[166] Other evidence points to political pressure exerted on behalf of the St. Petersburg teachers, one of whom was the daughter of a staff member in Christian's office. Investigator Strickland implied as much in a March 1961 memorandum to Johns Committee chair William O'Neill. Strickland took this opportunity to complain that the DOE had been slow to act on evidence he had submitted for certificate revocations, noting that some cases were more than a year old.[167] Kelley repeated this concern a year and a half later in internal DOE correspondence. In November 1962 Kelley fretted over the fact that the BOE had been slow to revoke certificates in cases where teachers obtained legal representation and had proved at times "quite uncooperative" in acting on the state superintendent's recommendations.[168]

One might dismiss these small acts of support for targeted teachers as commitment to the principle of due process or, as some suggested, ignorance that the cases involved charges regarding teachers' sexuality. But that was not the case in the most inspiring act of community support for teachers who ran up against the Johns Committee that I have found. In 1964 African American citizens of Bay County challenged the state to restore the credentials of an African American teacher whose homosexuality had led to dismissal in 1962. In September 1963 an attorney for the teacher asked for reinstatement on the grounds that a psychiatrist had pronounced the teacher "rehabilitated." There is no evidence that the BOE reversed its position and, in fact, Kelley doubted that the citizens knew that the teacher had been dismissed because of his sexuality.[169] That was a naïve perspective. In the citizens' letter sent to Governor Bryant in his role as chair of the BOE, ninety-five people based their argument on the fact that the teacher who had been dismissed was an excellent teacher whose contributions to the community were significant. The citizens stated, "If we had a dozen persons with the love and interest of our people as [this teacher] has—this would be a community second to none."[170] The group referenced the psychiatrist's recommendation that the teacher could work "without any harm or molesting of any kind" and argued that the teacher "knows the difference between what's right and what's wrong."[171] Clearly, the citizens were willing to put aside the issue of the teachers' sexuality in the interest of the man's welfare and an even higher priority—the education of their children. "The man has to make a living and teaching is the only thing he's been trained to do. . . . We are asking you prayerfully and religiously to please for the sake of our people to give Mr. [Teacher] another chance."[172] A handwritten note at the top of a second letter of support, this one with seventy-three signatures, underscored the point: "Please sign your name. We want Mr. [Teacher] back to work with music in our school."[173]

In a survey of the three most prominent gay and lesbian publications from 1956 to 1965, only *One* gave much attention to the Johns Committee. The *Mattachine Review* mentioned the University of Florida crackdown in a short piece that focused more on a similar undercover operation at the University of Michigan that led to thirty-four arrests on charges relating to homosexuality. The *Review* reprinted, without additional comment, an editorial that appeared in the *Michigan Daily*. The author of the editorial noted the issue of entrapment but focused more on why the arrests were a faulty approach to "the psychological problem of the homosexual."[174] The author of the original piece condemned laws that branded homosexuals as criminals, alleging that they were instead people "with serious psychological difficulties."[175]

Hal Call's 1964 "Open Letter to the 'Johns Committee'" was an important exception to the almost complete silence that characterized the *Mattachine Review*'s coverage of the Investigation Committee for nearly a decade. But even Call's otherwise painstaking critique stopped short of championing the right of lesbians and gay men to teach in public schools. Instead, his treatment of the teacher purge first underscored the fact that the dismissed teachers represented only 137 out of 40,000 teachers, and then charged that the Johns Committee did not publicize how many of those who lost their credentials on morals charges did so, in fact, due to homosexual acts. By highlighting the small percentage of teachers caught in the investigation and suggesting that even some of these were not actually gay or lesbian, Call refused to take up discussion of what the public should do with the very real existence of gay and lesbian schoolteachers.[176]

The Ladder made no mention whatsoever regarding the Johns Committee, although it did include a news brief about three FSU professors who had been arrested in an undercover homosexual investigation.[177] The first mention of the Johns Committee that appeared in the pages of *One* came through a letter to the editor in 1959. In a brief rundown of the key facts concerning the University of Florida investigation, the writer—"Socrates" from Gainesville—remarked, "Students were the only group that rose to the situation in a commendable and civilized manner."[178] *One* reported on the Johns Committee a dozen more times in the next five years, generally offering brief reports on developments such as the 1959 and 1961 legislative reports, changes in legal statutes, the *Neal v. Bryant* court challenge, and the 1963 legislative session. Letters to the editor continued. Writers called for legal protection against employment discrimination for homosexuals, a vacation boycott of Florida, likened the Johns Committee to Castro's style of communism, and referred to Florida as a police state.[179] A very short report, "No Guts in Florida?" highlighted the special attack on schoolteachers and charged the Johns Committee with flagrant violation of the U.S. Constitution. The column ended with a challenge to stand up and fight. *One*'s coverage of the release of "Homosexuality and Citizenship in Florida" included a brief

review of the purple pamphlet and the furor it had caused as well as statements attributed to politicians and newspaper writers around the state, and
turned the Johns Committee's public relations nightmare into a membership plea. "After watching the Florida situation since 1955 we at ONE begin
to believe that the whole mess there may continue for a long time if the only
weapons used against the Committee are words. . . . If the homosexuals in
Florida had given $1.00 each to ONE, rather than the thousands of dollars
they have given to lawyers and psychiatrists and blackmailers, how much
different things would be today."[180] From the broader perspective afforded the
historian, words of support for Florida's gay and lesbian schoolteachers were,
in fact, rare. But the writer at One was absolutely correct about the critical
importance of solidarity. No social movement could advance without it.

Conclusion

> I am confident, too, that the members of the committee will
> recognize their responsibility to all the people of Florida and not
> abuse the broad powers granted them.[181]
> —Governor LeRoy Collins, August 1956

> Prejudice and intolerance are peculiar things. They are like a mist
> or heavy fog that can surround an area, or penetrate the minds of
> people, and cloud over their reason and common sense. And like
> an evil cloud, prejudice does not stop in one area, but continues to
> infect other places as well. . . . Tragedy could be in the making if all
> of us are not watchful and alert.[182]
> —Ruth Perry, March 1957

Governor LeRoy Collins did not sign the bill that brought the Florida Legislative Investigation Committee to life in 1956. Without his veto, however,
the measure became law and the moderate governor, apparently, hoped for
the best. Civil rights activist Ruth Perry, assessing the political terrain from
a different standpoint than the governor, knew that broad powers unleashed
in a climate of prejudice and intolerance would, indeed, result in tragic consequences. The history of the Johns Committee validated her perspective. As
the committee probed into the work and lives of civil rights activists, then
lesbian and gay schoolteachers, and finally, USF professors, administrators,
and students, the fate of each depended on community vigilance. Lacking a
viable legal standing in the courts, without a supportive network to match
the strength of the NAACP, AAUP, or AAUW, and with no assistance from
the mainstream press, schoolteachers stood virtually alone against the Johns
Committee.[183] To be sure, there were some objections to the homosexual

purge, particularly at the university level. College students parodied the Johns Committee's pursuit of "deviant" sexuality through protest and performance, and UF yearbook editors included a dedication in 1959 to "those many students who for some reason leave the University of Florida, never to return. . . . The many tragedies at the University this year will never be forgotten or fully understood."[184] Some administrators at USF tried to evade, or at least complicate, the Investigation Committee's questions on sexuality. Nonetheless Dan Bertwell concludes that USF administrators "worked with the committee to expunge suspected homosexuals whenever possible" and Professor William Carleton recalled that public opposition to the UF investigation was "virtually non-existent."[185] Gay and lesbian educators' encounters with the legislative committee—while similar in some respects to those of civil rights activists and USF personnel targeted for political or academic reasons—differed significantly in the end.

Clearly, colliding with the Johns Committee was a difficult experience for all. The committee wantonly violated due process in its dealings with all types of witnesses. As a matter of course it relied on intimidation and hearsay during interrogations. Invasion of privacy was a central feature of the investigations as the Johns Committee and its agents stormed into the domains of private association, classrooms, and homes. Margaret Fisher remembered, "If there is anything about the Johns Committee, it was not artful. . . . [It was] acting out the Wyatt Earp or Eliot Ness, the Hollywood version of evil doing, and way off course so they rarely got any useful information. Hurt a lot of people who had done nothing except maybe to socially offend some people. . . . It was a good example of flagrant error in public life."[186]

The people caught up in this Cold War nightmare found similar ways to cope; the collective body of testimonies is a record of evasion, denials, and obfuscation. The courts, professional authority, and to some degree the public exonerated civil rights activists and USF personnel who employed these tactics, even as the Johns Committee was falling into disgrace. Vindication for lesbian and gay schoolteachers, however, awaited another time.

In the final analysis the NAACP disabled the Johns Committee with its Supreme Court victory in *Gibson v. Florida Legislative Investigation Committee*. Civil rights activists were riding the crest of their movement; the injustices meted out by the Johns Committee only fueled their fortitude. Ruth Perry explained, "The conviction that remains with me from that difficult experience is that we will continue our fight for first class citizenship with greater determination and courage than ever before."[187] And although the Johns Committee hammered USF, the young university was resilient. This was familiar terrain for professors who rallied to hold their own in battles over academic freedom. As it turned out, the USF investigation marked a critical turning point in the life of the Investigation Committee. As public criticism mounted, the Johns Committee became an embarrassing liability for Florida. Even schoolteachers won a technical victory over the Johns Committee with a 1962 Florida Supreme Court decision in which license revocations for three educators were reversed because the state had not followed its own legal procedures. This was, however, merely a reprieve while government officials sorted out bureaucratic details. The Florida teacher purge continued for three more years.

Differences in context explain why lesbian and gay schoolteachers, USF personnel, and civil rights activists countered the Johns Committee attack with varying degrees of success. In the context of the interrogations, the advantage of legal counsel and open hearings was significant. Fisher articulated the well-known modus operandi of the Johns Committee. It was "a free-wheeling search for likely offenders (to be heard in secret with no access to counsel and no appeal to a court of law) who can be induced to testify to misdoing by other[s]. . . . Such flagrant disregard of standard safeguards for participants in adversary proceedings amounted to blackmail, an offense against academic as well as constitutional standards on the principles of common law."[188]

NAACP members challenged the Johns Committee in the courts of law, refusing to allow the committee to disregard the standard safeguards that Fisher outlined. Taking the Investigation Committee to court was not a realistic option for USF from a political perspective as it would pit one arm of the state against another, but the university could demand open campus proceedings in accordance with academic standards. The university, in fact, offered the committee its facilities and services, and even provided the opportunity for volunteers to testify at the inquiry. This forced the Johns Committee "at least to make a show of following due process in its proceedings as well as examining some presuppositions and testing some of its findings for truth value."[189] Schoolteachers hauled before the Johns Committee alone, without counsel or time to think through a testimony strategy, could not demand an open hearing, either in court or within the halls of the academy. Public knowledge of their personal lives would have led to their certain dismissal from teaching and exposed them to physical danger. Had they insisted upon the right to a trial, legal statutes were not in their favor. The teacher would have faced the risk of prosecution for violating sodomy laws. Even the American Civil Liberties Union did not consider laws against homosexual activities violation of civil liberties until 1964, although it did oppose government sanctions based on one's sex identity status rather than overt acts, and it did claim to protect the right to due process for persons charged with homosexual acts. The ACLU lost its first challenge to employment discrimination based on sexual orientation in January 1964. In that case assistant U.S. attorney Gill Zimmerman argued that homosexuality was "so patently immoral" that people refused to work with homosexuals, causing a decrease in workplace efficiency.[190] The point is, while cultural resistance and unlawful arrests greeted civil rights activists at every turn, de jure segregation *had* been overturned and the First and Fourteenth Amendments *did* apply to their case. No laws existed to protect gay and lesbian citizens and, since the end of World War II, federal, state, and local governments had stepped up antigay harassment and prosecution. There was no legal recourse for lesbian and gay schoolteachers, and the Johns Committee knew it.

The schoolteacher purge occurred during the most virulent period of the twentieth century for lesbians and gay men. Postwar liberals such as Arthur Schlesinger Jr. began to link homosexuality with communism, a connection soon solidified by Republicans in the U.S. Senate hoping to discredit the Truman administration on national security issues. Robert J. Corber argues it would prove "difficult to exaggerate the significance" of the 1950 Senate Appropriations Committee investigation into same-sex behavior.[191] The federal government's purge of homosexual employees rested on the claim that gay men and lesbians could pass as heterosexuals and infiltrate government offices. But this contradicted the popular notion that homosexuals could be identified by stereotypical behavior and, according to Corber, "encouraged the medicalization of the juridical discourse on sex."[192] That is, stretching the medical definition of homosexuality to encompass emotional instability would provide justification for employment discrimination even if gay men and lesbians did not look or act like queers.[193] Corber observes, in the "unprecedented social and sexual upheaval" of the postwar years, the nexus drawn between homosexuality and communism not only allowed the government to trap people on the basis of behavior or politics, but it also helped to contain the sexuality of queers and straights alike.[194] Given this climate, it was unlikely that anyone would speak publicly in support of lesbian and gay teachers. Among those who challenged the Johns Committee's abuse of civil rights activists and USF professors, many would, like Carol Scott of the AAUW, be careful to separate their concerns from the committee's assault on homosexuals. The sense of outrage emanating from the small gay press in Los Angeles notwithstanding, the Johns Committee's campaign against homosexuals remained unchecked.

Gay men and lesbians were, collectively, just beginning to recognize and protest their minority status in the 1950s. Historian John D'Emilio explained why the homophile movement emerged when it did in his seminal work, *Sexual Politics, Sexual Communities: The Making of a Homosexual Minority in the United States, 1940–1970.* The book has become a classic in social-constructionist analysis. D'Emilio described the postwar period as a decisive phase "of a much longer historical process through which a group of men and women came into existence as a self-conscious, cohesive minority."[195] Embryonic organizations adopted an assimilationist strategy to claim individual civil rights. By 1955 both the Mattachine Society and the Daughters of Bilitis were headquartered in San Francisco; *One* was based in Los Angeles. These early activists were trying to establish a liberal framework for change as they campaigned for legal protections afforded other citizens and sought positive recognition by professional authorities. During the tenure of the Johns Committee, however, these gains were not yet in sight and, in spite of the work to create what Nan Boyd aptly termed "the necessary fiction of national community," California was a long way from Florida.[196] Consequently, the Florida schoolteachers forced to discuss intimate details concerning their sexuality with agents of the Johns Committee had little claim to a "oneness of purpose" such as that which sustained other witnesses. They did not carry the confidence of civil rights activists or professors who knew they had nothing to hide. Except for the occasional testimony in which a witness might defend lesbian or gay colleagues as "very respectable, wonderful teachers," the silence surrounding these targets of the Johns Committee was deafening.[197]

It is likely that schoolteachers and the homophile organizations maintained a distance from each other on mutual, if unspoken, terms. As middle-class professionals and employees of the state, most gay and lesbian teachers kept their sexuality hidden and avoided any public association with overt homosexuals. Calling on the homophile organizations for assistance would only provide the Johns Committee with more "evidence" to revoke teachers' credentials. And homophile organizations that made a practice of regulating members' behavior in order to project only "positive" images would not welcome the notoriety that would accompany a defense of the Florida teachers.[198] Both parties knew that as long as the political-economic system remained closed to gay men and lesbians it would be futile for gay rights groups to protest job discrimination against teachers. Two decades after the Johns Committee locked up its files, Supreme Court Justice William Brennan surveyed a political landscape that had changed little: "Because of the immediate and severe opprobrium often manifested against homosexuals once so identified publicly, members of this group are particularly power-less to pursue their rights openly in the political arena."[199]

The tragedy that a generation of schoolteachers associates with the Johns Committee antedated the defining event of the gay rights movement by a decade. Social movements require elements that did not yet exist for gay men and lesbians: "a mass base of individuals, groups, and organizations linked by social interaction" and "a shared collective identity."[200] Or, as D'Emilio put it, "Activists had not only to mobilize a constituency; first they had to create one."[201] Nevertheless, in the darkest days of state oppression against gay men and lesbians, it was important to move whatever cultural or politi-cal barriers might be budged, and the homophile organizations put their shoulder to the task where they could. The social stigma associated with homosexuality would have to be loosened before the alliances critical to a social movement could be formed.[202] Although a sense of desperation pushed some to seek their day in court, Mary Bernstein explains that re-sulting victories were piecemeal and therefore did not generate significant political change.[203] In spite of the failures of the homophile movement to change discriminatory laws and policies or to establish a large base of sup-porters, it did "rupture the consensus that shaped social attitudes toward homosexuality and society's treatment of gay people."[204]

Still, lesbian and gay teachers did not have the social tools or political leverage in 1959 to speak out collectively against assault in Florida. Rather, as Bernstein notes in her review of homophile politics from 1940 to 1964, "mere survival ruled the day."[205] It would fall to a poet of another generation, another political context, to assert "that what is most important to me must be spoken."[206] The legacy of the teachers pursued by the Johns Committee adds historical weight to Audre Lorde's great insight: "My silences had not protected me. Your silence will not protect you."[207]

4

Doing the Public's Business

As an American the dignity and worth of every individual is recognized. Each individual is equal before the law and has the law's protection. . . . Every man has the right to . . . work where he wants.

—Thomas D. Bailey, March 1961

Homosexuality is not an illness like chickenpox—you cannot see it by looking into another person's face. . . . The revocation of a teaching certificate is the public's business. . . . The presence of even one homosexual teacher in our schools is not to be tolerated.

—Thomas D. Bailey, 27 July 1961

Florida state superintendent of public instruction (SSPI) Thomas Bailey was probably unaware of the moral contradictions contained in these sentiments expressed in the space of four months. After all, both the patriotic rhetoric on individual dignity and civil equality and the homophobic discourse that supported the state's effort to remove gay and lesbian teachers from public schools were central elements in the dominant ideology of the United States in the mid-twentieth century. Moreover, Florida's "crime against nature" law stamped gay and lesbian schoolteachers as statutory felons beyond the law's protection.[1] Internal contradictions, moral or otherwise, weaken the validity of political philosophy, but that has rarely been enough to prevent acts of oppression and discrimination. The history of segregation is a powerful case in point. Bailey, who stood with Pork Choppers on the issues of segregation and sexuality, also was an advocate for due process and upholding the professional authority of school administrators. This makes him a central figure in understanding how an out-of-control Investigation Committee set in motion institutional changes that haunted lesbian and gay teachers in Florida long after the Pork Choppers' legislative mandate came to an end.

A native of Lugoof, South Carolina, Bailey moved to north Florida to accept a supervisory position at the Thomas Industrial Institute in DeFuniak Springs in 1920. He stayed in Pork Chopper territory for two decades, later taking positions at Ocala (1939) and Tampa (1943). In 1949 Bailey began the first of five consecutive terms as Florida's state superintendent of public instruction.[2] His retirement in 1965 coincided with the termination of the Johns Committee. It is unlikely Bailey would have held this cabinet position for so long had he challenged the Pork Choppers in any significant way. He was clearly in their camp regarding the defining issue of segregation.

In 1954 Bailey wrote an analysis of the *Brown v. Board of Education* decision that offered a telling mix of patriotic-tinged legalism and racism. He charged that the U.S. Supreme Court had handed the South its "greatest crisis since Reconstruction," and suggested that the *Brown* ruling threatened democracy itself by attacking "the public school systems of the several States."[3] After paying customary attention to states' rights, Bailey noted that segregation was a practice established by law and added that, prior to the Civil War, it had not been a "problem"—African Americans were slaves then, not citizens, and therefore had no legal claim to civil rights. He reminded his audience that during the nineteenth century it was, in fact, illegal to educate African Americans.[4]

Continuing his analysis, Bailey clarified that the Court had called for an end to compulsory segregation, not integration, and said he saw no difference between forced segregation and compulsory integration.[5] As the chief school officer in the state, Bailey took the path the Supreme Court left open by failing to set a definite timetable or specific procedures for desegregating schools: "When the Supreme Court issues its formal decree Florida can determine its plan of action relating to the issues of segregated public schools."[6] At times, disputes over strategy for maintaining segregation prompted politicians to reassure constituents that they were, indeed, protecting the racist cultural tradition. Such was the case in 1957 when Bailey addressed the House Committee on Education, declaring "Attorney General Ervin and I are both dedicated to a segregated public school system."[7] Bailey was not as direct when he reported to President Kennedy on the status of school desegregation in Florida in 1963. Nearly a decade after the initial *Brown* decision, Bailey summarized the familiar rationale for what amounted to resisting desegregation. First he stated that Florida had constructed new buildings, bringing "most" African American school facilities up to the quality of schools for white children in the state. In addition, Bailey claimed that the average salary for African American teachers was higher than the average salary of white teachers.[8] Florida, like other states, was hoping to stave desegregation by finally making an attempt to provide "equal" schooling but it was too little, too late. Without providing an exact number, Bailey added that "some" African American students had utilized the pupil-assignment law to gain admittance to white-majority schools. He suggested that more students could not be admitted without lowering standards, relying on an old chestnut to make his case: "I firmly believe that the chief function of schools is *education,* and that schools should not be used primarily as *social laboratories.*"[9] Bailey supported his racist assertions by citing standardized test data, making no mention of the disparity in educational opportunity established through decades of segregation. He was willing to project into the future, however, claiming that integration in schools would be a slow process best accomplished if "the educators of the two races in our state are allowed to work on this problem in education without too much outside interference."[10] Bailey was still railing against desegregation in 1971. In "Some Reflections on My Retirement after Five Years," Bailey extended his argument that mass secondary schooling dilutes the quality of education. "The school can no more transmute weakness into power, or mediocrity into excellence than a chemist can transmute lead into gold."[11] He singled out court decisions that made schools "an instrument to deal with social problems" as a particularly frustrating impediment to his vision of quality education.[12]

Bailey's influence was considerable in Florida and extended beyond state boundaries; at the time he wrote the 1954 essay on segregation, he had just been elected president of the Council of Chief State School Officers.[13] His papers reveal a zeal for his version of democracy and an allegiance to administrative expertise in the execution of the law. It is unlikely he expected his authority to be challenged. So when the Johns Committee charged that administrators in Florida were negligent in their "duty" to rid the schools of homosexuals, Bailey was, apparently, caught off guard. In a response that suggested the Investigation Committee was acting recklessly (and, perhaps more pointedly, intruding into his domain), Bailey defended the state school system. Teacher investigations were a complex matter and the law required a semblance of due process. All this took time. The task was especially complicated, Bailey explained, when teachers' "moral deficiencies" were difficult to detect. By classifying homosexuality as an illness but one markedly different from chickenpox, Bailey was drawing upon the emerging opinion that Robert Corber described as the "medicalization of the juridical discourse on sex."[14] Bailey needed to address the issue of sexuality in order to defuse the situation that the Johns Committee had created with the release of its 1961 legislative report, and he spoke in a language his constituents could understand. Bailey pledged to eradicate an "illness" that, if allowed to incubate, threatened to "spread" throughout the school system. He managed to wrest control of the "homosexuality problem" away from the Johns Committee, aided by the Florida Education Association (FEA) and the Florida Supreme Court. The result was to shift the locus of state oppression of gay and lesbian teachers from a renegade Investigation Committee to the Florida Department of Education (DOE). Institutionalizing the teacher purge allowed the practice to become a routine part of state governance, similar to antigay purges at the federal level. As David Johnson explains, once institutionalized within the national security state, antigay policies remained standard operating procedure in the federal government until the 1970s.[15] Just as there was more to the anticommunism movement than Joe McCarthy, the Florida teacher purge reverberated beyond the panic induced by Charley Johns and his colleagues.[16]

In this chapter I analyze the turf battle that erupted between the Johns Committee and the DOE in 1961 and eventually engaged all three branches of state government. In brief, the Florida Legislative Investigation Committee accused an executive cabinet department of failing to protect a state interest—banning gay and lesbian personnel from public schools. But the legislature had only recently granted the DOE authority to investigate charges against teachers. The judicial branch was drawn into the public quarrel when the Florida Supreme Court heard a case brought by three teachers who lost their teaching credentials on charges stemming from a Johns Committee investigation. The *Neal v. Bryant* decision established the importance of due process in purging gay and lesbian teachers from Florida schools and shifted this burden to the bureaucracy of the DOE. The FEA collaborated with the DOE on teacher investigations as the Johns Committee faded from the scene.

In the pages that follow I place the DOE in political context and discuss evidence that indicates education officials were concerned with eliminating gay and lesbian teachers as early as summer 1958, a year after the Hillsborough County sheriff's investigation but before the Johns Committee's investigation at the University of Florida. Then I trace the action of the public battle between the Johns Committee and the DOE, examine the genesis and impact of the *Neal v. Bryant* case, and document the FEA's complicity in purging gay and lesbian teachers from the profession. Although the Johns Committee is most infamously linked with the surveillance of teachers' private lives during the Cold War, and rightly so, a number of others had a hand in "doing the public's business."

Pork Chop Government

A writer for the *Florida Times-Union* wrote in 1960, "Education provides one of the best examples of the centralized nature of Florida's government."[17] The Florida State Board of Education (BOE) consisted of four of the six elected cabinet members—secretary of state, attorney general, treasurer, and the state superintendent of public instruction—and the governor. Florida's strong cabinet system diminished the power of the governor, who had to share decision making with six others.[18] Further, the governor was not allowed to serve consecutive terms, unlike the cabinet members. In a 1954 letter explaining this structure, Bailey noted that since 1861 only two members of the Florida state cabinet had been defeated in reelection bids.[19] This practice allowed cabinet members to create long-standing connections with county officials who were critical political players in a one-party state. Although state funds were apportioned to counties based on an average daily student-attendance formula, some worried that the cabinet wielded too much power in school matters. The trend in most states was to elect a board of education separate from the state cabinet; in 1958 Bailey acknowledged, "So far as I know there is no organizational pattern exactly like ours in Florida."[20]

The BOE oversaw three educational bodies: the Department of Education, the Board of Control (BOC), and the State Advisory Council on Education. As SSPI, Bailey was the chief administrator at the DOE, which consisted of the Division of Administration and Finance and the Division of Instruction. County superintendents of public instruction were the administrative links between the DOE and local schools. J. Broward Culpepper administered the BOC. The BOC and its Council of Presidents enforced policy regarding public universities and other postsecondary institutions in Florida. In 1964 the BOC became the Board of Regents. The State Advisory Council on Education met twice a year to review educational policy and advise the BOE. Seven citizens appointed by the governor served four-year terms and the SSPI was executive secretary. Other statutory groups included the Teacher Education Advisory Council, which made yearly reports to the BOE concerning teacher education and certification, and an Interim Committee on Education. The president of the Senate, Speaker of the House, and governor appointed members of this group. All in all, Superintendent Bailey wielded a good deal of influence on state educational policy.

The Florida Senate was the real center of power in the state, however, as established in the 1885 Constitution, "the first disfranchising constitution after Reconstruction" among the southern states.[21] It was this reactionary document that weakened the governor's office, established a "home rule" system to protect county patronage, and diminished the impact of African American votes by adding a poll tax. In 1925 the Senate cast off population-based representation established by the 1868 constitution and established the configuration for disproportionate representation that would cycle through the following decades.[22] Officials revisited the apportionment map every decade but Pork Choppers controlled the Florida Senate for most of the twentieth century and thereby maintained their disproportionate representation in the legislature by pushing through their favored apportionment plans.[23] Establishing the Johns Committee was one of the Pork Choppers' last victories before the U.S. Supreme Court ordered Florida to implement an apportionment plan based on population that would align with the federal Constitution. The 1968 elections brought Pork Chopper dominance in Tallahassee to an end.

In 1956, however, Charley Johns and his fellow Pork Choppers retained a powerful presence in the Senate that enabled them to push through the bill to establish the Investigation Committee. The group was not yet concerned with teachers, except those who supported desegregation. It is difficult to determine with precision the moment that the Johns Committee took up its crusade against gay and lesbian teachers. But before the Investigation Committee issued its first public statement on the matter, the issue of teacher morality was already under discussion in the Interim Legislative Committee on Education (ILCE), one of the special advisory groups in the state educational system.

A Gestapo to Police Teachers?

At its June 1958 meeting the ILCE noted that there was no system in place for identifying or removing teachers on the basis of perceived moral deficiencies. Members noted that school administrators were reluctant to share information on teachers who moved from district to district because of liability concerns; the committee considered establishing a state agency to "investigate, promulgate and regulate standards of ethical and moral conduct for teachers of Florida."[24] In the discussion Ed Henderson, executive secretary of the FEA, stated that his organization was willing to conduct investigations of teachers if given legal status. Although one might have expected the FEA to protect teachers' interests rather than volunteer to run investigations against them, the history of the FEA's collusion with the Johns Committee suggests otherwise, as noted in chapter 3.[25] In a document prepared for the members of the

ILCE, the FEA enumerated its purposes. "Advancing the welfare of teachers" appeared sixth on the list of eight objectives that included conducting studies of Florida schools, informing the public and working with citizens on educational issues, recommending laws and representing the profession in the legislature, and improving the quality of teaching.[26] Representatives Surles and Mann argued against establishing a state agency, refuting the notion that administrators might be liable for information they shared about teachers in a professional setting. Surles was cited in the minutes as seeing no need for "setting up any Gestapo to police teachers."[27]

When the committee met again in November 1958 they picked up the discussion regarding an agency for screening teachers and raised the issue of fingerprinting teachers. J. T. Kelley, director of the Division of Teacher Education, DOE, maintained that it was difficult to revoke teachers' certificates and argued that the law must be strengthened "to clear out these undesirables."[28] In the aftermath of the University of Florida investigation, M. L. Stone, dean of the College of Education at Florida State University (1956–67) reported that educators in higher education were doing everything in their power to prevent students "inclined toward communism, or any number of derogatory personality traits" from becoming teachers.[29] Senator John Rawls, who had cosponsored the bill to establish the Johns Committee, objected to a statewide screening system, noting that local control of the situation was preferable. The superintendent of public instruction (SPI) for Dade County countered that different sections of the state dealt with different problems, and argued that Florida should adopt the California plan for screening teachers. He added, "You can not tell by [teachers'] looks, or by their list of recommendations, or by their intelligence, or any other facility, what objectionable trait or belief or condition exists in the applicants."[30] Rawls held the line against instituting "such Gestapo methods," but Senator Pope argued that when it came to "people who are shaping the minds of future citizens" he could not see why anyone would object to fingerprinting. "We know," he continued, "there has been a substantial amount of communist infiltration. . . . Everyone concerned with education should be adequately screened."[31] Discussion continued until Senator Dickenson commented that there would be little objection to a fingerprinting bill if it were applied to the whole state system. "If this were approached studiously, quietly, the legislature would probably look favorably on this process of screening."[32] The committee passed a motion to recommend the legislature pass a bill to provide for the fingerprinting of teachers statewide. One member clarified that the information would only be available to the DOE and county superintendents. Senator Rawls responded that he "had yet to see any Gestapo information that is sacrosanct. If you have clerks, . . . it will spread."[33] It is interesting to note that three of the five legislators engaged in this discussion opposed screening mechanisms that would increase state surveillance of teachers, initiatives that were promoted by the representatives of the DOE, county superintendents, higher education, and the FEA. Professional educators were leading the assault on teacher privacy while Representatives Surles and Mann and Senator Rawls preferred to tend to issues at the local level.

In a March 1959 report in a section titled "Protection of Schools against Subversion and Immorality," the ILCE called for a fingerprinting bill. The committee tried to soften its position—likely considered an affront by many—noting, "The vast majority of school personnel are dedicated, loyal Americans with a commendable professional attitude toward their responsibility."[34] The ILCE also implied that its recommended policy was directed toward unknown "others"—not its own people. A population boom in Florida was causing a teacher shortage and 80 percent of new hires came from outside the state, "where integrity and reputation are more difficult to check than with our homefolk."[35]

Turf War

When the Johns Committee presented its report to the 1959 session of the legislature, it adopted Senator Dickenson's tack of suggesting all state employees be fingerprinted, to avoid any resistance educators might mount as a targeted group. The recommendations regarding ways to systematize state surveillance of teachers that the committee offered in 1959, however, were *only* suggestions—or more accurately, a warning shot. The Johns Committee expected state educational institutions to clamp down on teachers and warned that if an "effective program for coping with this problem [homosexuality] is not immediately brought forth and put into practice," the legislature should take "whatever action is necessary to bring this problem to an absolute minimum and maintain it there."[36]

The centerpiece of the Investigation Committee's report was its sensationalized summary of "salient facts" concerning homosexuality. Based upon testimony it had taken, the Johns Committee stated that homosexuals were to be found at all levels in Florida's educational system and that homosexuality was more prevalent among those with advanced formal education. This, along with the belief that homosexuality was the product of environment and training, justified state scrutiny of teachers' personal lives, according to the committee. It repeated the powerful lie that has kept teachers in the closet for years: "A surprisingly large percentage of young people are subject to be influenced into homosexual practices if thrown into contact with homosexuals who desire to recruit them."[37] Although the committee was not prepared to introduce legislation at this point, the 1959 report made its agenda clear. Without a centralized system of records, there would be "absolutely no way of assuring [*sic*] that homosexual teachers who are caught are not merely reshuffled from one institution to another." Collecting photographs and fingerprints of all teachers would enable investigators "to quietly ferret out concrete proof on the vast majority of all practicing homosexuals" in schools.[38]

Eleven days before the Johns Committee presented its report, Senator Carraway introduced a bill that would enable the BOE to investigate teachers, search for "any misconduct," and file charges against teachers who would be entitled to a public hearing. While the BOE already had the power to dismiss teachers for cause, it lacked procedural authority to collect evidence; the bill would give the BOE investigative and subpoena powers. The 1959 legislature adopted Section 229.08 into law, greasing the skids for revoking teachers' certificates on the basis of moral misconduct.[39] This, of course, was *after* the Johns Committee had recklessly invaded the private lives of many teachers. Scores of investigations would follow.

In its 1961 report to the legislature, the Johns Committee reviewed its court battles with the NAACP, its investigation of "subversive" organizations such as the Southern Conference Educational Fund, and its findings regarding an adoption ring in Gainesville. The part of the report that grabbed major media attention, however, centered on "Homosexual Conduct on the Part of State Employees, Particularly in the Field of Education." The committee claimed that the "problem" was more serious and extensive than first imagined, and repeated the "salient facts" that laced the 1959 report. The committee stated that the number of homosexual instructors at all levels of schooling was much more substantial than generally believed and reminded legislators that the "practicing homosexual is, almost entirely, the product of environment." Pitching its rhetoric at near-panic levels, the Johns Committee declared, "Practicing homosexuals almost invariably turn to the recruitment of young people as sex partners. . . . Practically all children are susceptible to being recruited into homosexual practices at one stage or another of their development . . . [and a] homosexual teacher, having direct supervision over numerous children, can and does do tremendous damage to quite a large group of children when the teacher turns to the recruitment of young sex partners."[40] Apparently committee investigators turned up one teacher who was a pedophile and erroneously conflated pedophilia with homosexuality. The report went on to scold school administrators for attitudes and actions that, from the committee's perspective, contributed to their problem. The Johns Committee charged that administrators closed their eyes to the matter of homosexual teachers in schools, due either to a lack of knowledge or too little appreciation for the scope of the situation. The committee was incensed that administrators allowed homosexual teachers to slip away with resignations without facing criminal prosecution or revocation of their teaching certificates. Then the committee made the comment that newspapers picked up around the state: "The combination of administrators ignoring the problem and his [administrator's] lenient dealing with the individual when caught makes the public educational system in Florida a veritable refuge for practicing homosexuals."[41]

The release of the 1961 report caused the state superintendent of public instruction and the chair of the Johns Committee to "bump heads," as a reporter for the *Ft. Lauderdale Daily News* put it. The paper quoted Bailey as saying the allegations in the report were "out of proportion," with Investigation Committee chair William O'Neill responding that school officials were "naïve." Although Bailey did not plan to initiate a DOE investigation regarding the cases in the committee's report, he did emphasize that the BOE would continue to revoke teachers' certificates and "'put them out of business' in Florida." Bailey charged that the Johns Committee report was hurting the state's image, which led O'Neill to shoot back, "I don't run the newspapers." Bailey was in the position of defending his department's handling of the homosexual "problem" without causing additional damage to Florida's national reputation. Unlike the Johns Committee and its agents, Bailey embraced the importance of due process even as he rejected gay and lesbian teachers. "I don't think the committee intended to infer that we're reeking with this type of thing, but it has given this erroneous impression throughout the country. . . . I don't countenance this sort of thing, and we've been revoking certificates on the basis of the evidence and will continue to do so."[42]

As school officials feared, some citizens seized upon the Johns Committee's claims to attack the entire education profession. "BELIEVER IN CHRIST" connected a $200 increase in salary for Florida teachers to the alleged lack of cooperation the Investigation Committee was getting from school officials in purging homosexuals from the schools. The writer wondered if the actions of the state would call down another Sodom and Gomorrah calamity.[43] Another writer chastised school officials for their inattention to the supposed homosexual problem: "The charges, whether true or not, are revolting. . . . As is too often the case, school administrators and officials of the law are too willing to retreat to a head-in-the-sand position on these 'delicate' matters. They beg off pressing their investigations or bringing formal charges by saying that the resulting publicity would be damaging to the school system or that 'these things are just too hard to prove.'"[44]

To his credit Bailey held the line on due process, noting "You can't accuse a person of something like this unless you have all the evidence. This is very serious."[45] Of course, he had no problem stripping teaching certificates from gay and lesbian educators once "something like this" was determined to the satisfaction of the state. And the insistence on due process provided a defense for administrators who moved too slowly according to the Johns Committee and members of the public who shared the perspective of the editorial writers. Pinellas County superintendent of public instruction Floyd Christian told a reporter from the *St. Petersburg Independent* that his schools were not "'harboring' teachers guilty of homosexuality." Strickland had focused heavily on the Tampa Bay area in the early phases of the schoolteacher interrogations and Christian probably felt the heat of the 1961 report more keenly than other county superintendents. He assured the newspaper's readers that "Pinellas teachers 'police their own ranks.'"[46] The next day in the *Tampa Tribune* Christian criticized the Johns Committee report as drastic and damaging to the morale of teachers throughout the state. "'It is a shame to put a cloud over the entire profession by innuendo or implication. . . . So few of the teachers are involved." The BOE had revoked five certificates from teachers in Pinellas County since 1959, out of a staff of 5,000 people. "Five out of 5,000 isn't very bad," Christian maintained.[47]

After the initial flurry following the 1961 report subsided, Bailey wrote a lengthy statement on the BOE's position regarding homosexual teachers in Florida. He emphasized the point that the BOE "was and is" cooperating with the Johns Committee, using some form of the word "cooperate" six times in the three-page document. Bailey noted he had initiated a meeting with Senator Cliff Herrell and Investigator Strickland in 1959 to "develop a cooperative plan of action." They agreed that the Johns Committee would "serve as the investigative arm of the state" and present evidence to the BOE for action. The BOE revoked teaching certificates in all forty-five cases presented to the department.[48] Bailey pointed to procedural issues in his defense. He underscored the fact that the BOE had been revoking certificates for "immoral activity" for many years, but since the investigations could not be carried out in the public "limelight," most often cases were conducted quietly and went unnoticed. He explained that the "discovery of immoral activity and the building of a legal case to prove such activity is a long and tedious process." If a teacher did not plead "guilty," the state could not rely on hearsay or anonymous charges; facts that would stand up in court were difficult to obtain. In all of this, Bailey noted, the rights of the individual must be protected.[49] Bailey took issue with the Johns Committee's claim that administrators were deficient in rooting out homosexuals, again referring to their "full cooperation." In fact, he surmised that because of this diligence the percentage of homosexuals in education was likely to be less than in other occupations.[50]

A year later Bailey looked back on the turbulent 1961 legislative session with frustration, commenting that there had been few, if any, open lines of communication between the legislature and the DOE. The FEA made a similar report in its summary "The 1961 Legislature and Education." The writer of the review charged that legislators had introduced many bills detrimental to education, causing FEA lobbyists to expend energy in defensive action, rewriting legislation and working on amendments.[51]

In 1961 the Florida legislature cleaned up the procedure for revoking teacher certificates on morals charges so that it would not violate due process rights. Previously the hearing officer had served the dual function of prosecutor and jury. The new law required the BOE to appoint a hearing officer to serve as judge and a county-based state attorney to present evidence against the accused teacher. Teachers were allowed a hearing in which they could be represented by counsel and call witnesses. The hearing officer would then present findings of fact and conclusions based on law to the BOE who would take final action. The Hillsborough County representative who introduced the 1961 bill explained that the earlier version of the law had resulted in "'witch hunts' in investigating charges against teachers."[52]

After the 1961 session the state continued to refine its process for revoking teachers' certificates. The Johns Committee took testimony from Director Kelley of the DOE, who explained that charges against teachers might be initiated by Strickland, county superintendents, newspaper accounts, or departments of education in other states. If Kelley believed the evidence at hand was sufficient to proceed with the case, he would have the county superintendent or Superintendent Bailey sign a petition to revoke the teacher's certificate. At that point Kelley would present the evidence and petition to the BOE and notify the teacher of a hearing date. Kelley added that if he couldn't depend on Strickland or the FEA to collect evidence, "I would be lost."[53] The revocation process could be completed within four weeks if the teacher did not request a hearing; in the few cases where teachers did request hearings, the ordeal could last for eight months. Kelley and members of the Investigation Committee discussed snags in the process regarding the standard of proof for a person's "guilt," such as the contradiction between one's denial and polygraph test results, or cases where a person might have "confessed" to Strickland or a school official but denied the "confession" at the hearing.[54]

The assistant attorney general who had been acting as the hearing officer in these cases spoke with the Johns Committee next. He suggested additional legislation that would make "voluntary" admission of homosexual conduct during a preliminary interrogation sufficient basis for revoking certificates. It is clear that these officials were concerned with due process for teachers only to the point of avoiding a constitutional violation that would nullify the revocation. The assistant attorney general explained that officers of the state already had the legal muscle to deal with "recalcitrant" teachers in a "left-handed" way: the hearing officer could simply adjourn the hearing if a witness refused to talk and then the prosecuting state attorney could subpoena the teacher under normal contempt powers. Johns Committee legal counsel Mark Hawes mused that perhaps the committee should consider an amendment to short-circuit this process by giving the hearing officer contempt power over witnesses who refused to talk.[55] The Johns Committee and the BOE would be taken to task for their disregard of due process, retroactively, when three courageous teachers demanded their day in court.

Straighten Up and Fly Right

The 1959 amendment to the Florida statutes that granted the BOE authority to investigate teachers was double-edged: it *required* the BOE to conduct an investigation before initiating revocation proceedings. Specifically, the law mandated that either BOE employees or an FEA committee conduct an investigation to determine probable cause regarding a teacher's misconduct before sending a revocation case on to the hearing officer for review. Accused teachers were to be allowed a chance to explain their actions or refute evidence during the investigation phase. Then, if the investigation committee determined that the bar of probable cause had been met, the case would be reviewed by the hearing officer who would submit a report of findings and recommendation for legal action to the BOE.[56]

The BOE deviated from this procedure by relying upon Strickland to conduct the preliminary investigations—a fact Bailey and Kelley freely admitted. Yet the chief investigator of the Johns Committee was not an employee of the BOE, as Bailey clearly knew. In an exchange of letters with an attorney representing a teacher who had been questioned by Strickland in 1960, Bailey stated, "Mr. R. J. Strickland is not employed by the State Board of Education, but is employed by the legislative investigating committee which works as an arm of the Legislature, entirely independent of the executive department of government."[57] Bailey explained he had no authority regarding Strickland's work, a point Strickland himself emphasized in his reply to the attorney: "Inasmuch as the State Department of Education has no jurisdiction over this [Investigation] Committee or its activities or personnel, I wish to advise you that such charges as you made in your letter to [Bailey] were placed before the wrong Department."[58] The attorney's point was that Strickland's interrogation of this teacher violated the procedure for revoking a certificate on the basis of moral turpitude. The attorney inquired "why no charges were made, no hearing was held, no opportunity to defend was given, and yet this teacher has been condemned and has suffered this humiliation with no chance to be heard."[59] This particular teacher was well placed, politically. He was the son of a former county SPI and a brother-in-law of a recently elected state senator. Knowledge of Strickland's freewheeling approach to these cases was beginning to spread, suggesting another reason the 1961 legislature voted to amend Section 229.08(16) of the Florida statutes to clean up the process for revoking certificates. But by then another case regarding the BOE's inattention to due process was simmering that would eventually land in the Florida Supreme Court.

In October 1960 Strickland interrogated five employees of the Pinellas County School System, four white women and one African American man. Following the interrogation SPI Floyd Christian suspended the teachers on grounds of moral turpitude, pending action by the BOE. On 6 December Christian sent a letter to Kelley, pushing for a hearing date for the accused teachers. Christian was concerned because the lengthy gap between the suspensions and the teachers' hearings allowed public unrest to grow, making it "very difficult to keep down the rumors" and disturbing the "peace of mind of other teachers who are fearful of this Legislative Investigation Committee."[60] Rather than face the DOE alone as many of their colleagues did, these teachers employed attorneys and enlisted the National Education Association (NEA) in their defense. The school system in Pinellas County was recognized as progressive and one of the accused was the daughter of a member of Christian's staff, which might help explain why these teachers decided to challenge their dismissal more vigorously than others.[61] The critical break in the cases came when hearing officer George Georgieff cited

Strickland's reports as the basis for his recommendation to proceed to a hearing on revocation. Recognizing the problem, Kelley fired off a notice to Georgieff to alert him to the "rather grave error" that he was certain counsel would raise at the hearing: "The Legislative Investigating Committee is not the investigating body of the State Department of Education."[62] In March Bailey sent a memorandum to the other members of the BOE detailing how testimony the five teachers gave before Georgieff differed from the transcripts of their interrogation by Strickland. The teachers retracted earlier admissions of homosexual acts and stated that they had made those statements under duress.[63] Nevertheless, the BOE voted unanimously to revoke all five certificates on 4 April 1961 and the teachers were fired. Three of the teachers appealed and on 19 October 1962, two years after their ordeal began, the Florida Supreme Court reversed the revocations on the single ground that the BOE did not comply with the procedural mandates of the law. Referring to the "so-called investigation" conducted by Strickland, the Court observed that "Mr. Strickland was not an employee of the State Board of Education. . . . He did not purport to conduct his investigation in accordance with the provisions of the statute, nor did he advise the petitioners that he was conducting a proceeding in conformity with the statute."[64] Although the ruling focused on the point that Strickland's investigation could not serve as the legal preliminary investigation called for by law, depriving the teachers of a chance to refute the charges against them, the Court also noted that Strickland went beyond the legislative mandate established for the Investigation Committee by questioning teachers about their sexuality. "Actually, the Committee had no such power to investigate these people at that time. The statements which they allegedly made were obviously extracted from them under a threat of publicity which might result from the threatened exercise of power which the Committee did not possess."[65] In response the BOE acknowledged it did not follow the statutory procedure for revoking certificates but argued that the omitted preliminary investigation was directory rather than mandatory. The Court disagreed. Then the BOE argued that the preliminary investigation was not necessary because it served no useful purpose. The Court dismissed this rationale, writing: "It is not the province of an administrative body, nor indeed of this court, to weigh the wisdom of an enactment of the legislature."[66] Although the 1961 legislature had just altered the law to give the BOE discretion regarding preliminary investigations, the Court was bound to rule on the law in place at the time of the action against the teachers. By a 5–2 vote the Florida Supreme Court reversed the revocations but remanded for "further proceedings to be conducted in compliance with the statute."[67] That is, the teachers won the case but the BOE simply could initiate a new process to deprive these same teachers of their certificates. Less than a month later Kelley reported to Bailey that Pinellas County SPI Christian was "very anxious to keep working on these cases."[68] The BOE vacated its revocations of the three certificates in March 1963. Christian informed Kelley that he would fight full reinstatement and back salary for the teachers but would agree to a modest settlement if the teachers would resign. Bailey advised the BOE that if the Pinellas County School Board instituted new proceedings to revoke the teachers' certificates, the matter would come before the BOE once again.[69] Evidently the two women tried to find teaching jobs in the West. Kelley replied to inquiries from state officials in Arizona and California, noting that the Florida certificates had been revoked and then restored by order of the state Supreme Court but he was unable to provide further information. Although that was probably enough to keep the women out of public schools, a handwritten note on one of the letters suggested that Kelley might send a copy of the Supreme Court decision as a way of providing additional information that would surely seal the deal.[70]

Most teachers did not contest the loss of their certificates at BOE hearings. When three Pinellas County educators did, they exposed the illegal maneuvers and tactics of intimidation that characterized the teacher purge. The Supreme Court's ruling loosened the grip the Johns Committee had on the teacher investigations and replaced Strickland's bare-knuckles tactics with refined state policy. The Investigation Committee might still pass information along and the FEA could help collect evidence, but from here on out the DOE would process its dealings with deviant teachers pretty much by the book. The process for stripping gay and lesbian teachers of their professional credentials had settled into routine bureaucracy.

Scandal! And Business as Usual

Hamstrung in court, the Johns Committee worked with other state agencies to advance its homophobic agenda. In 1962 the Investigation Committee moved on to a broader analysis of the "homosexual problem" and considered fingerprinting all state employees, adopting a uniform policy regarding homosexuality for all state agencies, discontinuing retirement benefits for homosexuals, and adding surveillance checks within the state personnel system. As mass arrests were made in Hillsborough and Polk counties and in Panama City, Tallahassee, and other cities, the Florida Children's Commission initiated a program of public education on "the dangers of homosexualism."[71] Embarrassed by the fiasco at the University of South Florida and its political fallout, the Johns Committee pledged to cooperate with law enforcement agencies and give up the practice of taking the law into its own hands. In 1963 counsel Mark Hawes and chief investigator R. J. Strickland, freewheeling agents identified with the egregious excesses of the Investigation Committee, resigned.[72] In what would be its last term, the Johns Committee appointed John Evans staff director. Evans, too, would tangle with Bailey as the DOE tried to manage all the teacher investigations the Johns Committee had dumped into its lap.

In January 1964 the Johns Committee instructed Evans to have Bailey hire someone in the Teacher Certification Division to handle investigations against gay and lesbian teachers. The committee was worried about the magnitude of the situation—approximately eighty revocation cases and more than a hundred files to investigate. Although the Florida Supreme Court had placed the authority for investigating teachers squarely with the BOE, Evans assured Bailey that he would continue to offer direct assistance. The Johns Committee "intends to be most active in seeking control of dangerous homosexual practices within the state," but it could no longer provide "the nearly full-time attention to this problem that its gravity demands."[73] In a response written two weeks later Bailey suggested that the FEA do all the investigative work on gay and lesbian teachers, since the responsibility for processing all cases referred to the BOE was enough to stress its resources. Evans responded that Bailey knew best and asked him to remind the FEA that the Johns Committee was ready to pass along information in its files.[74]

This polite exchange paralleled the release of the Johns Committee's scandalous publication, "Homosexuality and Citizenship in Florida." The pamphlet exposed the crudity that fueled the Johns Committee's attacks on teachers and severed support from constituents and politicians who couldn't distance themselves fast enough from the floundering Investigation Committee. Printing the booklet (at taxpayer expense) was a serious miscalculation.[75]

Staff Director Evans addressed the annual convention of the Florida Federation of Women's Clubs on 15 April in the midst of this uproar, devoting his talk to a defense of the Johns Committee and the purple pamphlet. Women's organizations were significant players in Florida politics, as the action of the American Association of University Women regarding the USF investigation illustrated.[76] It is likely that Evans, former press secretary to Governor Bryant, was well aware of the potential influence of such groups. Toward the end of his presentation Evans expressed his "dismay as a parent" regarding an aspect of the Johns Committee report that "has been almost totally ignored" and told the gathering of women that he hoped to "arouse your concern."[77] Whether Evans was motivated more by the point expressed in his letters to Bailey regarding timely dispensation of the teacher investigations or a desire to deflect public criticism away from the Johns Committee, he called upon the tactic his predecessors had used in 1961: Evans suggested that the BOE was negligent in its duty to expel homosexual teachers from the profession.

Evans reminded his audience that Johns Committee files dating to 1961 contained allegations against 123 teachers. For the sake of the "thousands of fine Florida teachers who are cast under a cloud of suspicion" and the "well being of the youngsters who are daily exposed to these individuals," Evans said the allegations needed to be refuted or affirmed.[78] But, Evans charged, no agency was following up—not the Johns Committee, or the DOE, or the FEA Professional Practices Committee. Evans asserted that the contents of the files would surely "sicken" the women of the Florida Federation of Women's Clubs, just as it had sickened him, and professed amazement at the silence of the media. "So far we have found no official agency which believes it is properly constituted to undertake the necessary investigation and action, which leads one to wonder if it is all right for this affliction to flourish in Florida but improper to call for action to control it."[79] This time, however, when a spokesman for the Johns Committee suggested that homosexuality was "flourishing in Florida," the impact was weaker than it had been in 1961. Such cries of alarm were becoming stale and ineffective. An editorial in the *Miami Herald* put Evans's claims into context: "It's a shame our educators have to waste time defending themselves against the reckless shotgun attacks by the discredited Legislative Investigations Committee. . . . Yet we have to endure the headline-hunting director of the 'Johns Committee' and its baseless accusation that Bailey is floundering in a sea of apathy and naivete. . . . If the committee doesn't have anything better to do with its time, let it go back to printing obscene books."[80]

Commentary such as this compelled Evans to offer a press release on 18 April in which he argued that "the majority of Florida's citizens are cognizant that in exposing the rapid spread and insidious aspects of homosexuality the Committee is neither crying wolf nor palming off a pipe dream."[81] But he did retreat a bit from the bold statements delivered to the women's club. Evans acknowledged the arrangements that he and Bailey had worked out in February—that the information from the 123 files would be released to the Professional Practices Commission as soon as it was organized and the Johns Committee would forward information to the BOE upon request.

Evans added that the Investigation Committee was not suggesting that homosexuality was peculiar to the teaching profession, even though it had implied as much in the 1959 and 1961 reports to the legislature.[82]

Robert Sherrill of the *St. Petersburg Times* reported that Evans's speech "caused a spasm of alarm" among BOE and FEA officials; he connected this most recent turmoil to the commotion that accompanied the release of the purple pamphlet, and used both examples to highlight the ineptitude of the Johns Committee.[83] Sherrill's report also ran in the *Miami Herald,* prompting committee chair Richard Mitchell to prepare a document of "fact" for legislators in the St. Petersburg and Miami areas. In the document Mitchell emphasized the Investigation Committee's cooperation with the BOE and Superintendent Bailey, noting that the two groups enjoyed "a good working relationship."[84] According to the document, Bailey described his exchange with Evans as one of "continuous and cordial contact."[85] Evans and Bailey met on 1 May to discuss how to deal with the remaining teacher investigations. Bailey suggested starting with a few cases to work out procedures; evidently the Professional Practices Commission was not yet ready to begin investigations and the work would fall to J. T. Kelley in the Certification Division of the DOE. Evans sent the first cases to Bailey on 4 May and on 19 May Bailey got BOE approval to refer some cases to the FEA. Other cases went to local school boards for investigation. On 2 June the Johns Committee sent the remainder of the teacher files to Bailey.[86] After six years the Florida Legislative Investigation Committee's persecution of gay and lesbian teachers had come to an end.

Between 1963 and 1965 the Investigation Committee trained its sights primarily on legislation. The committee's 1965 report included proposed bills for a sexual behavior act, an academic freedom law, new teacher certification revocation procedures, and a fingerprint bill. The Sexual Behavior Act included definitions of sexual deviation and deviate sexual conduct, and penalties for violating the law. The academic freedom law sought "safeguards against those who would ignore the responsibility inherent in academic freedom and who would use that freedom as a vehicle for propagandistic efforts of any sort."[87] Even though the Johns Committee was not suggesting Florida was vulnerable to subversion activities on campus, it recommended vigilance to ward off such possibilities. The Investigation Committee also called for increased internal security measures and stronger personnel screening systems in the university system.[88] The Johns Committee suggested amending chapter 229 of the Florida statutes yet again to allow the SSPI to suspend the certificate of accused teachers while an investigation was ongoing to prevent suspected teachers from teaching in another county in the interim. Florida had been fingerprinting state employees by administrative order since 1962; the Johns Committee proposed writing this action into state law in 1965.[89]

None of the proposed bills passed. Conceivably the Investigation Committee might have continued throughout the decade with a renewed emphasis on rooting out "un-American" activities on college campuses, but the homophobia that sustained the Johns Committee in 1961 tripped it up in 1965. In a letter to a constituent, Governor Haydon Burns recalled the "most despicable pamphlet on homosexuals which was a disgrace to this state. . . . This project in itself brought upon the committee such disrespect as to render any other efforts completely ineffectual. . . . This committee is of no further value."[90] The legislature let the Johns Committee expire with the 1965 session.

Conclusion

Until 1957 gay and lesbian teachers in Florida worked in a climate characteristic of schools across the nation. If administrators found teachers' sexuality suspect, the teachers would lose their jobs through dismissal or resignation. Such a possibility created a professional environment of self-monitoring and uncertainty. This uneasy arrangement changed when the Hillsborough County sheriff's office exposed more than thirty teachers in its investigation of a gay and lesbian subculture in the Tampa Bay region. Although it is difficult to pinpoint the genesis of the Johns Committee's interest in homosexuality, both the Investigation Committee and education groups such as the ILCE and the FEA took up the matter within months of the Hillsborough County investigation. The Johns Committee focused its energies on a statewide search for gay and lesbian teachers with a scope and intensity unequaled in American educational history. Agents exceeded the mandates of the Investigation Committee in their pursuit and intimidation of teachers, exhibited a blatant disregard for due process and legal procedures, and charged the DOE with negligence. The Johns Committee's reprehensible behavior places it among the most appalling examples of abuses of state power during the Cold War, but the Investigation Committee did not change the climate for teachers in the Sunshine State single-handedly. To understand the full force of Florida's homosexual purge, one must consider the transition of institutional authority regarding scrutiny of teachers, from a renegade legislative committee to a centralized state bureaucracy.

The Florida political system positioned a strong legislature against a weak executive branch. Although the governor was limited in his ability to challenge Pork Choppers (if he were so disposed), other members of the state cabinet carried the clout that comes with incumbency. Sitting atop the DOE with its numerous advisory groups, Thomas Bailey maintained ties to county superintendents of public instruction and other educational groups, most significantly the FEA. It is interesting to note that when the ILCE met in 1958, DOE and FEA representatives argued in favor of establishing a centralized system to collect information on teachers, signaling the emergence of a battle for authority regarding oversight of teachers. But the Johns Committee had latched onto the "homosexual problem" and it was not yet ready to relinquish this effective mechanism for stirring public opinion. It strong-armed the DOE, pushing the entire educational network of Bailey's department, local county superintendents, and the FEA to pronounce its denunciation of homosexuality. FEA officials promoted the 1959 and 1961 bills that strengthened the state's position against gay and lesbian teachers, and volunteered to run investigations against members of the profession. Hungry for the respect of the political establishment, the FEA advocated a share of increased state control over members of the teaching profession. With the Johns Committee pushing from one direction and the FEA pulling from another, the Florida legislature gave the BOE subpoena and investigative powers to use against gay and lesbian teachers. Minutes from a meeting of the FEA's Personnel Problems Committee note that the 1959 legislature expanded the power of the BOE to revoke teachers' certificates in two significant ways: allowing the board to search for evidence of moral turpitude and adding a new category of offense for which certificates could be revoked. Before the board had investigative authority, revoking certificates required either conviction or admission of guilt, both hard to come by in many instances. In addition, the 1959 law allowed for certificates to be revoked on the "lesser" but equally vague grounds of "grossly unethical" behavior.[91] Without an investigative staff of its own, the DOE simply processed the revocation cases forwarded by the Johns Committee. The blistering 1961 report that criticized administrators' negligence regarding the "homosexual problem" then surely infuriated Bailey, who found himself having to reassure the public that the DOE was vigilant in rooting out homosexual teachers. The state's top educational administrator articulated the importance of due process, concentrating on its roles in maintaining order and protecting the profession at large.

The Johns Committee's reckless disregard for due process caught up with it in October 1962 when the Florida Supreme Court overturned certificate revocations in *Neal v. Bryant.* Although the Court majority and Bailey insisted upon following due process in these proceedings, whether gay and lesbian teachers should be expelled from the profession was never the point of debate. The state simply refined its procedures for revoking credentials in a series of steps beginning in 1959 to make the process legal and efficient.

In theory, and sometimes in practice, legislative investigation committees serve an important function in guiding responsible legislation. From beginning to end, the Florida Legislative Investigation Committee can claim no such service. Bigotry, anti-intellectualism, and reckless disregard for due process of law constitute its legacy. Nevertheless, the Johns Committee set in motion the public panic that ignited critical legislative and executive action. It brought the "homosexual problem" to public attention, prompted the passage of homophobic laws, and pushed the educational establishment to expand its bureaucracy to encompass antigay policies and procedures. In response the DOE, joined quite enthusiastically by the FEA, claimed the professional authority to police its own. The political fallout from the Johns Committee's witch hunt cemented the amorphous fate of gay and lesbian teachers in legal and professional discourse.

When the Johns Committee overstepped its boundaries, a divided state Supreme Court slapped it down, insisting on purging teachers by the book. By the time Bailey resigned as state superintendent of public instruction, the book had been written, and all branches of government had a hand in it. Purging gay and lesbian teachers had become the public's business.

A Profession at Risk

In citing the cases of 123 teachers we were not
suggesting that homosexuality is an affliction peculiar
to that profession, for it is not. It happens that because
teachers are public employees, leaders of youth, they
have commanded special attention—attention we hope
will be turned to other segments of our society as we
move to control the sordid aspects of homosexuality.

—John E. Evans, staff director, Florida Legislative
Investigation Committee, 18 April 1964

Scholars who study our queer past have tracked an antigay trifecta
of beliefs that nonqueer forces have used to justify discrimination against
gay and lesbian citizens: Homosexuals are sinful, criminal, and medically
pathological.[1] This rationalization intensified during the Cold War with the
federal government's persecution of gay men and lesbians, an episode that
historian David Johnson argues "permeated 1950s political culture."[2] The
Johns Committee purge is a significant part of this history, for the swirl of
ideological currents that swept gay and lesbian teachers out of Florida classrooms emanated from particular standpoints on morality, crime, and illness,
and targeted a profession at the center of American culture.

Certain aspects of the teaching profession distinguish it from other types
of public employment such as government work and military service, leaving teachers especially vulnerable to homophobic persecution. For instance,
the expectation that educators act as exemplars for students has led to intense public scrutiny of teachers' personal lives and restricted professional
autonomy. The fact that schoolteachers work with children opened the door
to homophobic fears—unsubstantiated but persistent—that gay and lesbian
teachers would "recruit" students; this fear reinforced demands that teachers
act in accordance with a narrow standard of normative behavior. Analyses
of the feminization of teaching provide additional explanations for the rela-

tively low status of the profession, low levels of autonomy for its practitioners, and the great latitude the public has taken regarding supervision of teachers' lives in and outside the classroom. Public perceptions of schoolteachers as guardians of the dominant ideology along with restrictive professional structures, such as contracts that forbade specific personal behavior, engendered conservative thought and demeanor. Since most teachers who challenged the standards of normative behavior imposed upon them lost their jobs as a result, the workforce was depleted of its most radical members. Historically, teacher organizations have not supported colleagues who transgressed social norms and, thus, teachers have been easy targets for state suppression of gay and lesbian people. The intersection of these factors regarding public scrutiny, low levels of status and autonomy, and work with children locates teaching in a unique position—even among other public professions—in the crosshairs of antigay forces.

As the Florida purge demonstrates, teachers have been vulnerable to homophobic action in every sense of the word. They were exposed to damaging attack, liable to severe penalties, and constrained in their ability to resist. Teachers are deserving of special attention from gay and lesbian historians precisely because people such as John Evans gave teachers special attention in the Cold War persecution of homosexuals. Placing this study in the context of educational history, one can argue that teachers, out of the entire queer population, may be most vulnerable to antigay attacks. Through teachers, the state has sought to define conditions governing the queer presence, just as the Johns Committee articulated in 1964.[3]

A Mouthpiece for Antigay Rhetoric

The history of the Florida Legislative Investigation Committee provides searing evidence of the three-pronged rationale that school authorities used to brand gay men and lesbians as unfit educators and purge them from the teaching profession. The Investigation Committee released its most notorious statement on homosexuality in 1964, *after* the authority for investigating teachers had shifted to the Department of Education. "Homosexuality and Citizenship in Florida" drew immediate condemnation, apparently to the surprise of committee members who perceived their publication as a straight-from-the-shoulder report to Florida citizens on the moral climate within the state.[4] The report represented the committee's "findings" on the nature of homosexuality, its social manifestations, and the extent to which it existed in the population, drawn from the Investigation Committee's interrogations of gay and lesbian educators, interviews with law enforcement officers and medical personnel, and study of scientific and popular literature. The committee illustrated its report with photographs—of a boy in various poses, a frontal shot of a young man bound in ropes, a scene from a public restroom (with some elements blacked out)—and appended a glossary of "homosexual terms." The slick front cover of the state-sponsored publication was a photograph of two men embracing and kissing. This violet-colored image, combined with the unsophisticated analysis contained in the little booklet, handed critics a perfect turn of phrase. The "purple pamphlet" offended citizens and legislators who objected most often to the photographs and glossary. Many complained that the publication was an inappropriate use of tax money, and one states attorney charged that the purple pamphlet violated obscenity laws. Few critics argued with the antigay substance of the report, however. Most notable among the exceptions was Hal Call's "Open Letter" published in the *Mattachine Review*. Often, as a news editorial clarified, the public outcry against the purple pamphlet was directed at the Johns Committee's mishandling of a serious issue: "As usual, we don't criticize the objective of the investigation but rather the flamboyant procedures; the disregard of orderly procedures; the tactical indiscretions."[5] What the Investigation Committee had to say about homosexuality, quite clearly, accorded with the dominant ideology of the period. In spite of a weakened political position in the final months of the Johns Committee's appointed run, it still could wreak havoc with its rhetoric.

Noting that homosexuality had a historical context, the Johns Committee opened its report by acknowledging the dual explanations regarding twentieth-century views of homosexuality. "The origins of homosexuality are obscure, as is the question of whether it is sin or sickness. It is depicted in ancient cave drawings; was recognized in the culture of the Golden Age of Greece; figures in the controversy over Shakespeare's sonnets; is regularly debated in the scholarly seminars of forensic medicine; and figures prominently in security considerations in the highest echelons of today's world powers."[6]

Casting the complexity represented by a few thousand years of human history aside, the report did not deliberate over the sin *or* sickness question; according to the Johns Committee, homosexuality was sinful *and* sick *and* criminal. It turned to old-time religion for a catch-all descriptor, suggesting to readers "that the Biblical description of homosexuality as an 'abomination' has stood well the test of time."[7]

This fundamentalist doctrine resonated with many citizens. One mother wrote to the Johns Committee to express her appreciation for its efforts at "curb[ing] and control[ing] the spread of this filthy practice which seems to become more popular day by day." She supported the removal of any teachers who were even "suspect" regarding their sexuality. The writer worried that parents' influence over children would be overshadowed by professional educators' manipulation. "Certainly we as parents are guardians of our children's morals but there isn't much we can do when they are exposed to the homosexual 'fads' of people who have been trained to teach and reach the minds of the younger generation."[8]

Members of the Palm Beach Ministers Conference joined their concerns with those of area business and professional men and parents in a letter to committee chair Charley Johns in 1963. The group praised the Investigation Committee's work in "eliminat[ing] sex deviates from our schools," and asked Johns to step up investigations in Palm Beach County where, the petitioners believed, "lesbianism" was practiced by many teachers and running rampant among girls between the ages of twelve and eighteen. The ministers and their allies offered a number of reasons for suppressing what many deemed sinful behavior. "Certainly this is not only fertile ground in which to breed communism, but it is also against the very grain of marriage, normal life, and manhood."[9] Believing the moral foundations of their society at risk, and apparently their sense of gender identity, these citizens appended a list of names of people for the Johns Committee to investigate.

The purple pamphlet consistently treated homosexuality as a "threat to the health and moral well-being" of the citizenry.[10] Two of the five recommendations the committee offered toward the end of the report dealt with homosexuality as a pathological condition. The Investigation Committee urged lawmakers to revise Florida statutes, mandating a psychiatric examination prior to the sentencing of those convicted of homosexual acts with a minor, and giving judges discretionary power to order a psychiatric examination of anyone convicted of engaging in homosexual acts. The committee also recommended treatment in outpatient psychiatric centers for convicted homosexuals on probation or parole.[11] This last point suggests that the Johns Committee believed homosexuality was an illness one could treat, and the report cited a physician who held that homosexuality was a "curable disease." But the committee's position on sexuality was ambiguous, as noted by its frequent claims that homosexuality was a sinful, criminal act, and by debate on whether homosexuality could be "cured." In testimony transcripts chief counsel Mark Hawes recalled that, having spoken with many doctors, psychiatrists, and psychologists, the common understanding was that "even under the best conditions, with the youngest offenders who practice very little homosexual conduct, the prognosis for permanent, lasting cure can't be guaranteed."[12] The executive secretary of the Florida Education Association agreed, stating that was the reason gay men and lesbians should be barred from teaching: "Of all the activities of the government the most sacred trust we have is what happens to these children and, therefore, anyone who has shown any of these tendencies, since we know that the medical profession will not support any statement of cure—we think the youngsters ought to be protected from such influences."[13]

The notion of homosexuality as illness had so permeated mid-twentieth-century American culture that even self-described "happy" and "well-adjusted" people adopted the language of pathology. The purple pamphlet quoted a lesbian who took issue with the way authorities dealt with gay men and lesbians, treating all as criminals. She conceded, however, "Homosexuality is, as a total picture, a dread disease. It must be stopped from spreading rapidly."[14] Although this woman drew a distinction between illness and criminal behavior in her letter, the Johns Committee made no such distinction.

The Investigation Committee's stated purpose for publishing the study on "Homosexuality and Citizenship in Florida" was to present information in advance of proposed legislation. In its 1964 publication the committee recommended that the Teacher Certification Division of the Florida Department of Education hire personnel to investigate homosexual teachers, and noted that it had already begun to draft a "Homosexual Practices Control Act" for Florida. In addition to the recommendations regarding psychiatric treatment discussed above, the Johns Committee suggested that the Florida legislature create a central records repository that would contain information on people who had been arrested and convicted on charges of homosexuality. These records would be available to public-employing agencies. In addition, the Investigation Committee proposed a measure making a second homosexual offense a felony with the "appropriate" penalties upon conviction.[15] The Johns Committee believed it was locked in a battle of control over sexuality within the state and argued that "established procedures and stern penalties will serve both as encouragement to law enforcement officials and as a deterrent to the homosexual hungry for youth."[16] Chances are the Investigation Committee needn't have worried about lackadaisical enforcement of antigay laws; their own publication quoted an official who determined that homosexuality was "the most insidious crime of all."[17]

Indeed, antigay laws would meet no challenges in the Florida court system. When the state Supreme Court reversed a decision that stripped two lesbians and a gay man of their teaching credentials, it did so only because of procedural error. In handing down its decision in *Neal v. Bryant* the justice writing for the Court majority clearly stated that the law banning gay men and lesbians from teaching was not at issue. Given this perspective, the Investigation Committee's influence regarding legislation was of considerable weight. According to Florida's highest Court, the law was "the law" once established by the legislature; good judgment was inconsequential.[18]

As it turned out the "Homosexual Practices Control Act" and other recommendations that the Investigation Committee presented to the 1965 legislature did not pass. The committee lost nearly all credibility in the uproar over the purple pamphlet and finally the legislature shut it down. The general public had tired of the Johns Committee's bombastic rant but never seriously questioned its threefold premise that homosexuality was sinful, medically pathological, and criminal. On this point the Florida Legislative Investigation Committee was an unapologetic mouthpiece for the larger community. "In addition to the moral and legal problems engendered by the spread of homosexuality, its practitioners face a very real medical hazard. . . . The homosexual, subject to abnormal external and internal pressures, tends to neuroticism and mental imbalance, a predilection opening pathways to crime and conduct far beyond the veil of rationality. . . . Homosexuals pose a problem demanding of serious attention by all concerned with sound citizenship."[19]

A Most Vulnerable Profession

Teaching is a profession most vulnerable to antigay discrimination. As a long view of educational history attests, the public has defined schoolteachers as moral exemplars for students and this results in restrictions on teachers. The following excerpt from Horace Mann's *Fourth Annual Report* is perhaps the best-known statement on the subject; it has reverberated to generations of schoolteachers since first published in 1841. Mann intended local school committees to serve as "sentinels stationed at the door of every schoolhouse in the State, to see that no teacher ever crosses its threshold, who is not clothed, from the crown of his head to the sole of his foot, in garments of virtue. . . . [The committees speak] as a single voice coming from a single heart,—they urge, they insist, they demand, that the great axioms of a Christian morality shall be sedulously taught, and that the teachers shall themselves, be patterns of the virtues, they are required to inculcate."[20]

Mann's message was clear. The mission of public schools was to impress a common set of values on the state's children, modeled by their teachers. Observers have wrestled ever since with the many questions such a system raises in a pluralistic, allegedly democratic society and have debated the impact of this doctrine on student and teacher well-being. Yet people held the expectation that teachers serve as role models for students long before the establishment of a school system in the United States, a fact that enabled Mann and other school reformers to adopt the notion as part of their Common School crusade. When the responsibility for teaching literacy and moral ideology shifted from the institutions of family and church to the school, Karen Harbeck argues, the community felt not only a right but also an obligation to regulate the personal conduct of teachers.[21] This arrangement continued into the twentieth century, relatively unabated until a marked increase in teacher activism in the 1960s. Florida law, for instance, dictated that teachers "labor faithfully and earnestly for the advancement of the pupils in their studies, deportment and morals, and embrace every opportunity to inculcate, by precept and example, the principles of truth, honesty and patriotism and the practice of every Christian virtue."[22] As Howard Beale noted in his 1936 text on academic freedom, middle-class respectability for teachers depended upon strict conformity to a set of normative values, for the citizenry equated just about any expression of nonconformity with instability.[23] Historian Kate Rousmaniere summed up the standard thus: "If becoming a teacher meant anything, it meant literally becoming a certain kind of person. . . . [Once hired, a teacher's] very identity remained under constant public scrutiny."[24]

It became a truism that personal behavior weighed more heavily than professional competence in determining a teacher's fitness to serve in a given community. Documentary evidence combined with rich anecdotal data shore up this point. Contracts forbade women teachers from "fall[ing] in love" and getting married, and extracted promises to work in Sunday School, sleep eight hours a night, and remember one's obligations as "the willing servant of the school board and the townspeople."[25] Beale's review of school districts' restrictions on teachers attending the theater, playing cards, dancing, gambling, swearing, drinking, and engaging in sexual behavior offered plenty of evidence to support his claim that a "teacher's conduct outside of school is more likely to cause trouble than his teaching in school."[26] He went on to explain that charges of "immorality" are so vague and inconsistently defined as to cover almost any transgression imagined by school authorities. Even when tenure laws were established, "immoral conduct" provided legitimate grounds for a teacher's dismissal, regardless of whether the act in question involved one's professional duties or even took place in the local community. If charges involved sexual behavior, teachers usually were fired on the basis of hearsay without any concern for proof of the claims. Courts allowed such dismissals because, traditionally, the "fitness" of a teacher relied upon one's "*reputation* of good character."[27] Early twentieth-century sociologist Willard Waller acknowledged the public's unusual obsession with regulating the sexual behavior of teachers, poking fun at the extent to which even normative behavior was prohibited. "With regard to sex, the community is often very brutal indeed. It is part of the American credo that school teachers reproduce by budding. . . . The community prefers its male teachers married, but if they are unmarried, it forbids them to go about marrying. . . . Sex prejudice against school teachers . . . [is] almost without parallel in modern life. Women teachers are our Vestal Virgins."[28]

During the twentieth century, school officials surveyed the sexuality of schoolteachers with increased vigor. Drawing on a century's worth of material, Jackie Blount provides a comprehensive historical account for how "schools attempted to regulate the gender and sexual orientation of their workers—and by extension students" in her landmark work, *Fit to Teach*.[29]

Historians have noted a critical shift in the ways the public supervised teachers during the interwar years, when "the most intimate parts of teachers' lives became subject to systematic surveillance and evaluation."[30] In the years surrounding the Great Depression, school districts continued to demand strict obedience and oaths of loyalty from teachers as salaries fell and paydays might be skipped altogether. In addition, teachers were called upon to be "hygienic models" for their students, examined for signs of physical and psychological health. Jonna Perrillo explains how this new type of administrative control over teachers replaced community control to a degree, in exchange for increased status for teachers as "professionals." Still, teachers possessed little autonomy and knew they had to "conform their lives, their bodies, and their ideas to the public will."[31]

Waller wrote in 1932 that the moral principles society saddled schoolteachers with tended to be those most adults had abandoned for themselves but still expected others to practice. The notion of making the school a "museum of virtue" put teachers in the company of "the helpless" and children, Waller claimed.[32] His observation that teachers were "paid agents of cultural diffusion" confirmed that the philosophy Mann advanced nearly one hundred years before had taken root.[33] And yet, these agents to whom the community entrusted such a central cultural role lived more often than not on the social periphery. Margaret Nelson explores this paradox, explaining that some scholars have addressed the issue by arguing that the community's prescriptive control of teachers' lives represented ideal rather than typical behavior, as Waller suggested. She offers an alternative dual explanation, first describing the teacher in this situation as a "symbolic representative of a specific standard" that relies on a "pure embodiment" of the educational ideal.[34] Nelson also posits a sociopolitical interpretation that considers community restraints on teachers as a reaction to the authority teachers represented by virtue of their knowledge—knowledge gained from obtaining more formal education than most community members and knowledge of intimate aspects of children's lives that comes from working with them in the classroom over a period of time. That is, the community recognized schoolteachers as a potentially powerful force and imposed restrictions on their personal behavior to maintain control of the predominately female labor pool.[35]

Teachers learned to guard their thoughts and actions, as illustrated by a woman who simply stated, "Because I am a teacher I dare not be frivolous and outspoken in my conversation."[36] The intense public scrutiny of teachers' lives meant that schoolteachers had to contend with restraints not experienced in other professions. Richard Quantz asserted, "The respected status teachers received could only be maintained by having two selves—a public self, who tried to live up to the community expectations, and a private self, who needed to allow her own humanness to develop."[37] Individual teachers juggled these competing selves with more or less acuity. For some, a place in the profession just wasn't worth the personal costs. Beale maintained that the many restrictions placed on teachers tended to "drive the ambitious, the independent, and the unconventional away from teaching."[38] And, of course, one might question the sort of respect one could hope to obtain when its price was loss of personal autonomy. Beale wasn't at all sure the bargain was feasible: "One reason that children and their parents do not have more respect for teachers is that they so meekly submit to dictation from every one who wishes to give it."[39]

In editing an important collection of essays on the history of teachers, Richard Altenbaugh summed up the consequences facing American educators who were measured according to how well they fulfilled the prescribed role of moral exemplar. The historical record reveals that "communities scrutinized what teachers taught in the classroom and monitored their behavior outside of it. . . . Teachers served as role models, thus often causing community members to prescribe higher moral standards for classroom instructors than they placed on themselves. . . . [These same people] usually shunned personal associations with teachers because they seemed somewhat less than adult, represented effeminacy, and symbolized failure. These attitudes were reflected in modest salaries and low status for teachers, regardless of the community's size or economic standing."[40]

Feminization

If one were pressed to name the single most influential person behind the feminization of teaching in the United States, Emma Willard would be a likely candidate. In 1819 she argued that, if "properly fitted by instruction, [women] would be likely to teach children better than the other sex; they could afford to do it cheaper; and those men who would otherwise be engaged in this employment, might be at liberty to add to the wealth of the nation, by any of those thousand occupations, from which women are necessarily debarred."[41] While her address to the New York legislature failed to get a financial commitment from an assembly more focused on building canals than supporting girls' schooling, Willard's argument remains a classic example of the style of rhetoric that called forth a cultural sea change: making women teachers. More importantly, as founder and head of the Troy Female Seminary, Willard oversaw the preparation of hundreds of teachers and directed a network of Troy graduates who established their own schools for educating women and preparing teachers.[42] A generation later Horace Mann addressed the subject of women teachers, utilizing the same general argument that Willard had put forward. Tapping into the ideology that historian Linda Kerber termed "Republican Motherhood," Mann made the case that women citizens were equipped by nature to do the kind of teaching he had observed in Prussian schools. Mann wanted teachers who would nurture children, appeal to their best behavior, and instill moral values; he didn't expect teachers to exercise too much rational authority or raise an intellectual challenge to the state curriculum. And if the idea of a state system of schools were to be successful, Massachusetts would need many more teachers. Women provided a cheaper source of labor than men; they were the perfect teachers for supplying the Common School movement. As many scholars have noted, Mann was the consummate salesman, pitching his educational ideology in a place and time ripe for reform. By the middle of the nineteenth century, teaching was widely recognized as "women's work."[43] The transformation exposed the profession to even more public oversight matching the parameters set for women in a sexist culture.

The feminization of teaching in the United States accelerated after the Civil War. Postwar economies put a strain on public wages, states were beginning to require more formal preparation and certification for the profession, and teachers were increasingly subjected to administrative supervision that cut into their job autonomy.[44] All of these conditions made teaching less attractive to men, who had more options in obtaining employment than women.

As the nineteenth century came to a close, the men who remained in the profession were reminded by a gender-conscious public that they worked in an occupation primarily staffed by women, with a corresponding lower status—as if they had forgotten what many regarded as the unfortunate facts of the feminization of teaching. Blount concludes, "As women took up the work of teaching, communities shifted the conditions of the classroom to align more closely with societal expectations for women rather than men."[45] In fact, in their essay addressing "Historical Perspectives on the Changing Appeal of Teaching as a Profession," Michael Sedlak and Steven Schlossman stated, "No single subject is more central to the history of the teaching profession than the changing role of women in American society."[46]

Historian Kathleen Weiler examined the notion of the "woman schoolteacher" as an ideological construct. She argued that when elements in the nineteenth-century political economy shifted to make it not only feasible but also economically necessary to hire women as teachers, economic need collided with separate-spheres ideology. The dominant ideology—that men were to occupy the public sphere of work and politics, and women were to occupy the private sphere of domestic life and work—was not an accurate reflection of reality; nevertheless it wielded significant influence in how many nineteenth-century Americans imagined and explained their culture and their places in it. As Weiler observed, hiring women schoolteachers would challenge this thinking since teaching was work in the public sphere. Employing women as teachers would be considered acceptable, however, if teaching were defined as "women's true profession" bestowed upon them by nature, and if the public viewed the school as an extension of the family.[47] Such rhetoric supported an important transformation in the separate-spheres ideology; in effect, the private sphere was expanded to encompass schoolwork. Since the public sphere carried more status than the private sphere, the shift was detrimental to society's perception of teaching. Thomas Woody recorded this sentiment in his early history of women's education by quoting a Massachusetts school committee: "As there is neither honor nor profit connected with [teaching], we see no reason why it should not be filled by a woman."[48] Male teachers found themselves trapped in a profession that had, figuratively, shifted beneath their feet and suddenly marked them as "unmanly." As these realizations settled, more and more men left the profession. Cries of alarm regarding the feminization of teaching reached a crescendo by the end of the nineteenth century when a major backlash against women whipped through the field of education. New models of professionalization took root in the early decades of the twentieth century, featuring a "male model of administrative control."[49] As the emphasis on professionalization supplanted some of the control the community had exerted over teachers, Weiler argues that "by 1950 women teachers were firmly fixed in subordinate roles and schools were rigidly divided into gender hierarchies."[50]

In assessing the authority commanded by schoolteachers in the United States, Jurgen Herbst noted that they have been regarded "as little more than hired help."[51] This philosophy stretched back to the earliest days of the first state-supported normal schools, founded in Massachusetts at the behest of Horace Mann. In their discussion of early teacher-preparation institutes in the United States, Steven Tozer, Paul Violas, and Guy Senese traced the influence the two-tier Prussian school system had on nineteenth-century American educators such as Mann. The Prussian normal schools produced teachers for the *volkschules,* elementary schools for the common people where children learned to respect God, emperor, and country in a nationalistic curriculum, basic literacy, and little more. The state-defined objectives for the children were loyalty and obedience; intellectual development and academic excellence were reserved for students in the *vorschules,* gymnasiums, universities, and military institutes. The educational philosophy in place held that *volkschule* teachers required little knowledge beyond what they were to impart to their students, so the course of study at the normal schools emphasized pedagogical methods over academic content. Tozer, Violas, and Senese note that this sort of normal school approach "defined teacher education [in the United States] for the subsequent century," to devastating effect. They argue that the relatively low level of respect the American public maintains for teachers today is partly due to the normal-school approach designed to "train technicians" rather than "educate scholars."[52] The requirements for teaching as emphasized in the Common School period merged neatly with the views of many nineteenth-century American educators who believed women possessed a limited capacity for rational thought but were especially well-suited to work with children, providing yet another reason to support the feminization of teaching. Mann himself proclaimed "one of the clearest ordinances of Nature, that woman is the appointed guide and guardian of children."[53]

Women constituted the majority of public school teachers by the end of the nineteenth century when a new model of schooling based on Frederick Taylor's notions of scientific management emerged. The indomitable leader of Chicago's elementary school teachers, Margaret Haley, delivered a classic critique of the structural design in Progressive Era schooling that distanced teachers even further from professional autonomy. Speaking before the National Education Association in 1904, Haley denounced twentieth-century schools for "lack of recognition of the teacher as an educator in the school system, due to the increased tendency toward 'factoryizing education,' making the teacher an automaton, a mere factory hand, whose duty it is to carry out mechanically and unquestioningly the ideas and orders of those clothed with the authority of position, and who may or may not know the needs of the children or how to minister to them."[54]

A generation later, according to journalist Stephen Ewing, the still prevalent "petty regulations" teachers faced were a key reason that "the best" of college women avoided a career in education. Ewing told his readers, "No individual of spirit will choose to work in a milieu where her professional initiative will be curbed at every turn and where her personal activities will be under constant surveillance."[55]

Beyond the strictures on professional autonomy, marriage bans offer the most prominent example of restrictions aimed at women teachers. School boards barred women teachers from marriage throughout North America for half of the twentieth century although racism determined how this played out in different contexts. Given the extent of race discrimination in the labor market, African American women's economic contributions were critical to family support. Often African American teachers continued to work after marriage with the support of their communities.[56]

Although the National Educational Association began to challenge marriage bans earlier in the century, by 1940 only 13 percent of school districts nationwide would hire married women and 70 percent of the districts fired women teachers who married. Prohibitions against granting tenure to married women continued until the mid-1960s.[57] Just as the bans were falling, however, school authorities stepped up their efforts to force teachers to exhibit gender identities aligned with heterosexual traits. Blount documents how the well-worn practice of community oversight regarding teachers' behavior carried over to the mid-twentieth century when school authorities assumed a responsibility for policing teachers' gender presentation and sexual orientation. For instance, administrators considered ways to gauge the likely sexuality of job candidates on the basis of gender presentation during interviews. Blount delineates how "public perception shifted from regarding spinster teachers as good, upstanding members of their communities to castigating them as sinister, deviant women who corrupted children," a shift that paralleled the movement to drop the marriage bans against women teachers.[58]

Low levels of autonomy and gendered restrictions are two of the interlocking reasons teachers have struggled for professional status. This is not to suggest that teachers *accept* the gender stereotypes or that the profession simply rolls along in a deterministic fashion within narrow parameters.[59] But gender dynamics played an important role in twentieth-century teachers' activism because gendered ideology permeated the structure of schools. Lawrence Cremin explained the route that teachers of Haley's generation took to enhance the status of their profession. "Predominantly women, they saw themselves as exploited by predominantly male administrators and boards of education, with no job security, no rights to academic freedom, and salary scales at approximately half of those for men of equivalent rank, training, and experience; and they made salaries, working conditions, and job security their primary concerns, believing that once salaries, working conditions, and job security improved, professional status would inevitably follow."[60]

Few events in life, however, are inevitable. Although teachers did gain some critical improvements eventually—equalizing salary schedules for women and men and dismantling overt race discrimination in compensation, establishing tenure laws, bringing collective bargaining to the negotiations table—much of the twentieth-century history of efforts to improve status and working conditions for teachers is a record of disappointment.

A number of historians have studied the failure of teacher unions to mount strong campaigns for teachers' rights in the period between the successes of Haley's Chicago Federation of Teachers at the beginning of the twentieth century and those of the American Federation of Teachers and National Education Association in the 1960s. Marjorie Murphy cites a number of factors that contributed to the frustrating history of teacher unions, "gender differences" in the workforce among them. She also incorporated "recurrent seasons of red-baiting," "chronic fiscal crisis in education," and the "ideology of professionalism" in her analysis.[61] Joel Spring pointed to the power of corporations and conservatism of teachers, David Tyack discussed administrative coercion and the professionalization impulse among teachers, Wayne Urban focused on the shortcomings of an interest group concerned primarily with material interests, and Richard Quantz attributed the disappointing performance of unions to "the force of subjectivity in human life"—the fact that individual teachers made labor choices that best fit personal needs at given times.[62]

In any case, without a strong cohesive network to protect professional autonomy and guard against erosion in work conditions, teachers were left to contend with whatever policies the public might set. And professional status, as Geraldine Clifford astutely observed, generally followed the status of clients. In the United States, children have rarely been accorded high status, beyond high-sounding rhetoric. One need only look to the persistence of appalling numbers of children in poverty or the lack of comprehensive health care for examples. "Odes to home and child to the contrary notwith-standing," Clifford noted, "domestic activities confer small status or power to either sex."[63] Her conclusion is apparent: Since schooling embraced the domestic functions of child rearing, work "parents have always done without special qualifications," teaching would share the undervalued status associ-ated with women's "traditional" duties.[64]

Conservative Response

In his 1839 attack on the centralized school structures being developed by Common School reformers, Orestes Brownson charged that the system built for uniformity would produce conservative teachers. He warned that educa-tional leaders in the normal schools and state bureaucracies would get teachers to "respect and preserve what is, to caution them against the licentiousness of the people, the turbulence and brutality of the mob, the dangers of anarchy, and even of liberty; but they will rarely seek to imbue them with a love of lib-erty, to admonish them to resist the first encroachments of tyranny, to stand fast in their freedom. . . . They will but echo the sentiments of that portion of the community, on whom they are the more immediately dependent, and they will approve no reform, no step onward, till it has been already achieved in the soul of the community."[65] Later in the century, prominent schoolman Francis Parker opined, "We are a servile set, thinking too much of our bread and butter."[66] Without tenure laws to guard against arbitrary dismissal, living under the strict surveillance of the community, and for a long time with the majority of teachers without even the power of a vote, teachers were indeed a conservative lot. Howard Beale emphasized what he considered the real problem with a lack of personal and intellectual freedom for American teach-ers: multiple repressions (short of dismissal) that led to self-censorship. He noted that teachers preferred to speak of "discretion" when explaining their choices to speak out (or not) on issues. Beale observed that it was "difficult to determine when discretion ceases to be discretion and becomes expedi-ency or even fear."[67]

Historians agree that teachers, generally, have responded to the restrictions placed upon them with a sense of resignation. Correspondents in Courtney Vaughn-Roberson's study of 547 twentieth-century women teachers explained that they considered it a "duty" to comply with conservative notions of wom-anhood that permeated the cultures in which they taught, "question[ing] little."[68] Wayne Urban argued that teachers adopted a passive posture prior to the 1890s and even after "big city teachers began to flirt with activism in that decade," remained compliant almost everywhere else.[69] It is important to note that the "big city" activism was directed at "bread and butter" issues. In her study of New York City teachers, Kate Rousmaniere described union activity as "notoriously conservative" and clarified that "teacher associations were not radical political organizations but self-interested protective groups that held mainstream views about the role of schools and teachers."[70] Historian Joseph Newman confirmed this perspective, suggesting that teachers are as likely to support the dominant ideology in a community as members of any other occupation: "Most teachers, like other workers, hold the dominant values of the community. Because most teachers find it hard to imagine having to defend their views or actions to the community, they will not stick their necks out to defend co-workers who come under attack because they are different."[71]

Not only did teachers themselves acquiesce to the stringent demands society placed on members of their profession, they were quick to turn on colleagues suspected of violating the moral code of the community. The Brooklyn Teachers Association, for example, supported the investigations of teachers whose loyalty to the U.S. government was questioned in the Red scare that followed the Bolshevik Revolution.[72]

Although a general pattern of conservative behavior holds for the teaching profession overall, it would be a mistake to think that all teachers fit that mold. Historians of teachers are clear that schoolteachers have led "complex and ambiguous work lives" and some "have demonstrated an uncanny, though often overlooked, ability to shape events."[73] Patricia Carter, for instance, studied coalitions between teachers and women's political groups during the first decades of the twentieth century and determined that these groups were able to "break the stereotype of the submissive and apolitical woman teacher" through their joint attack on "sex discrimination in the labor market." Carter adds an important point: The effectiveness of this campaign lay with the political savvy of the women activists who took a tack that "stretched, but did not threaten, the traditional boundaries of the family unit."[74] The teachers would go only so far in challenging the status quo.

Vanessa Siddle Walker's recent work explores the role that nineteenth- and twentieth-century black educators played as advocates for equality, action that has been minimized if not ignored in historical scholarship. Teachers and administrators took an "activist, political stance" as important as the more celebrated efforts of the NAACP, and "often worked in concert with civil rights organizations."[75] As Siddle Walker shows, there was considerable overlap in membership records of black teacher organizations and civil rights groups. Black educators risked their jobs, and their lives, by working to equalize salaries, contest poor teaching conditions, and fight for desegregation. But the "resistance of Black educators . . . was intentionally vested in their professional organizations, rather than in the easily recognized behavior of individual Black teachers."[76] This strategy included inviting other professionals from the private sector to join the teacher groups, thus creating a shield of protection for the teachers who most certainly would be fired for their activism. Although all civil rights activists faced the danger of physical harm and other types of retaliation, teachers risked loss of income if fired from their city, county, and state jobs.[77] But by filtering their activism through professional organizations, black educators established "the most primary, most consistent, and best organized mechanism advocating for change" in the difficult decades that launched the twentieth century.[78]

For all of the important work that individual teachers, and especially black teacher organizations, have done to secure civil rights, promote equal educational standards, protect academic freedom, and maintain professional integrity, there simply have not been enough colleagues willing to share the burden—or the risks. Chicago teacher Lillian Herstein observed as much when she surmised, "You know what the schools need is not more freedom but more teachers who want freedom. Almost none of our teachers [have] a social philosophy."[79] The theme that many teachers were ill prepared to debate political issues or articulate a strong argument for the role of education in a democracy was one Beale gave a good deal of attention to in his study on academic freedom. Situating part of the problem in the normal-school training most teachers experienced, Beale found that few had had much access to scholarship that challenged the conventional opinions they held. Teachers who did express concern about restricted liberties often were too afraid to confront school authorities. Acknowledging "good reason for their fear," Beale nevertheless found lack of courage one of the most effective brakes on teachers' freedoms.[80]

In her landmark study on the legal history of gay and lesbian teachers, Karen Harbeck argued that teachers' propensity to be "self-regulating" is due to the widely known consequences of "displeasing their communities." Courts only began to rule against restrictions that violated teachers' rights to freedom of speech, association, religion, and privacy in recent decades; for most of the twentieth century, courts held that public employment was a privilege "subject to whatever conditions the government wished to impose."[81] As a group, schoolteachers have not been forceful in protecting the standard of academic freedom. Even if they had been so disposed, they had no legal defense against hostile school systems until the end of the twentieth century.

It is little wonder, then, that sociologist Waller concluded, "Radicals cannot usually hold teaching positions, and even moderately sophisticated views greatly limit the range of a teacher's choice of jobs."[82]

To some degree, teachers' reluctance to oppose restrictions regarding their employment can be explained by events in the political economy that affected many workers. Thousands of teachers were fired during the Red scares following World Wars I and II, creating a climate of extreme vulnerability for anyone who would challenge the system, and of course, workers did all they could to avoid losing jobs during the Great Depression. Both a new ideological emphasis on consumerism and entertainment in the 1920s and the patriotic fervor that swept through the nation during and after World War II correlated with a decline in white teacher activism even as black teachers were finding ways to combat racist school policies.[83]

The tendency toward conservatism among teachers was reinforced by factors specific to the field of education. The imposition of the new "professionalization" that accompanied the buildup of centralized educational bureaucracies in the twentieth century alienated urban teachers from their neighborhood communities, created divisions among colleagues, and cultivated a "self-conscious timid[ity]" in teachers who were "under public pressure" to "behave 'professionally.'"[84] A more persistent explanation for the conservative behavior of teachers, however, can be traced to the social class composition of the teaching force. Historically, schoolteachers in the United States have come from the lower-middle class and practitioners have used teaching as a means for social mobility. Again making allowance for exceptions, most teachers in this economic position would not want to risk losing a position that represented increased status in the community. As Marvin Lazerson put it, "There was little to be gained by waging war with the hierarchy when one's goal was to join it. In the end, teachers gave up their rights of citizenship. They accepted the notion that education should be non-political and that as teachers they should refrain from agitating for the right to determine policy. In return, despite the ambiguities of their position they were pretty much left alone in their classrooms."[85]

As we have seen, however, teachers were not "left alone" in their lives outside the classroom.

Purging the Homosexual Menace

In her landmark study Jackie Blount states that teachers, "long expected to adhere to rigid and highly restrictive codes of acceptable moral behavior," encountered conditions in the mid-twentieth century that led to intensified scrutiny concerning sexuality.[86] To be sure, similar attacks on teachers preceded the Cold War purges, but documented cases are few and often based on claims that teachers engaged in sexual relationships with students, behavior not to be confused with same-sex attraction in general. Two of the most cited cases involved Walt Whitman and Horatio Alger (who had given up teaching for the ministry at the time of the charges).[87] Buffeted between the entrenched professional practice of monitoring personal behavior and the excesses of postwar containment ideology, schoolteachers were particularly vulnerable to the 1950s witch hunts.

Working for the government was precarious employment for gay men and lesbians in mid-twentieth-century America. Although the U.S. military has drummed individuals out of service because of their sexuality since the Revolutionary War, an explicit policy banning homosexuals from the armed forces was not formally established until World War II.[88] Allan Bérubé's important work traces the impact of this antigay policy, largely ignored or circumvented during the crisis of war but pursued with abandon once victory was secured. Postwar purges drove hundreds of women from the Women's Army Corps in occupied Japan and sent thousands of servicemen home on special "queer" ships, all with dishonorable discharges.[89] Dismissals (averaging more than 1,000 per year after the war) brought special hearings, loss of veteran benefits, and diminished civilian job opportunities; psychiatric hospitalizations, court-martials, and prison sentences were not infrequent.[90]

Cold War politicians whipped up fears of a "homosexual menace" in lockstep with the military purge. A defining moment came in February 1950 when a State Department official told a Senate committee probing the loyalty of government workers that most of a group of federal employees recently dismissed were homosexuals. As historians John D'Emilio and David K. Johnson have demonstrated, Republicans seized the opportunity to link homosexuals with communism and then charge the Truman administration with lapses in national security. Johnson explained the Cold War distinction between a loyalty risk—a person with "a willful desire to betray secrets"—and a security risk—a person exhibiting "behaviors or associations that might lead one inadvertently or unwillingly to betray secrets in the future."[91] Although politicians routinely named alcoholics, those who talked too much, and homosexuals as security risks, they focused their attention on "perverts," and "security risk" quickly became a euphemism for "homosexual."[92] In June 1950 the Senate authorized a study on homosexuals in government and released its findings before the year was out. The themes of immorality, pathology, and crime surfaced, leading to demands that homosexuals be barred from employment with the federal government. An average of five civilians per month lost their jobs in the executive branch due to charges of homosexuality between 1947 and April 1950 but when the Senate report was released eight months later the average had climbed to sixty dismissals per month.[93] When Republicans regained the White House in 1953, President Eisenhower issued Executive Order 10450 that explicitly denied federal employment to "sexual perverts." Over the next sixteen months an average of forty employees per month were fired on the basis of sexual orientation.[94] By then, persecuting gay and lesbian federal employees was a practice firmly embedded in the "bureaucracy of the national security state."[95]

As the purges circulated to state and local levels of government, teachers—like military and other governmental workers—became vulnerable to homophobic witch hunts. As public employees they were susceptible to the full force of state repression.[96]

Gay and lesbian teachers, military personnel, and federal employees became targets during the Cold War for symbolic reasons. As guardians of the culture, defenders of the nation, and trustees of the state, these men and women were held to a normative standard of behavior. Since many people equated homosexuality with sin, sickness, and criminal activity, the citizenry assumed a right to purge "perverts" from professions that served the public. Critics charged that gay men and lesbians were "incompatible with military service" because homosexuality "undermines military discipline, creates security risks, and gives the military a bad reputation."[97] The 1950 Senate report *Employment of Homosexuals and Other Sex Perverts in Government* argued that homosexuals were unfit for government service due to their weak character and the danger they posed to national security. D'Emilio summed up the charges: "Immature, unstable, and morally enfeebled by the gratification of their perverted desires, homosexuals lacked the character to resist the blandishments of the spy."[98] An overseeing public intended to keep the character and reputation of its workers under surveillance and circumscribed any activity that it thought might disrupt discipline or threaten security. Fears that homosexuality would spread—from soldier to soldier and sailor to mate, within government offices, or from teacher to student—added fervor to the crusade. Yet, for all of the similarities regarding oversight of these public professions—the emphasis on character, reputation, discipline, and security—schoolteachers were vulnerable to antigay persecution in a unique way.

Unlike federal government employees and members of the military, teachers work with children. They are, in fact, expected to serve as role models for their students under the panoptic gaze of the local community. In addition, teaching has long been a feminized profession in contrast with the traditionally male preserves of the military and federal offices, making teachers even more susceptible to public oversight in a sexist society. The public has drawn upon a combination of these factors to justify its control over teachers in private as well as professional behavior. Although professional constraints restrict the behavior of other government workers and that control is quite rigid in the case of the military, public surveillance of teachers' private lives takes place to a degree unparalleled in other occupations.

Conclusion

> Florida is a magnet. . . . This peninsula is, in almost every respect, the most pleasant and favorable place to live on the North American continent.[99]
>
> —"How to Obtain and Hold Good Teachers in Florida's Schools," 1957

> The Florida Education Association [FEA] is seriously concerned about [homosexuality]. It has always been our policy to do everything possible to discourage grossly immoral persons from teaching in the schools. If they have been found, we have supported efforts to remove them permanently from the classrooms of the state and nation.[100]
>
> —Ed Henderson, executive secretary, FEA, 1961

The Florida Legislative Investigation Committee's purge of gay and lesbian teachers began during a teacher shortage. The combination of industrial expansion and the 1950s baby boom engendered a 62 percent increase in the number of students in grades 1 through 12 in Florida's schools between 1946 and 1955. In less than a decade the student population went from 428,489 to 697,776. School officials expected the figure to climb to 1,084,369 by 1961.[101] The postwar boom in Florida was part of what historian Gary Mormino refers to as "one of the great population shifts in history."[102] Moderate climate, increased numbers of retirees, a relatively strong economy, and technological advancements that supported the military-industrial complex and transportation expansion, not to mention the advent of air conditioning, drew people to the Sunbelt. Florida, in particular, capitalized on media promotion. The state's population grew from 2.7 to almost 5 million in the 1950s.[103] In 1959 state superintendent of public instruction Bailey reported to Governor Collins that Florida needed 7,000 new teachers each year to keep up with the "mushrooming population."[104]

Members of the FEA were concerned that some of the people hired to fill the ranks demonstrated "undesirable morals" and engaged in "unethical acts." The Ethics Committee met in 1957 to recommend that the FEA board establish a committee to "handle problems concerned with unethical practices among teachers." A note in the margin prescribed revoking certificates.[105] The FEA seized whatever leverage it might have had during the teacher shortage to ratchet up its control of the profession and gain status for practitioners. Apparently sensing that the window of opportunity was narrow, in 1959 FEA committees recommended "the profession move as rapidly as possible toward the time when it polices its own ranks" and tied the elusive desire for greater professional esteem to public awareness of the teachers' commitment to "a high code of ethics."[106] Four years later the FEA commanded the legal authority to investigate teachers but the Johns Committee's obsession with teachers' sexuality had spoiled collective expectations for professional eminence. In 1963 the president of the FEA Board of Directors noted it would "take a great deal of constructive work on the part of the Board in the next two years to prove to the Legislature and to the teachers of Florida that the profession is willing to establish and maintain high professional standards."[107] As discussed in chapter 4, the FEA did not hesitate in building its case for professionalism on the expulsion of gay and lesbian teachers. The episode fits neatly in the contours of education history.

The history of teaching lays bare a profession most susceptible to community oversight, even when compared to other occupations in the public sector. Two deeply rooted factors—the expectation that schoolteachers serve as role models for children and the set of consequences that spring from a predominately female workforce in a sexist culture—have circumscribed teachers' autonomy. The effects on teachers' lives have been profound.[108] Most apparent is the fact that teachers who transgress the boundaries of community expectations regarding their behavior usually have been fired. Joseph Newman's reflection on the example of Atlanta teacher Julia Riordan is, as he put it, a "dramatic" case in point, "but hardly exceptional. . . . Throughout the United States, teachers who stood out as different often found themselves in the same position—out of work and out of luck."[109]

It follows that teaching has developed a reputation as a conservative occupation. In noting a more serious threat in the form of self-censorship, Beale argued that many teachers would yield to pressures that eroded their self-expression and intellectual freedom. The majority of teachers, however, simply shared the conservative worldview of their communities.[110] Whether due to self-inclination, fear of reprisal, or the expulsion of those who did stick their necks out, the profession has consisted of practitioners unlikely to challenge the dominant ideology. Black educators who confronted racist school policies constitute the obvious exception to this pattern but as Siddle Walker found, these teachers usually shared the culture and beliefs of the communities in which they taught, and they did not challenge the social expectations of the community.[111]

Measured on intellectual, political, and social axes, the conservative bearing of the profession has meant that teachers have failed to form strong networks of support for those among their number who didn't fit the public's perception of the model schoolteacher. The Florida Education Association's pledge to "do everything possible" to help purge gay and lesbian teachers from the nation's classrooms should be seen in this context, reflecting a general pattern in educational history.[112] When the Personnel Problems Steering Committee met in 1961 to discuss the "homosexual cases," one member suggested that the FEA support teachers in civil cases "to the fullest extent, regardless of whether the teacher is the plaintiff or the defendant."[113] The motion did not go forward. Following the release of the purple pamphlet, Johns Committee chair Richard Mitchell sent a letter of appreciation to the president of the FEA, acknowledging the strong support Florida teachers provided the Investigation Committee. Mitchell wrote, "That so many of your members have recognized that [homosexuality] is a problem which must be faced squarely and frankly . . . is to us clear evidence of a major breakthrough toward the control of rampant homosexuality affecting and threatening the youth of Florida. . . . We seek and are grateful for the interest, concern, cooperation and guidance of your association and its membership."[114]

Lacking organizational support from their colleagues, queer teachers found it difficult to shield themselves from public scrutiny or claim the civil rights protections due all citizens. Little had changed a generation later when Anita Bryant led a successful effort to rescind a nondiscrimination ordinance in Miami. In 1977 the Dade County Metro Commission moved to include sexual orientation in its antidiscriminatory law regarding employment, housing, and public accommodations, incurring the wrath of the nascent Christian Right political movement. Bryant, who converted her 1959 Miss Oklahoma title into a singing/orange juice sales career, traded on her credentials as a mother in the infamous "Save Our Children" campaign. She directed the force of her crusade against gay men and lesbians at teachers, motivated by the same flawed rationale that the Johns Committee had disseminated two decades earlier. If teachers could not be fired on the basis of their sexuality, Bryant feared, "First, public approval of admitted homosexual teachers could encourage more homosexuality by inducing pupils into looking upon it as an acceptable life-style. And second, a particularly deviant-minded teacher could sexually molest children."[115]

Bryant revived the tired Cold War refrain but this time a gay liberation movement was in place to challenge the absurdities. No doubt preaching to the choir, a writer for *Lesbian Tide* summarized that Bryant's "ignorance of homosexuality was so complete, her prejudice so simplistic, she seemed a ludicrous parody of 1950s style American 'womanhood.'"[116] Nevertheless, Bryant tapped into a deep reserve of antigay sentiment, and the public referendum to overturn the antidiscrimination ordinance passed by a two-to-one margin. The defeat spurred a national mobilization of gay and lesbian activists, including teachers who began to organize to end school employment discrimination. Battle lines were drawn with teachers at the center. As historian Jackie Blount perceptively explained, "LGBT teachers effectively had become the wedge issue that divided public support for gay civil rights."[117]

Another generation would pass before the Miami-Dade County Commission reauthorized the law banning discrimination based on sexual orientation in 1998. Elizabeth Birch, executive director of the Human Rights Campaign, called the 7–6 vote a "watershed victory for gays and lesbians nationally."[118] Currently, there are no statewide laws to guard against employment discrimination on the basis of sexual orientation or gender identity in Florida, leaving gay and lesbian teachers vulnerable to the whims of local school boards.[119] The 2007 Florida Education Code states that instructional staff may be dismissed on charges pertaining to immorality or conviction of a crime involving moral turpitude, the Education Practices Commission maintains the authority to revoke teaching licenses on these grounds as well as personal conduct considered to reduce one's effectiveness as a school board employee, and district school superintendents are required to file a report with the Department of Education regarding anyone dismissed due to "conduct involving any immoral, unnatural, or lascivious act."[120] Even though the U.S. Supreme Court invalidated Florida's law banning "unnatural or lascivious" acts in 2003, the Education Code still contains language that provides cover for school boards to fire teachers because of their sexual orientation. As Catherine Lugg has argued, *Lawrence* will go only so far in establishing job security for gay and lesbian teachers because public schools regulate sexuality under myriad state laws and policies.[121] Four decades removed from the Johns Committee investigation, teaching remains a risky business for gay men and lesbians in Florida.

Conclusion

> It behooves us all to come to know the nature of the
> homosexual, for he is with us in every area of the state.
> It behooves us, too, *to define* for him, and for ourselves,
> *the conditions which govern his presence.*
> —Florida Legislative Investigation Committee, 1964

> I wish the homosexual revolution would hurry
> up! It is so desolate, this hiding in the catacombs.
> —J. M., Florida, 1963

As Robert J. Corber noted, the history of the Florida Legislative Investigation Committee should not be interpreted as an aberration of American democracy but understood as an example of state power "integral to its workings."[1] He explains that the Florida teacher purge, like other witch hunts during the Cold War, "enabled the state to consolidate its power to regulate both homosexuality and heterosexuality in moments of national crisis when that power has been threatened."[2] Shifting notions of sexuality kindled the mid-twentieth-century emergence of the regulatory state as laws increasingly recognized homosexuality as a "totalizing identity."[3] The Johns Committee engaged in every element of William Eskridge's succinct summary of this aspect of American history: "The regulatory state not only policed but increasingly sought to flush out the homosexual through toilet stakeouts, decoy operations, and witch hunts. The state also sought to expunge homosexuality from the public culture through censorship, terrorizing raids and surveillance, and license revocations."[4] No profession was more critical to the state's ill-conceived efforts to eliminate homosexuality from American culture than teaching. The Cold War battle between Florida teachers and the Johns Committee occupies an important place in twentieth-century American history.[5]

It would be a mistake, though, to characterize the Florida teacher purge as nothing more than an example of the oppressive force of state power in repressive times. The teachers under interrogation resisted in whatever ways they could, making for a dynamic, embattled history. That the teachers' various actions did not alter the outcome of the investigations—and that organizations did not advocate on their behalf—does not negate their significance. As historians of African American history have established, "Any effort by oppressed people to affirm their humanity can be characterized as an act of resistance."[6] And no act of resistance is inconsequential. Vanessa Siddle Walker's scholarship confirms that even when the struggle yields little structural change in a given political-economic context, it may set an important foundation for more successful sociopolitical movements that follow.[7] Eskridge picks up the argument from a legal perspective. He explains that as long as a social consensus denigrates a minority, little help can be expected from the courts. But even when individuals lose legal battles to assert political rights, over time the action may destabilize the social consensus against the group. Once the social prejudice begins to fade, judges are more likely to rule in favor of the minority group. Legal advancement for religious and ethnic minorities, women, and sexual minorities fits this circular pattern.[8] The teacher purge occurred just a few years before the Stonewall rebellion and the political movement that followed. Although we are unlikely to know the extent of any long-term effect generated by the fated teachers' resistance, it surely mattered: "The world is moved by diverse powers and pressures creating cross currents that unpredictably . . . determine the outcome of events. Often invisible in their influence, these forces shape our destinies."[9]

A decade after the Florida purge ended, gay and lesbian teachers joined the vanguard of those who challenged employment discrimination, usually at severe personal cost. But as John D'Emilio explained, "Before the movement could become a significant social force, the consciousness and the conditions of daily life of large numbers of lesbians and homosexuals had to change so that they could take up the banner carried by a pioneering few."[10] Harbeck paints a vivid picture of the forces that merged to create the Cold War climate that gave rise to the Florida Legislative Investigation Committee: "When the historical constraints upon teachers' personal lives and the fear of ideological and social corruption of youth were combined with the perceived link between communism and homosexuality, conservatives easily asserted their views in the social and legal struggle."[11] Teachers were easy targets for nonqueer oppressors—always in the public eye and with unique legal status that separated them from workers in other occupations. As Harbeck found, in most states teachers who were arrested on charges involving homosexuality "faced immediate job termination, regardless of the disposition of their criminal case."[12] The laws allowed teachers to be fired for conduct not related to their job, even if the arrests were illegal and even if they were found not guilty.[13] Courts relied on the well-established tradition that put reputation above all else to justify this action; educators whom society deemed of questionable character were judged unfit to teach. Until queer teachers could break through this legal tradition, they remained trapped in a cycle of oppression unique to the profession.

The teachers who found themselves in the sights of the Johns Committee could do very little, then, to protect themselves from attack. The legislators who claimed the schools had become a "refuge for practicing homosexuals" and vowed to rid the system of teachers they considered immoral were acting well within the strictures of American educational practice.[14] It would take collective dissent on a massive scale to alter aspects of the political economy that kept queer citizens' lives in check, and that day had not yet come. Until progressive elements forced changes in the medical structure, homosexual teachers would be fired because they were "sick." Until political forces demanded change in the legal statutes, gay and lesbian teachers would be fired because they were "criminals." Given the history of teaching as it developed in the United States, it is not surprising that teachers, collectively, did not take a more active role in dismantling discriminatory policies and laws against gay men and lesbians.

The rationale for firing gay and lesbian teachers and revoking their certificates that the Johns Committee relied upon was cut from the same ideological cloth that school administrators and politicians have used against teachers since the 1930s.[15] But the single-mindedness that fueled the Florida investigation, the intensity with which Johns Committee agents pursued their subjects, the extent of state support, and the number of people investigated over the nine-year period mark this episode as unique in the annals of education history and put it on a par with the better-known witch hunts of the Cold War era.

This study of the Florida purge enhances both the history of teaching and queer history by underscoring the role of dominant ideology in education and the larger culture. For years the dominant ideology in the United States reinforced beliefs that homosexuality is "sinful, criminal, and medically pathological." These beliefs along with the laws and policies they generated barred gay men and lesbians from teaching, disqualified them from obtaining professional educational credentials, and kept gay and lesbian teachers in the closet. In a climate of mounting oppression during the Cold War, the homophile movement of the 1950s and other civil rights advances in the 1960s shook up the dominant ideology and roused people to political action. Cracks in the dominant ideology created fissures in homophobic political structures. By 1973 mainstream medical authorities no longer considered homosexuality pathological. Beginning with Illinois in 1961, states began to decriminalize homosexuality. The effort was piecemeal until 2003 when the U.S. Supreme Court handed down its decision in *Lawrence v. Texas*. Over time, legal decisions that restricted gay men and lesbians from teaching or kept queer teachers from coming out eroded, marking a significant transformation in the political economy. Yet many queer teachers remain in the closet, at once illustrating the hold ideology has on schoolteachers and suggesting the necessary part schoolteachers will need to play if queer people are to claim full human rights.

Until Americans let go of the notion that homosexuality is "sinful," queer teachers will be regarded as "immoral," in spite of pronouncements to the contrary by medical and legal authorities. Advances in the political economy notwithstanding, it is a difficult thing to change the ideology of a nation. Queer victories in the political economy, in fact, may spur nonqueers to increase their surveillance over the sexuality of teachers. Since Americans have made schoolteachers guardians of the dominant ideology, public oversight of teachers' sexuality will remain intense as long as the battle is fixed. To accept queer schoolteachers, after all, is to accept a queer nation.

This last point is critical. Putting the history of discrimination against queer teachers in the context of a broader history of teachers, it becomes apparent that queer rights cannot be gained in full until queer teachers are fully accepted. At some level, the Florida Legislative Investigation Committee must have known this. "It behooves us," the committee argued in regard to the queer teacher, "to define . . . the conditions which govern his presence."[16] To control teachers is to control the dominant ideology. Does it not follow, then, that to free teachers from antigay discrimination is to take a crucial step in dismantling homophobia in our society? The history of education in the United States demonstrates—and current practice still exhibits—that it is the province of the schoolteacher to serve as moral exemplar for the nation.

Notes

Preface

1. Testimony, 19 October 1960, p. 3, File 42, Box 10, S1486 Florida Legislative Investigation Committee, State Archives of Florida, Tallahassee (hereafter, S1486). Names of witnesses (other than public officials) who appeared before the Florida Legislative Investigation Committee are not a matter of public record.

2. Testimony, 19 October 1960, p. 4, S1486.

3. Testimony, 19 October 1960, p. 4, S1486.

4. Testimony, 19 October 1960, p. 5, S1486.

5. Testimony, 19 October 1960, p. 5, S1486.

6. Testimony, 19 October 1960, pp. 8–9, S1486.

7. Testimony, 19 October 1960, p. 9, S1486.

8. Testimony, 19 October 1960, p. 10, S1486.

9. Testimony, 19 October 1960, p. 11, S1486.

10. Testimony, 19 October 1960, p. 12, S1486.

11. Testimony, 19 October 1960, p. 11, S1486.

12. Testimony, 19 October 1960, p. 13, S1486.

13. Testimony, 19 October 1960, p. 13, S1486.

14. Testimony, 19 October 1960, p. 14, S1486.

15. Testimony, 19 October 1960, p. 14, S1486. Emphasis in the original.

16. "Report of Florida Legislative Investigation Committee to 1959 Session of the Legislature," pp. 8–9, File 21, Box 1, S1486.

17. In this historical analysis I use the terms *gay* and *lesbian* to refer to the men and women under interrogation since my emphasis is not on a broader conception of queer sexuality. Overall, this is a record of what happened to men who were gay and women who were lesbians, or those assumed to be gay men or lesbians. The specific

terms seem appropriately descriptive. I use the term *homosexual* when referring to the language used by agents of the Investigation Committee, other state agencies, the media, witnesses, and others from the period under review, since that word was the term most often used at the time.

18. See David K. Johnson, *The Lavender Scare: The Cold War Persecution of Gays and Lesbians in the Federal Government* (Chicago: University of Chicago Press, 2004).

19. Scholars owe James A. Schnur gratitude for his efforts to make the Investigation Committee's records available for study. For a review of the Florida legislature's support of the Investigation Committee, see Bonnie Stark, "McCarthyism in Florida: Charley Johns and the Florida Legislative Investigation Committee, July, 1956 to July, 1968" (master's thesis, University of South Florida, 1985). For a comprehensive study on the way the Investigation Committee framed its mission within Cold War parameters, see Stacy Lorraine Braukman, "Anticommunism and the Politics of Sex and Race in Florida, 1954–1965" (PhD diss., University of North Carolina at Chapel Hill, 1999) On civil rights, see Steven F. Lawson, "The Florida Legislative Investigation Committee and the Constitutional Readjustment of Race Relations, 1956–1963," in *An Uncertain Tradition: Constitutionalism and the History of the South,* ed. Kermit L. Hall and James W. Ely Jr. (Athens: University of Georgia Press, 1989), 296–325; Caroline S. Emmons, "Flame of Resistance: NAACP in Florida, 1910–1960" (PhD diss., Florida State University, 1998); Robert W. Saunders Sr., *Bridging the Gap: Continuing the Florida NAACP Legacy of Harry T. Moore, 1952–1966* (Tampa: University of Tampa Press, 2000); and Judith G. Poucher, "One Woman's Courage: Ruth Perry and the Johns Committee," in *Making Waves: Female Activists in Twentieth-Century Florida,* ed. Jack E. Davis and Kari Frederickson (Gainesville: University Press of Florida, 2003), 229–49. For political and legal analyses of the Investigation Committee's attack on homosexuals, see William N. Eskridge Jr., "Privacy, Jurisprudence, and the Apartheid of the Closet, 1946–1961," *Florida State University Law Review* 24 (Summer 1997): 703–838, and Gerard Sullivan, "Political Opportunism and the Harassment of Homosexuals in Florida, 1952–1965," *Journal of Homosexuality* 37, no. 4 (1999): 57–81. On the university investigations, see James A. Schnur, "Cold Warriors in the Hot Sunshine: USF and the Johns Committee," *Sunland Tribune* 18 (November 1992): 9–15; James T. Sears, *Lonely Hunters: An Oral History of Lesbian and Gay Southern Life, 1948–1968* (Boulder, Colo.: Westview Press, 1997), 12–107; James A. Schnur, "Closet Crusaders: The Johns Committee and Homophobia, 1956–1965," in *Carryin' On in the Lesbian and Gay South,* ed. John Howard (New York: New York University Press, 1997), 132–63; Allyson A. Beutke and Scott Litvack, *Behind Closed Doors: The Dark Legacy of the Johns Committee* (Gainesville: Documentary Institute in the College of Journalism and Communications, University of Florida, 2000); Dan Bertwell, "'A Veritable Refuge for Practicing Homosexuals': The Johns Committee and the University of South Florida," *Florida Historical Quarterly* 83, no. 4 (2005): 410–31; and Karen Graves, "Confronting a 'Climate of Raucous and Carnival Invasion': The AAUW Takes on the Johns Committee," *Florida Historical Quarterly* 85, no. 2 (Fall 2006): 154–76.

20. Published works in the Florida Legislative Investigation Committee historiography that focus on the schoolteacher purge consist of Stacy Braukman, "'Nothing Else Matters but Sex': Cold War Narratives of Deviance and the Search for Lesbian Teachers in Florida, 1959–1963," *Feminist Studies* 27, no. 3 (Fall 2001): 553–75; Karen L. Graves, "Doing the Public's Business: Florida's Purge of Gay and Lesbian Teachers, 1959–1964," *Educational Studies* 41, no. 1 (February 2007): 7–32; and Karen Graves, "Containing the Perimeter: Dynamics of Race, Sexual Orientation, and the State in the 1950s and 60s," in *The History of Discrimination in U.S. Education: Marginality, Agency, and Power,* ed. Eileen H. Tamura (New York: Palgrave Macmillan, 2008).

21. See John D'Emilio, "Not a Simple Matter: Gay History and Gay Historians," *Journal of American History* 76, no. 2 (September 1989): 439, 441–42; Martin Bauml Duberman, Martha Vicinus, and George Chauncey Jr., eds., *Hidden from History: Reclaiming the Gay and Lesbian Past* (New York: New American Library, 1989), 1; Henry Abelove, "The Queering of Lesbian and Gay History," *Radical History Review* 62 (1995): 46; Carolyn Dean, "Queer History," Review of *Queer Fictions of the Past: History, Culture, and Difference* by Scott Bravmann, *History and Theory* 38, no. 1 (February 1999): 130; and Alex P. Kellogg, "Report Reveals Tight Job Market for Historians of Gay Topics," *Chronicle of Higher Education,* July 6, 2001.

22. See Lisa Duggan, "Lesbianism and American History: A Brief Source Review," *Frontiers* 4, no. 3 (1979): 81.

23. Karen M. Harbeck, *Gay and Lesbian Educators: Personal Freedoms, Public Constraints* (Malden, Mass.: Amethyst Press and Productions, 1997).

24. Jackie M. Blount, *Fit to Teach: Same-Sex Desire, Gender, and School Work in the Twentieth Century* (Albany: State University of New York Press, 2005), 5, 15, 184.

25. Anonymous, informal conversation with author, 9 July 2005, Tampa.

Chapter 1: Politics of Intimidation in the Sunshine State

Testimony, 19 October 1960, p. 10, File 42, Box 10, S1486.

1. Stark, "McCarthyism in Florida," 10–12; David R. Colburn, "Florida's Governors Confront the *Brown* Decision: A Case Study of the Constitutional Politics of School Desegregation, 1954–1970," in *An Uncertain Tradition: Constitutionalism and the History of the South,* ed. Kermit L. Hall and James W. Ely Jr. (Athens: University of Georgia Press, 1989), 333.

2. "NAACP Probing Law Is Indicated," Associated Press news report, 5 August 1956, File 2, Box 16, S1486; Stark, "McCarthyism in Florida," 12–14.

3. "NAACP Probing Law Is Indicated."

4. Jeff Woods, *Black Struggle, Red Scare: Segregation and Anti-Communism in the South, 1948–1968* (Baton Rouge: Louisiana State University Press, 2004), 2.

5. Woods, *Black Struggle,* 5–6; Emmons, "Flame of Resistance," 219–22; Lawson, "The Florida Legislative Investigation Committee and the Constitutional Readjustment of Race Relations," 298; Amilcar Shabazz, *Advancing Democracy: African Americans and the Struggle for Access and Equity in Higher Education in Texas* (Chapel Hill:

University of North Carolina Press, 2004), 180–95; Ellen Schrecker, *Many Are the Crimes: McCarthyism in America* (Boston: Little, Brown, 1998), 389–95.

6. "NAACP Probing Law Is Indicated"; "NAACP Probing Bill Becomes Law," Associated Press news report, 21 August 1956, File 2, Box 16, S1486; Stark, "McCarthyism in Florida," 6–9, 15–16. From this point forward, I use "Florida Legislative Investigation Committee," "Investigation Committee," and "Johns Committee" interchangeably.

7. Braukman, "Anticommunism and the Politics of Sex and Race in Florida," 17–18; Jack E. Davis, introduction to *Making Waves: Female Activists in Twentieth-Century Florida,* ed. Jack E. Davis and Kari Frederickson (Gainesville: University Press of Florida, 2003), 2; Kevin N. Klein, "Guarding the Baggage: Florida's Pork Chop Gang and Its Defense of the Old South" (PhD diss., Florida State University, 1995), 1–20; Stark, "McCarthyism in Florida," 3, 15–16.

8. "Anti-NAACP Committee Hires Tampan," *Tampa Tribune,* 18 October 1956.

9. Stark, "McCarthyism in Florida," 17–18; Attorney General Richard W. Ervin to Henry Land, 4 October 1956, File 6, Box 3, S1486.

10. Mark Hawes, "Confidential State of Florida Legislative Investigation Committee Progress Report," 17 January 1957, p. 13, File 21, Box 1, S1486.

11. Stark, "McCarthyism in Florida," 27–31; Braukman, "Anticommunism and the Politics of Sex and Race in Florida," 90–91; Sears, *Lonely Hunters,* 56–57. For detailed accounts of the Johns Committee attack on the NAACP, see Poucher, "One Woman's Courage," 229–49, and Saunders, *Bridging the Gap.* See Lawson's analysis of the Johns Committee's strategy to tie the NAACP to communism in "The Florida Legislative Investigation Committee and the Constitutional Readjustment of Race Relations."

12. Testimony, 6 February 1959, p. 9, File 18, Box 7, S1486.

13. Testimony, 6 February 1959, pp. 11–12, File 18, Box 7, S1486.

14. Testimony, 6 February 1959, pp. 34 and 38, File 18, Box 7, S1486.

15. Quoted in Dal McIntire, "Tangents: Trouble in Tampa," *One* 5 (October–November 1957): 18.

16. McIntire, "Tangents," 18; "Board Asks Parley on 'Strict' Law Aimed at Perverts," *Tampa Tribune,* 12 June 1957.

17. Quoted in Harry Robarts, "Dr. Cline's Firing Leads to Probe of 'Personal Habits, Morals' of Teachers Here," *Tampa Tribune,* 6 July 1957. Although Farnell initially said he would release the names of fired teachers to the press, the school board voted unanimously to withhold the names two weeks later. Farnell explained that families were involved and that the teachers' removal rested on claims others made that the teachers were "deviates." News accounts noted only seven teachers were listed in the sheriff's report; of these, four teachers left the district before the report was released, one was soon to leave, and the other two would be dismissed. See "School Board Withholds Names in Morals Probe," *Tampa Tribune,* 24 July 1957.

18. Chuck Hendrick, "13 Nabbed in Crackdown on Morals Offenders Here," *Tampa Tribune,* 13 July 1957.

19. Quoted in Hendrick, "13 Nabbed in Crackdown."

20. Quoted in Hendrick, "13 Nabbed in Crackdown."

21. Quoted in Sears, *Lonely Hunters,* 17.

22. Quoted in Sears, *Lonely Hunters,* 22–23. See Sears's account of the crime and political reaction, pp. 12–24, and Lyn Pedersen, "Miami Hurricane," *One* 2 (November 1954): 3–8.

23. Pedersen, "Miami Hurricane," 8.

24. Braukman, "Anticommunism and the Politics of Sex and Race in Florida," 131–35; Schnur, "Closet Crusaders," 134–35; Schnur, "Cold Warriors in the Hot Sunshine," 10.

25. Poucher, "One Woman's Courage," 230–31.

26. See Poucher's account of the hearings in Poucher, "One Woman's Courage," 235–45.

27. Quoted in Lawson, "The Florida Legislative Investigation Committee and the Constitutional Readjustment of Race Relations," 311.

28. Emmons, "Flame of Resistance," 221, 234, 236–37; Saunders, *Bridging the Gap,* 170; Lawson, "The Florida Legislative Investigation Committee and the Constitutional Readjustment of Race Relations," 316.

29. Letter to the editor, *One* 6 (February 1958): 30.

30. Stark, "McCarthyism in Florida," 64.

31. Braukman, "Anticommunism and the Politics of Sex and Race in Florida," 159.

32. "Report of the Florida Legislative Investigation Committee to the 1961 Session of the Legislature," pp. 6–7, File 21, Box 1, S1486.

33. "Report of the Florida Legislative Investigation Committee," 19–20.

34. Quoted in Schnur, "Closet Crusaders," 141; Stark, "McCarthyism in Florida," 165.

35. Stark, "McCarthyism in Florida," 110, 118.

36. Stark, "McCarthyism in Florida," 192–209; Braukman, "Anticommunism and the Politics of Sex and Race in Florida," 276.

37. Quoted in Braukman, "Anticommunism and the Politics of Sex and Race in Florida," 272.

38. Board of Control, "Statement of Policy on Academic Freedom and Responsibilities," 7 December 1962, p. 3, File 2, Box 1, S1486.

39. *Neal v. Bryant,* 149 So. 2d 529 (1962 Fla. LEXIS 3332; 97 A.L.R. 2d 819); Harbeck, *Gay and Lesbian Educators,* 179–86.

40. Braukman, "Anticommunism and the Politics of Sex and Race in Florida," 279–81. According to Lawson, the balance in the Court shifted when Justice Felix Frankfurter became ill, deliberations were held up, and Frankfurter's replacement on the Court, Justice Arthur Goldberg, sided with the new majority. See Lawson, "The Florida Legislative Investigation Committee and the Constitutional Readjustment of Race Relations," 314.

41. Quoted in Mary L. Dudziak, *Cold War Civil Rights: Race and the Image of American Democracy* (Princeton, N.J.: Princeton University Press, 2000), 79.

42. Derrick Bell, *Silent Covenants:* Brown v. Board of Education *and the Unfulfilled Hopes for Racial Reform* (Oxford: Oxford University Press, 2004), 49.

43. Bell, *Silent Covenants,* 9. See chapter 6, "*Brown* as an Anticommunist Decision," 59–68.

44. Stark, "McCarthyism in Florida," 202, 82–87, 192–209.

45. Braukman, "Anticommunism and the Politics of Sex and Race in Florida," 282–90; Sears, *Lonely Hunters,* 94–98; Schnur, "Closet Crusaders," 148–52.

46. Quoted in Stark, "McCarthyism in Florida," 226–27.

47. Stark, "McCarthyism in Florida," 223–24, 228–29.

48. Quoted in Sears, *Lonely Hunters,* 106.

49. Quoted in Richard T. Jones, "Sodomy—Crime or Sin?" *University of Florida Law Review* 12 (Spring 1959): 85.

50. Jones, "Sodomy—Crime or Sin?" 85, 92.

51. McIntire, "Tangents," 20.

52. Braukman, "Anticommunism and the Politics of Sex and Race in Florida," 180.

53. The following information is based on my examination of the transcripts of eighty-seven schoolteachers who testified before the Johns Committee, S1486.

54. Klein, "Guarding the Baggage," x–xi, 119–20. For a discussion of the distinction between north and south Florida, see Klein's preface, vii–xi. Ironically, Professor Dietrich was one of the UF faculty members targeted by the Johns Committee in its 1958 investigation. Events regarding his experience with the Johns Committee are related in Beutke and Litvack, *Behind Closed Doors.*

55. Federal Writer's Project of the Work Projects Administration for the State of Florida, *Florida: A Guide to the Southernmost State* (New York: Oxford University Press, 1939), 3. The rendering of such a north-south divide is, of course, an imprecise art. Some historians stress the point that "vast sections of South Florida . . . conform to no such neat categories." See Gary R. Mormino, *Land of Sunshine, State of Dreams: A Social History of Modern Florida* (Gainesville: University Press of Florida, 2005), 6–7.

56. Information compiled from records in File 20, Box 4; Files 19 and 20, Box 5; Files 12 and 13, Box 6; Files 11–14, 16–17, Box 13, S1127 Florida. State Department of Education, Superintendent of Public Instruction, Thomas D. Bailey, Subject Files, 1949–1965, State Archives of Florida, Tallahassee (hereafter S1127).

57. Braukman, "Anticommunism and the Politics of Sex and Race in Florida," 34–35, 90–91, 151; Schnur, "Closet Crusaders," 134; Stark, "McCarthyism in Florida," 13, 30, 64–65.

58. Schnur, "Closet Crusaders," 141; Stark, "McCarthyism in Florida," 88–89.

59. Stephen Preskill, "Contradictions of Domestic Containment: Forestalling Human Development during the Cold War," in *Inexcusable Omissions: Clarence Karier and the Critical Tradition in History of Education Scholarship,* ed. Karen Graves, Timothy Glander, and Christine Shea (New York: Peter Lang, 2001), 182.

60. Preskill, "Contradictions of Domestic Containment," 182–86. Important texts on domestic containment include Dudziak, *Cold War Civil Rights;* Elaine Tyler May,

Homeward Bound: American Families in the Cold War Era (New York: Basic Books, 1988); and Ellen W. Schrecker, *No Ivory Tower: McCarthyism and the Universities* (New York: Oxford University Press, 1986).

61. Nan Alamilla Boyd, *Wide Open Town: A History of Queer San Francisco to 1965* (Berkeley: University of California Press, 2003), 71–72.

62. John D'Emilio, *Sexual Politics, Sexual Communities: The Making of a Homosexual Minority in the United States, 1940–1970* (Chicago: University of Chicago Press, 1983), 40–53; John D'Emilio, *Making Trouble: Essays on Gay History, Politics, and the University* (New York: Routledge, 1992), 57–73.

63. Johnson, *The Lavender Scare*, 3–10.

64. Quoted in D'Emilio, *Making Trouble*, 59.

65. Daniel J. Robinson and David Kimmel, "The Queer Career of Homosexual Security Vetting in Cold War Canada," *Canadian Historical Review* 75 (1994): 328.

66. Boyd, *Wide Open Town*, 116–18; Allan Bérubé, "Marching to a Different Drummer: Lesbian and Gay GIs in World War II," in *Hidden from History: Reclaiming the Gay and Lesbian Past*, 383–84, 388, 392; D'Emilio, *Sexual Politics, Sexual Communities*, 44; Lillian Faderman, *Odd Girls and Twilight Lovers: A History of Lesbian Life in Twentieth-Century America* (New York: Penguin, 1991), 118–30.

67. D'Emilio, *Sexual Politics, Sexual Communities*, 46; Henry Abelove, "New York City Gay Liberation and the Queer Commuters," in *Deep Gossip* (Minneapolis: University of Minnesota Press, 2003), 74–77. Abelove reports that the Library of Congress investigated more than 2,200 employees between 1947 and 1956, looking for "subversives or sexual perverts."

68. Boyd, *Wide Open Town*, 120–21; Sears, *Lonely Hunters*, 21–24. See also D'Emilio, *Sexual Politics, Sexual Communities*, 49–53.

69. Boyd, *Wide Open Town*, 163; Faderman, *Odd Girls and Twilight Lovers*, 164–66; and Elizabeth Lapovsky Kennedy and Madeline D. Davis, *Boots of Leather, Slippers of Gold: The History of a Lesbian Community* (New York: Penguin Books, 1993), 55–64.

70. Catherine Lugg brought this point to my attention. See her scholarship on the contemporary status of queer citizens, particularly "The Religious Right and Public Education: The Paranoid Politics of Homophobia," *Educational Policy* 12, no. 3 (May 1998): 267–83; "Sissies, Faggots, Lezzies, and Dykes: Gender, Sexual Orientation, and a New Politics of Education," *Educational Administration Quarterly* 39, no. 1 (2003): 95–134; "Our Straightlaced Administrators: The Law, Lesbian, Gay, Bisexual, and Transgendered Educational Administrators, and the Assimilationist Imperative," *Journal of School Leadership* 13, no. 1 (2003): 51–85; and "Thinking about Sodomy: Public Schools, Legal Panoptics, and Queers," *Educational Policy* 20 (2006): 35–58.

71. Eskridge, "Privacy, Jurisprudence, and the Apartheid of the Closet," 703–838.

72. Quoted in Blount, *Fit to Teach*, 89, 91. See chapter 5, "The New Moral Menace to Our Youth," pp. 80–107; Braukman, "Anticommunism and the Politics of Sex and Race in Florida," 186–88.

73. Quoted in Boyd, *Wide Open Town*, 93–94, 98.

74. Boyd, *Wide Open Town,* 96–97.

75. Quoted in Blount, *Fit to Teach,* 94–95. See John Gerassi, *The Boys of Boise: Furor, Vice, and Folly in an American City* (New York: Macmillan, 1966).

76. Boyd, *Wide Open Town,* 92–93.

77. Blount, *Fit to Teach,* 81.

Chapter 2: A Stealth Investigation

Mark Hawes to unnamed witness, p. 2, File 149, Box 11, S1486; testimony, 26 January 1960, p. 17, File 41, Box 7, S1486.

1. Blount, *Fit to Teach,* 80–81. See also Harbeck, *Gay and Lesbian Educators,* and Lugg, "Sissies, Faggots, Lezzies, and Dykes," 105–10. The emphasis on the explicit nature of public oversight of teachers' sexuality is important here. As Blount documents, schools in the United States have regulated the gender presentation and sexual behavior of teachers since the nineteenth century; overt policing of same-sex desire, however, developed in the post–World War II period.

2. Lugg, "Thinking about Sodomy," 36.

3. Eskridge, "Privacy, Jurisprudence, and the Apartheid of the Closet," 750.

4. Percentage compiled from Samuel Schloss and Carol Joy Hobson, "Statistics of State School Systems 1957–58: Organization, Staff, Pupils, and Finances," chapter 2 of *Biennial Survey of Education in the United States, 1956–58* (Washington, D.C.: U.S. Government Printing Office, 1961), 30. The percentage of male teachers in Florida rose slightly during the intense years of the teacher purge, from 26 percent in 1957–58 to 27.2 percent in 1959–60 to 28.8 percent in 1961–62. Percentages compiled from Carol Joy Hobson and Samuel Schloss, "Statistics of State School Systems 1959–60," Circular No. 691 (Washington, D.C.: U.S. Government Printing Office, 1963), 35 and Carol Joy Hobson and Samuel Schloss, "Statistics of State School Systems 1961–62 Final Report," Circular No. 751 (Washington, D.C.: U.S. Government Printing Office, 1964), 36.

5. Phyllis Lyon, quoted in Boyd, *Wide Open Town,* 156.

6. Blount, *Fit to Teach,* 78–79.

7. Testimony, 6 February 1959, p. 38, File 18, Box 7, S1486.

8. The worst examples involved witnesses beyond this data set: students at Florida Agricultural and Mechanical University, faculty at Gibbs Junior College, and non-school workers caught in a Tallahassee dragnet. See Braukman, "Anticommunism and the Politics of Sex and Race in Florida, 1954–1965," 176–79, and Schnur, "Closet Crusaders," 140.

9. The *Biennial Survey of Education in the United States, 1950–52* recorded data on segregated African American schools "in addition to" information gathered "for the total school system." Assuming that the figures given for the total school system include African American schools and that (only) African Americans staffed these schools, 4,540 African American teachers were among the 18,929 Florida teachers in

1951–52, representing 23.9 percent of the total. This comports with the 1949 Bureau of Labor Statistics finding that, in Florida, "Over a fourth of all elementary pupils, a fifth of all high school students, and similar proportions of classroom teachers were Negroes." Similar government documents compiled after the *Brown v. Board of Education* decision do not provide disaggregate data on African American teachers. See Samuel Schloss and Carol Joy Hobson, "Statistics of State School Systems: Organization, Staff, Pupils, and Finances 1951–52," chapter 2 of *Biennial Survey of Education in the United States, 1950–52* (Washington, D.C.: U.S. Government Printing Office, 1955), 20–23, 36–37, 88; U.S. Department of Labor, Bureau of Labor Statistics, *Employment Outlook for Elementary and Secondary School Teachers,* Bulletin No. 972 (Washington, D.C.: U.S. Government Printing Office, 1949), 24.

10. D'Emilio, *Sexual Politics, Sexual Communities;* D'Emilio, *Making Trouble;* John D'Emilio, *The World Turned: Essays on Gay History, Politics, and Culture* (Durham, N.C.: Duke University Press, 2002). Kinsey died in 1956, the same year that the Johns Committee was established.

11. "Report of Florida Legislative Investigation Committee to 1959 Session of the Legislature," 13 April 1959, pp. 3–9, File 21, Box 1, S1486.

12. Florida Legislative Investigation Committee memorandum, n.d., File 9, Box 3, S1486.

13. Testimony, 6 October 1959, pp. 3–4, File 28, Box 7, S1486.

14. Testimony, 6 October 1959, p. 4, File 28, Box 7, S1486.

15. Testimony, 24 May 1961, pp. 8–9, File 127, Box 8, S1486.

16. Testimony, 10 October 1962, p. 3, File 149, Box 10, S1486.

17. Testimony, 10 October 1962, pp. 8–9, File 149, Box 10, S1486.

18. Testimony, 31 December 1959, p. 3, File 48, Box 7, S1486.

19. Testimony, 26 January 1960, pp. 16–17, File 41, Box 7, S1486.

20. Testimony, 12 March 1960, p. 5, File 34, Box 7, S1486.

21. Testimony, 7 March 1961, p. 5, File 98, Box 8, S1486.

22. Testimony, 13 October 1960, p. 11, File 35, Box 8, S1486.

23. Testimony, 7 December 1959, pp. 8, 11, File 51, Box 7, S1486.

24. Testimony, 19 October 1960, p. 2, File 40, Box 8, S1486.

25. Testimony, 11 January 1961, p. 15, File 72, Box 8, S1486.

26. Testimony, 30 October 1962, p. 19, File 16, Box 11, S1486.

27. Testimony, 6 June 1962, p. 4, File 35, Box 10; Testimony, 31 December 1959; Testimony, 24 May 1961, p. 11, S1486.

28. Testimony, 6 October 1959, p. 4, File 29, Box 7; 17 September 1962, p. 2, File 92, Box 10, S1486.

29. See, for instance, Robinson and Kimmel, "The Queer Career of Homosexual Security Vetting in Cold War Canada," 335.

30. Estelle B. Freedman, "'The Burning of Letters Continues': Elusive Identities and the Historical Construction of Sexuality," *Journal of Women's History* 9, no. 4 (Winter 1998): 185.

31. Freedman, "'The Burning of Letters Continues,'" pp. 184–85, 193–94.

32. Strickland to Herrell, 15 December 1959, pp. 1–2, File 9, Box 3, S1486.

33. Strickland to Herrell, 15 December 1959, p. 2, File 9, Box 3, S1486.

34. Testimony, pp. 951–52, File 10, Box 5, S1486.

35. Testimony, p. 7, File 36, Box 8, S1486.

36. Testimony, 6 October 1959, p. 1, File 28, Box 7, S1486.

37. Testimony, pp. 4–5, File 149, Box 11, S1486. See also Testimony, 7 December 1959, p. 6, File 51, Box 7 and Testimony, 20 October 1960, p. 8, File 42, Box 8, S1486.

38. Memorandum: Norman B. Sikes to File, 7 April 1962, File 11, Box 1, S1486.

39. Testimony, 2 October 1959, pp. 2–3, File 30, Box 7, S1486. Also see Testimony, 19 August 1959, p. 195, File 33, Box 7, and 13 January 1960, p. 13, File 40, Box 7, S1486.

40. Testimony, 2 October 1959, pp. 3–21, File 30, Box 7, S1486.

41. Testimony, 4 December 1959, p. 21, File 53, Box 7, S1486. Also see Sears, *Lonely Hunters,* 35.

42. Testimony, 22 October 1962, pp. 1–2, File 9, Box 11, S1486.

43. Testimony, 19 January 1959, pp. 1147–49, File 10, Box 7, S1486.

44. Testimony, 19 January 1959, pp. 1151–52, File 10, Box 7, S1486.

45. Testimony, 19 January 1959, p. 1153, File 10, Box 7, S1486.

46. Testimony, 19 January 1959, pp. 1192–94, File 10, Box 7, S1486.

47. Testimony, 19 January 1959, pp. 1199–1200, File 10, Box 7, S1486.

48. Testimony, 19 January 1959, p. 1225, File 10, Box 7, S1486.

49. Testimony, 19 January 1959, pp. 1225–26, File 10, Box 7, S1486.

50. "Report," March 1960, File 1, Box 2, S1486.

51. Testimony, 16 April 1962, p. 136, File 102, Box 9, S1486.

52. Jenkins to Johns, 16 November 1961, p. 1, File 17, Box 2, S1486.

53. Testimony, 24 October 1962, p. 9, File 14, Box 11, S1486.

54. Testimony, 29 September 1960, p. 6, File 25, Box 8, S1486.

55. Testimony, 11 October 1962, pp. 5–7, File 147, Box 10, S1486.

56. Testimony, 13 June 1963, File 63, Box 11, S1486.

57. Document, State of Florida, County of Hardee, pp. 1–2, Box 8, S1486. See letters to Bailey, 22 June 1960, and Strickland to Herrell, 18 July 1960, File 11, Box 3, S1486.

58. Letter to Bailey, 22 June 1960, p. 1, File 11, Box 3, S1486.

59. Letter to Bailey, 22 June 1960, p. 2, File 11, Box 3, S1486.

60. Strickland to Herrell, 12 September 1960, File 11, Box 3, S1486.

61. Strickland to Hawes, 7 October 1960, pp. 1–2, File 12, Box 3, S1486; Strickland to O'Neill, 30 May 1961, p. 3, File 12, Box 1, S1486.

62. Testimony, 11 January 1961, p. 10, File 73, Box 8, S1486.

63. Testimony, 7 March 1961, p. 2, File 100, Box 8, S1486.

64. Testimony, 7 March 1961, p. 14, File 100, Box 8, S1486.

65. Testimony, 7 March 1961, p. 15, File 100, Box 8, S1486.

66. Testimony, 7 March 1961, pp. 15–16, File 100, Box 8, S1486.

67. Testimony, 23 May 1960, p. 19, File 12, Box 8, and Testimony, 6 October 1959, p. 8, File 29, Box 7, S1486.

68. Testimony, 7 December 1959, p. 10, File 52, Box 7, S1486.

69. Testimony, 20 October 1960, pp. 8–9, File 42, Box 8, and Testimony, 10 October 1960, p. 22, File 31, Box 8, S1486.

70. Testimony, 20 October 1960, p. 11, File 42, Box 8, S1486.

71. Testimony, 18 October 1960, pp. 4–5, File 38, Box 8, S1486.

72. Testimony, 18 October 1960, pp. 7–8, File 38, Box 8, S1486.

73. Testimony, 18 October 1960, p. 8, File 38, Box 8, S1486.

74. Testimony, 7 October 1959, pp. 3–4, File 26, Box 7, S1486.

75. Testimony, 7 October 1959, p. 9, File 26, Box 7, S1486.

76. Testimony, 7 October 1959, p. 9, File 26, Box 7, S1486.

77. Testimony, 20 October 1960, p. 9, File 43, Box 8, S1486.

78. Testimony, 20 October 1960, p. 9, File 43, Box 8, S1486.

79. Testimony, 26 January 1961, pp. 48–49, File 74, Box 8, S1486.

80. Testimony, 6 October 1959, pp. 5–6, File 28, Box 7, S1486.

81. Testimony, 6 October 1959, p. 6, File 28, Box 7, S1486.

82. Testimony, 10 October 1962, p. 3, File 151, Box 10, S1486.

83. Testimony, 10 October 1962, p. 13, File 151, Box 10, S1486.

84. Testimony, 11 October 1962, p. 7, File 148, Box 10, S1486.

85. Testimony, 11 October 1962, p. 8, File 148, Box 10, S1486.

86. Florida Legislative Investigation Committee document, 30 August 1961, File 14, Box 3, S1486.

87. Quoted in Boyd, *Wide Open Town,* 153.

88. Boyd, *Wide Open Town,* 152–53.

89. Sigmund Diamond, "Surveillance in the Academy: Harry B. Fisher and Yale University, 1927–1952," *American Quarterly* 36, no. 1 (Spring 1984): 43.

90. Diamond, "Surveillance in the Academy," p. 43.

91. Freedman, "'The Burning of Letters Continues,'" 182, 194.

92. Clarence J. Karier, *The Individual, Society, and Education: A History of American Educational Ideas,* 2nd ed. (Urbana: University of Illinois Press, 1986), 359.

Chapter 3: Silence Will Not Protect You

Pearl Mitchell to Ruth Perry, 26 May 1959, File 8, Box 1, Ruth Perry Papers, Special Collections Department, University of South Florida Tampa Library (hereafter, Perry Papers); "Report and Resolution: Tampa Area AAUW Study of Aspects of Academic Freedom and of Legislative Investigation of Florida Universities," pp. 4–5, File 2, Box 2, Egerton Papers, Special Collections Department, University of South Florida Tampa Library (hereafter, Egerton Papers); Lewis Bailey to Charley Johns, 11 November 1961, File 17, Box 2, S1486.

1. Audre Lorde, "The Transformation of Silence into Language and Action," in *Sister Outsider: Essays and Speeches by Audre Lorde* (Freedom, Calif.: Crossing Press, 1984), 42.

2. Lorde, "The Transformation of Silence," 44.

3. Saunders, *Bridging the Gap,* 98.

4. Testimony, 7 February 1957, pp. 670–71, File 1, Box 4, S1486.

5. Testimony, 18 February 1957, pp. 715–16, File 2, Box 4, S1486.

6. Testimony, 18 February 1957, p. 720, File 2, Box 4, S1486.

7. Saunders, *Bridging the Gap,* 175–76.

8. Testimony, 18 February 1957, p. 732, File 2, Box 4, S1486.

9. Testimony, 18 February 1957, p. 770, File 2, Box 4, S1486.

10. Testimony, 18 February 1957, p. 779, File 2, Box 4, S1486.

11. Testimony, 25 February 1957, pp. 124–25, File 6, Box 4, S1486.

12. Testimony, 25 February 1957, p. 125, File 6, Box 4, S1486.

13. Emmons, "Flame of Resistance," 80.

14. See Emmons, "Flame of Resistance," 30–84; and Poucher, "One Woman's Courage," 230–31.

15. File 9, Box 1, "Broadcast Comments," Perry Papers.

16. Poucher, "One Woman's Courage," 235; "The Daring Plot against Miami Negroes," *Jet Magazine* (28 March 1957): 12–15.

17. Poucher, "One Woman's Courage," 236.

18. Poucher, "One Woman's Courage," 236–37.

19. Poucher, "One Woman's Courage," 239; "Before the Florida Legislative Investigation Committee, Transcript of Testimony," 10 February 1958, p. 3, File 13, Box 4, S1486.

20. Poucher, "One Woman's Courage," 240.

21. "Preliminary Statement," 26 February 1958, File 6, Box 1, Perry Papers.

22. Quoted in Poucher, "One Woman's Courage," 240–41.

23. Quoted in Elliott J. Pieze, "Legislative Communist Investigation Flops," *Miami Times,* 1 March 1958.

24. Pieze, "Legislative Communist Investigation Flops."

25. "Report of Florida Legislative Investigation Committee to 1959 Session of the Legislature," 13 April 1959, pp. 1–2, File 21, Box 1, S1486.

26. Pieze, "Legislative Communist Investigation Flops."

27. Schnur, "Cold Warriors in the Hot Sunshine," 9.

28. "Strictly Confidential Memorandum," 18 April 1962, File 1, Box 1, S1486; Schnur, "Cold Warriors," 10.

29. Steve Raymond, "Politics Denied in USF Probe," *Tampa Tribune,* 22 May 1962; Stark, "McCarthyism in Florida," 136–38.

30. Fred Smith, "'Politics Denied in USF Row," *Tampa Tribune,* 20 May 1962.

31. Testimony, 1 June 1962, pp. 1428–33, File 14, Box 5, S1486.

32. Testimony, 1 June 1962, pp. 1415–16, File 14, Box 5, S1486.

33. Sam Mase, "Homecoming Skits Lampoon Johns, Kennedy, Smathers," *Tampa Tribune,* 21 October 1962.

34. Testimony, 28 May 1962, p. 54, File 5, Box 5, S1486.

35. Schnur, "Cold Warriors," 12–13.

36. Memorandum, Millard F. Caldwell to Farris Bryant, 16 March 1960, File 17, Box 1, C. Farris Bryant Papers, Department of Special and Area Studies Collections, George A. Smathers Libraries, University of Florida, Gainesville (hereafter, C. Farris Bryant Papers).

37. Memorandum, Caldwell to Bryant, 16 March 1960, File 17, Box 1, C. Farris Bryant Papers.

38. "Policy on Morals and Influences," 9 December 1961, p. 1, File 2, Box 1, S1486.

39. "Policy on Morals and Influences," 9 December 1961, pp. 1–2, File 2, Box 1, S1486.

40. Bertwell, "'A Veritable Refuge for Practicing Homosexuals,'" 419–29.

41. Stark, "McCarthyism in Florida," 166–73.

42. Testimony, 1 June 1962, pp. 1522–23, File 15, Box 5, S1486.

43. Testimony, 1 June 1962, p. 1525, File 15, Box 5, S1486.

44. Testimony, 1 June 1962, p. 1527, File 15, Box 5, S1486.

45. Testimony, 6 June 1962, pp. 120–21, File 19, Box 5, S1486.

46. Testimony, 6 June 1962, pp. 125–27, File 19, Box 5, S1486.

47. Testimony, 6 June 1962, pp. 127, 130, File 19, Box 5, S1486.

48. Testimony, 30 May 1962, p. 1167, File 11, Box 5, S1486.

49. Testimony, 30 May 1962, pp. 1165–66, File 11, Box 5, S1486.

50. Margaret B. Fisher and Jeanne L. Noble, *College Education as Personal Development* (Englewood Cliffs: Prentice-Hall, 1960), 45.

51. Fisher and Noble, *College Education as Personal Development,* 45, 52–53.

52. Fisher and Noble, *College Education as Personal Development,* 280.

53. Testimony, 30 May 1962, pp. 1177–79, File 11, Box 5, S1486.

54. Testimony, 30 May 1962, pp. 1123–24, 1121, 1157, File 11, Box 5, S1486.

55. Testimony, 30 May 1962, pp. 1150–51, 1154–57, File 11, Box 5, S1486.

56. Testimony, 30 May 1962, p. 1184, File 11, Box 5, S1486.

57. Testimony, 30 May 1962, p. 1184, File 11, Box 5, S1486.

58. "Homosexuality and Administrative Attitude," p. 51, File 22, Box 1, S1486.

59. Ruth Perry, "Along Freedom's Road," 9 March 1957, File 3, Box 1, Perry Papers.

60. Quoted in Sears, *Lonely Hunters,* 75.

61. See *Lawrence v. Texas,* 539 U.S. 558 (2003); Lugg, "Thinking about Sodomy," 46–49.

62. Braukman, "Anticommunism and the Politics of Sex and Race in Florida," 50–51; Poucher, "One Woman's Courage"; Saunders, *Bridging the Gap,* 159–70; Stark, "McCarthyism in Florida," 21–23.

63. Quoted in "NAACP Hearings Canceled in State," *Miami News,* 1 August 1958.

64. "Report of Florida Legislative Investigation Committee to 1959 Session," p. 2.

65. "NAACP Hearings Canceled In State."

66. Perry, "Along Freedom's Road," 9 March 1957.

67. Ruth Perry, "Along Freedom's Road," 8 March 1958, File 3, Box 1, Perry Papers.

68. Perry, "Along Freedom's Road," 9 March 1957.

69. Perry, "Along Freedom's Road," 9 March 1957.

70. Perry, "Along Freedom's Road," 8 March 1958.

71. Certificate of Appreciation, File 8, Box 1, Perry Papers.

72. Ruth Perry, "Along Freedom's Road," 22 February 1958, File 3, Box 1, Perry Papers.

73. Quoted in Ruth Perry, "Along Freedom's Road," 4 June 1960, File 4, Box 1, Perry Papers.

74. See Bell, *Silent Covenants;* Dudziak, *Cold War Civil Rights.*

75. Confidential memorandum, James J. Love to members of the Board of Control, 3 June 1958, "UF Law" file, Box 31, J. Broward Culpepper Papers, Department of Special and Area Studies Collections, George A. Smathers Libraries, University of Florida, Gainesville (hereafter, J. Broward Culpepper Papers).

76. Confidential memorandum, Love to members of the Board of Control, 3 June 1958, pp. 1, 3.

77. Confidential memorandum, Love to members of the Board of Control, 3 June 1958, p. 1.

78. Confidential memorandum, Love to members of the Board of Control, 3 June 1958, p. 2.

79. Confidential memorandum, Love to members of the Board of Control, 3 June 1958. Fenn's tenure as dean of the University of Florida School of Law ended in 1958.

80. C. Vann Woodward, "The Unreported Crisis in the Southern Colleges," *Harper's Magazine* 225 (October 1962): 89.

81. Woodward, "The Unreported Crisis," 82, 84, 89.

82. Woodward, "The Unreported Crisis," 89.

83. Iredell Jenkins, quoted in Woodward, "The Unreported Crisis," 89.

84. Interview with the author, 18 August 2004; notes from interview with author, 1 July 2005, pp. 2, 6.

85. Interview with author, 18 August 2004.

86. William G. Carleton, *Free Lancing through the Century: A Memoir,* ed. Herbert J. Doherty (Gainesville, Fla.: Carleton House, 1988), 148.

87. "AAUP News Digest," 29 July 1963, pp. 1–2, File 3, Box 2, Egerton Papers (paraphrased).

88. "Report of the Special Committee of the Board of Control," 14 September 1962, p. 5, File 2, Box 1, S1486.

89. "Report of the Special Committee of the Board of Control," 14 September 1962, pp. 1–5, File 2, Box 1, S1486.

90. "A Statement Addressed to Our Colleagues at the Florida State University by

Seventeen Members of the Faculty of the Department of Physics Assembled on 1 November 1962," p. 2, File 16, Box 2, S1486.

91. "New Application of Principle," *St. Petersburg Times,* in Memo from Hendrix Chandler to Broward Culpepper, "Clippings 11/26/62" file, Box 13, J. Broward Culpepper Papers.

92. "A Non-Academic View of Freedom," *Tallahassee Democrat,* in memo from Hendrix Chandler to Broward Culpepper, "Clippings 11/26/62" file, Box 13, J. Broward Culpepper Papers.

93. "A Non-Academic View of Freedom," *Tallahassee Democrat.*

94. "Statement of Policy on Academic Freedom and Responsibilities," 7 December 1962, p. 3, Box 1, S1486.

95. Notes, File 5, Box 1, Egerton Papers.

96. Mrs. Stockton Smith, June 1962 document, p. 2, File 5, Box 1, Egerton Papers.

97. "Resolution: The Women's Republican Club of St. Petersburg, Florida," 10 April 1963, File 1, Box 25, Terrell Sessums Papers, Special Collections Department, University of South Florida Tampa Library (hereafter, Sessums Papers).

98. Johns, quoted in Wayne Thomas Jr., "To Members of the Plant City Conservative Club," 4 April 1963, p. 1, File 5, Box 1, Egerton Papers.

99. Johns, quoted in Thomas, "To Members of the Plant City Conservative Club," p. 1, Egerton Papers.

100. Thomas, "To Members of the Plant City Conservative Club," p. 1, Egerton Papers. Emphasis in the original.

101. Letters dated 27 April 1963, 3 May 1963, 4 May 1963, n.d., 27 April 1963, File 1, Box 25, Sessums Papers. Emphasis in the originals.

102. Jane Smith to Terrell Sessums, File 2, Box 25, Sessums Papers. Emphasis in the original.

103. "Sparks on Campus," *Tampa Tribune,* 19 May 1962.

104. John Egerton to Emmett B. Peter Jr., 27 March 1963, File 12, Box 2, Egerton Papers.

105. Emmett Peter Jr., "Johns Committee: A Balance Sheet," *Daily Commercial,* 31 March 1963, p. 2, File 12, Box 2, Egerton Papers.

106. Edward P. Morgan, 24 July 1962, p. 2, File 12, Box 2, Egerton Papers.

107. Stewart, quoted in Egerton's notes, April 1964, File 7, Box 1, Egerton Papers.

108. "Climate of Anti-Intellectualism," *Orlando Sentinel,* 24 April 1963; "Academic Freedom," WLOF-TV News Editorial, 4 February 1963, File 2, Box 2, Egerton Papers.

109. Interview with author, 18 August 2004.

110. Interview notes, 1 July 2005, p. 3; AAUW Minutes, 5 June 1962, AAUW Tampa Records, Special Collections Department, University of South Florida Tampa Library (hereafter, AAUW Records).

111. AAUW Minutes, 4 October 1962, 7 February 1963, AAUW Records.

112. Carol Scott to John Allen, 18 November 1962, File 16, Box 2, Egerton Papers.

113. Carol Scott to John Egerton, 13 January 1963, File 12, Box 2, Egerton Papers.

114. Mrs. Swift to John Egerton, 7 February 1963, File 12, Box 2, Egerton Papers.

115. Betty Hohnadel to Terrell Sessums, File 1, Box 25, Sessums Papers; AAUW Minutes, 4 April 1963, AAUW Records; Academic Freedom Committee AAUW to Florida Legislature, 24 April 1963, File 15, Box 2, Egerton Papers.

116. AAUW, "Report and Resolution," p. 1, File 2, Box 2, Egerton Papers.

117. AAUW, "Report and Resolution," p. 1. Emphasis in the original.

118. AAUW, "Report and Resolution," pp. 2–3.

119. AAUW, "Report and Resolution," pp. 4–5.

120. Interview with author, 18 August 2004.

121. Interview with author, 18 August 2004.

122. Interview with author, 18 August 2004.

123. Egerton to Kerns, 28 November 1962, File 12, Box 2, Egerton Papers.

124. Morgan, 24 July 1962, File 12, Box 2, Egerton Papers; "Informal Report #1," 16 September 1963, p. 1, File 1, Box 25, Sessums Papers.

125. "Informal Report #1," pp. 2–4.

126. Knowles quoted in "Put It in Uniform," *Tampa Tribune,* 27 May 1963.

127. "Put It in Uniform," *Tampa Tribune,* 27 May 1963.

128. Egerton to Scott, 31 May 1963, File 13, Box 2, Egerton Papers.

129. Scott to Egerton, 2 June 1963, File 15, Box 2, Egerton Papers.

130. "Report of Florida Legislative Investigation Committee to 1959 Session," 3, 5–7.

131. Charles O. Weaver, superintendent, Board of Public Instruction, De Sota, to Strickland, 18 September 1959, File 9, Box 3; Deane H. Bishop, chief counselor, County of Hillsborough, to Strickland, 4 November 1960, File 12, Box 3; Griffin Bishop, superintendent, Board of Public Instruction, Madison, 13 November 1961, File 17, Box 2, S1486.

132. Jenkins to Johns, 16 November 1961, File 17, Box 2, S1486.

133. Testimony, 16 April 1962, pp. 240–41, File 102, Box 9, S1486.

134. Godby to Johns, 15 November 1961, File 17, Box 2, S1486.

135. FLIC Minutes, 24 June 1960, p. 2, File 16, Box 1, S1486. Analysis of the nexus that developed between the DOE and the Johns Committee is presented in chapter 4.

136. Florida State Department of Education, "Office Memorandum," 12 September 1961, File 13, Box 13, S1127.

137. Kelley to Bailey, Office Memorandum, 28 December 1962, File 12, Box 13, S1127.

138. "Meeting of Steering Committee of Personnel Problems Committee, Florida Education Association, Tallahassee, Florida, January 23, 1959," p. 1, File "Personnel Problems Committee 1957–1963," Box 192, M86–011, I.1, Florida Education Association, State Archives of Florida, Tallahassee (hereafter, M86–011).

139. "Meeting of Steering Committee of Personnel Problems Committee, Florida Education Association," pp. 1–2, M86–011.

140. W. T. McFatter to Jack Stevens, 29 April 1959, pp. 3–4, File 8, Box 157, M86–011.

141. A. J. Stevens to W. T. McFatter Jr., 6 May 1959, p. 1, File 8, Box 157, M86–011.

142. Stevens to McFatter, 6 May 1959, p. 1.

143. A. J. Stevens to Robert E. Jones, 27 May 1959, File 8, Box 157, M86–011.

144. "Florida Education Association Meeting of Steering Committee of Personal [sic] Problems Committee, Tallahassee, Florida, January 7, 1960," pp. 1–2, File 1, Box 57, M86–011. See also FEA Board of Directors minutes, 11 March 1960, pp. 41–42, File 1, Box 57, M86–011.

145. "Florida Education Association Meeting of Steering Committee of Personal [sic] Problems Committee, Tallahassee, Florida, January 7, 1960," p. 2, File 1, Box 57, M86–011.

146. Hugh B. Ingram Jr., "Personnel Problems," in *Florida Education* (May 1960), File 1, Box 16; "Minutes of Meeting of the Board of Directors, Florida Education Association, Fort Harrison Hotel, Clearwater, Florida, August 8–10, 1960," pp. 54–55, File 1, Box 57, M86–011.

147. Harbeck, *Gay and Lesbian Educators,* 38–81, 188–91.

148. "Personal [sic] Problems Steering Committee, Florida Education Association, Tallahassee, Florida, November 6, 1961," pp. 2–3, File 1, Box 16, M86–011.

149. Robert Glenn to Charley E. Johns, 28 November 1961, File 8, Box 22, M86–011.

150. Ed Henderson to Lewis H. Treen, 7 November 1961, File 11, Box 10, M86–011.

151. "Report of the Palm Beach County Investigation," n.d., File 7, Box 7, M86–011.

152. Ed Henderson to R. J. Strickland, 23 March 1962, p. 1, File 19, Box 29, M86–011.

153. Henderson to Strickland, 23 March 1962, p. 1.

154. Henderson to Strickland, 23 March 1962, pp. 1–2.

155. Testimony, n.d., pp. 338, 340, File 103, Box 7, S1486.

156. Testimony, n.d., pp. 351–52, File 103, Box 7, S1486.

157. Testimony, 16 April 1962, pp. 148–51, File 102, Box 9, S1486.

158. Ed Henderson to Charley E. Johns, 17 May 1962, File 14, Box 22, M86–011.

159. "Minutes of Meeting, Personnel Problems Steering Committee, FEA Building, January 28, 1963," pp. 1–2, File 1, Box 16, M86–011.

160. Robert B. Turner Jr., "Convention Report: Professional Rights and Responsibilities Committee, Thursday, April 23, 1964," p. 3, File 3, Box 58, M86–011.

161. Testimony, 4 September 1960, p. 4, File 19, Box 8, S1486.

162. Cole to Strickland, 9 October 1962, File 16, Box 2, S1486.

163. Manning to Johns, 15 November 1961, File 17, Box 2, S1486.

164. Floyd T. Christian to J. T. Kelley, 6 December 1960, File 13, Box 13, S1127.

165. Floyd T. Christian to Richard Barnes Kennan, 3 January 1961, p. 2, File 13, Box 13, S1127.

166. J. T. Kelley to Thomas Bailey, 24 March 1961, p. 2, Box 13, S1127.

167. Strickland to O'Neill, 6 March 1961, p. 2, File 13, Box 3, S1486.

168. Kelley to Bailey, 8 November 1962, File 12, Box 13, S1127.

169. J. T. Kelley to William A. Norris Jr., 7 August 1964, File 12, Box 13, S1127.

170. The Citizens of Bay County to (Honorable) Governor Farris Bryant, 27 July 1964, p. 1, File 12, Box 13, S1127.

171. Citizens of Bay County to Bryant, 27 July 1964, p. 1.

172. Citizens of Bay County to Bryant, 27 July 1964, p. 1–2.

173. Letter from Queen Ester Wise Chapter #22, Order of Eastern Star, 27 July 1964, File 12, Box 13, S1127.

174. Thomas Hayden, quoted in "Homosexual Purges on at Two Universities," *Mattachine Review* 6, no. 3 (March 1960): 19. The *Mattachine Review* ran from 1955 to 1966, reaching about 2,500 readers per issue. *One* ran from 1953 to 1965 with an estimated 5,000 readers per month. See Sullivan, "Political Opportunism and the Harassment of Homosexuals in Florida," 75–77.

175. Hayden, "Homosexual Purges on at Two Universities," 20.

176. Hal Call, "Open Letter to the Florida Legislature's 'Johns Committee,'" *Mattachine Review* 10, no. 11 (1964): 6–7.

177. *The Ladder* 6, no. 5 (February 1962): 13, 22.

178. Letter to the editor, *One* 7, no. 9 (September 1959): 31–32.

179. See *One* 8, no. 4 (April 1960): 17–18; *One* 9, no. 7 (July 1961): 18–19; "Florida Still Very Warm for Mae," *One* 10, no. 5 (May 1962): 18; *One* 10, no. 7 (July 1962): 30–31; "Florida, Inquisitionland, Not Vacationland," *One* 11, no. 6 (June 1963): 17; "Florida Homo Hunt on for 2 More Years," *One* 11, no. 8 (August 1963): 14 (see also p. 30); *One* 12, no. 1 (January 1964): 30; *One* 12, no. 2 (February 1964): 30.

180. "'John' Like Report of the Johns Committee," *One* 12, no. 6 (June 1964): 13.

181. Collins, quoted in Stark, "McCarthyism in Florida," 16. There is evidence to suggest that Collins was appalled at the abuse of civil liberties unleashed by the Johns Committee. In 1959 he invited Professor William Carleton of the University of Florida to address the National Governor's Conference, just one year after the UF investigation and a few months following the infamous 19-59 Investigation Committee Report. Carleton used the opportunity to contrast violations of civil liberties on the national level with similar abuses on the state level. See Carleton, *Free Lancing through the Century*, 149–50.

182. Perry, "Along Freedom's Road," 9 March 1957.

183. See Sullivan, "Political Opportunism and the Harassment of Homosexuals in Florida," 60–61, 72, 77.

184. Quoted in Beutke and Litvack, *Behind Closed Doors*.

185. Bertwell, "'A Veritable Refuge for Practicing Homosexuals,'" 413; Carleton, *Free Lancing through the Century*, 148.

186. Interview with author, 19 August 2004.

187. Perry, "Along Freedom's Road," 9 March 1957.

188. Notes from interview with author, 4 July 2005, p. 2.

189. Notes from interview with author, 4 July 2005, p. 2.

190. Quoted in "Attack on U.S. Job Bar to Homosexuals Slowed," *Washington Post* 15 January 1964, File 13, Box 16, S1486; see the editor's note on "Civil Liberties and Homosexuality," *Civil Liberties Record* (April 1964): 2, File 30, Box 19, S1486.

191. Robert J. Corber, *In the Name of National Security: Hitchcock, Homophobia, and the Political Construction of Gender in Postwar America* (Durham, N.C.: Duke University Press, 1993), 19–20, 61–62.

192. Corber, *In the Name of National Security,* 62.

193. Corber, *In the Name of National Security,* 62.

194. Corber, *In the Name of National Security,* 69.

195. D'Emilio, *Sexual Politics, Sexual Communities,* 4.

196. Boyd, *Wide Open Town,* 111–14, 162.

197. Testimony, 19 October 1960, p. 10, File 42, Box 10, S1486.

198. Boyd, *Wide Open Town,* 164, 179.

199. Quoted in Craig A. Rimmerman, *From Identity to Politics: The Lesbian and Gay Movements in the United States* (Philadelphia: Temple University Press, 2002), 5.

200. Rimmerman, *From Identity to Politics,* 6.

201. D'Emilio, *Sexual Politics, Sexual Communities,* 5.

202. Mary Bernstein, "Identities and Politics: Toward a Historical Understanding of the Lesbian and Gay Movement," *Social Science History* 26, no. 3 (Fall 2002): 533–37.

203. Important court victories include *One's* pornography case in 1954, bar owners securing the right to public assembly in the 1960s, and the Florida schoolteacher case, *Neal v. Bryant.* See Bernstein, "Identities and Politics," 541.

204. D'Emilio, *Sexual Politics, Sexual Communities,* 3.

205. Bernstein, "Identities and Politics," 542.

206. Lorde, "The Transformation of Silence," 40.

207. Lorde, "The Transformation of Silence," 41.

Chapter 4: Doing the Public's Business

Thomas D. Bailey, "I Am Proud to Be an American," p. 1, *Florida School Bulletin,* March 1961, "Papers 1939–1974," M1968-16, Thomas D. Bailey Papers, University of West Florida Special Collections (hereafter, M1968-16); Thomas D. Bailey, 27 July 1961, pp. 2–3, "Reports 1953–1974," Box 11, "Education in Florida" Series, Department of Special and Area Studies Collections, George A. Smathers Libraries, University of Florida, Gainesville (hereafter, "Education in Florida" Series).

1. Florida was one of fourteen states that still banned consensual sodomy in 2003 when the U.S. Supreme Court ruled sodomy laws unconstitutional in *Lawrence v. Texas.* In 1961 Illinois became the first state to decriminalize consensual sodomy. The Florida Supreme Court invalidated the "crime against nature" law for vagueness in

1971 but upheld the "unnatural and lascivious acts" law. The state legislature decriminalized the "crime against nature" law in 1974. See William N. Eskridge Jr., *Gaylaw: Challenging the Apartheid of the Closet* (Cambridge, Mass.: Harvard University Press, 1999), 109, 329–30; Lugg, "Thinking about Sodomy," 35, 51.

2. "Tom Bailey Becomes State School Superintendent," *School Director: A Magazine for School and College Administrators* 2, no. 5 (January 1949): 4, "Papers 1939–1974," M1968–16.

3. Thomas D. Bailey, "Segregation Decision," 2 December 1954, p. 1, "Speeches and Press Releases by Bailey, 1954–58 (Segregation)," Box 15, S1127.

4. Bailey, "Segregation Decision," 2 December 1954, pp. 1–2.

5. Bailey, "Segregation Decision," 2 December 1954, pp. 2–3.

6. Bailey, "Segregation Decision," 2 December 1954, p. 5.

7. Thomas D. Bailey, "Statement before House Committee on Education—Public Schools HB-671," 26 April 1957, p. 1, "Papers 1939–1974," M1968–16. See also Bailey to Edgar S. Anderson, 1 June 1956, H. C. Robertson to Bailey, 13 June 1956, and Bailey to W. 1. Wolfe, 3 May 1957, "Segregation, June 56–May 57," Box 14, S1127.

8. Bailey to John F. Kennedy, 26 June 1963, p. 1, "Correspondence with President Kennedy Concerning Race Relations," Box 19, J. Broward Culpepper Papers.

9. Bailey to Kennedy, 26 June 1963, p. 1. Emphasis in the original.

10. Bailey to Kennedy, 26 June 1963, p. 3.

11. Thomas D. Bailey, "Some Reflections on My Retirement after Five Years," 1971, p. 3, "Papers 1939–1974," M1968–16.

12. Bailey, "Some Reflections on My Retirement after Five Years," p. 7.

13. Bailey to Earline Mitchell, 2 July 1954, p. 2, "Organization and Function of State Board of Education," Box 15, S1127.

14. Corber, *In the Name of National Security*, 62. See chapter 3.

15. Johnson, *The Lavender Scare*, 4–5.

16. See Johnson, *The Lavender Scare*, 2–5; Schrecker, *Many Are the Crimes*, xi–xviii.

17. "Is Florida Government Being Decentralized?" *Florida Times-Union*, 7 May 1960, "Politics and Education 1949–1972," Box 11, "Education in Florida" Series.

18. The state cabinet also included a comptroller and a commissioner of agriculture. All seven members served on the Board of State Institutions and the State Budget Commission. Most other boards consisted of five members. See Bailey to Mitchell, 2 July 1954, p. 1; Allen Morris, *The Florida Handbook 1975–1976*, 15th ed. (Tallahassee, Fla.: Peninsular, 1975), 107–10.

19. Bailey to Mitchell, 2 July 1954, p. 2.

20. Bailey to D. B. Oxner, 17 September 1958, p. 1, "Organization and Function of State Board of Education," Box 15, S1127. See also Bailey to Mitchell, 2 July 1954, p. 2, and "State Cabinet Members Have Many Powers," March 1960, "Politics and Education 1949–1972," Box 11, "Education in Florida" Series. Morris notes that political scientists concur: the Florida system of state government was unique among all the states. Morris, *The Florida Handbook*, 108.

21. Davis, introduction, 2.

22. Klein, "Guarding the Baggage," 37, 158. The Florida Center of Political History and Governance, Tallahassee, displays an excellent exhibit noting significant aspects of Florida's political history.

23. See Klein, "Guarding the Baggage," for an in-depth analysis of this history.

24. Minutes, Interim Legislative Committee on Education, 7 June 1958, p. 13, "Interim Legislative Committee on Education—Minutes—1957–58," Box 17, J. Broward Culpepper Papers.

25. One should bear in mind that critical players in the Florida teacher purge were linked in a network of associations. Henderson had been supervisor of instruction at the DOE from 1946 to 1948. Bailey served as president and director of the FEA (1938–39) and secretary of public relations for the FEA in 1947. While a teacher at DeFuniak Springs, Bailey taught future governor Fuller Warren; Richard Ervin, who served with Bailey on the state cabinet as attorney general; and Justice Roberts, who served on the Florida Supreme Court. Floyd Christian, involved in the *Neal v. Bryant* case as SPI of Pinellas County, had been president of the FEA and served on its board of directors. He was selected by Governor Burns to succeed Bailey as SSPI in 1965. At least twenty-four SPIs, along with Bailey and Governor LeRoy Collins, were Masons. See "Tom Bailey Becomes State School Superintendent," 4; Allen Morris, "Supt. Bailey: Service, Action," *St. Petersburg Times,* 27 February 1965, M1968–16; Thomas D. Bailey, "Yesterday, Today and Tomorrow," 26 January 1973, M1968–16; "Ed Henderson," File 10, Box 20, M86–011; Henderson to Robert Hatch, 9 September 1964, File 16, Box 6, M86–011; and "Available Speakers in Connection with Americanism Committee of Florida Masons," n.d., File 9, Box 10, S1127.

26. Florida Education Association, "Citizen and Professional Advisory Councils, Committees and Organizations Studying Florida Education in a Continuing Program," 5 June 1958, pp. 3–4, "Interim Legislative Committee on Education—General—1957–58," Box 17, J. Broward Culpepper Papers.

27. ILCE Minutes, 7 June 1958, p. 13.

28. Quoted in ILCE Minutes, 7 November 1958, p. 1, "Interim Legislative Committee on Education—General—1957–58," Box 17, J. Broward Culpepper Papers.

29. ILCE Minutes, 7 November 1958, p. 13 .

30. Quoted in ILCE Minutes, 7 November 1958, p. 13.

31. Quoted in ILCE Minutes, 7 November 1958, p. 14. David Johnson argues, in spite of political efforts to link homosexuality and communism, very few communists remained in the federal government by 1950. Most federal employees dismissed as security risks during the Cold War were fired on the basis of sexuality, not political leanings. See Johnson, *The Lavender Scare,* 3–10, 38–39, 98–99.

32. Quoted in ILCE Minutes, 7 November 1958, p. 15.

33. ILCE Minutes, 7 November 1958, p. 16.

34. "Expanding Horizons for the Future of Florida through Education, Report of the Interim Legislative Educational Committee," March 1959, p. 16, "Bill to Establish Chancellor System—1959," Box 17, J. Broward Culpepper Papers.

35. "Expanding Horizons for the Future of Florida through Education," March 1959, p. 16.

36. "Report of Florida Legislative Investigation Committee to 1959 Session of the Legislature," 13 April 1959, pp. 9–9a, File 21, Box 1, S1486.

37. "Report of Florida Legislative Investigation Committee to 1959 Session of the Legislature," 13 April 1959, pp. 3–5, File 21, Box 1, S1486.

38. "Report of Florida Legislative Investigation Committee to 1959 Session of the Legislature," 13 April 1959, p. 7, File 21, Box 1, S1486.

39. "Bill Seeks Morals Probe of Teachers," *Tampa Tribune*, 18 April 1959, "Moral Education 1959–1961," Box 10, "Education in Florida" Series; "Report of the Florida Legislative Investigation Committee to the 1961 Session of the Legislature," p. 23, File 21, Box 1, S1486.

40. "Report of the Florida Legislative Investigation Committee to the 1961 Session of the Legislature," p. 20. See also pp. 18–20.

41. "Report of the Florida Legislative Investigation Committee to the 1961 Session of the Legislature," pp. 20–21.

42. "Prober Demands 'Deviates' Ouster," *Ft. Lauderdale Daily News,* 29 May 1961, "Morals," Box 10, "Education in Florida" Series.

43. "Shocked," *Ft. Lauderdale Daily News,* 3 June 1961, "Morals," Box 10, "Education in Florida" Series.

44. "A Shocking Charge," (Ft. Pierce) *News Tribune,* 28 May 1961, "Morals," Box 10, "Education in Florida" Series.

45. Bailey quoted in "Prober Demands 'Deviates' Ouster."

46. "Christian Hits Morals Report as 'Untrue,'" 25 May 1961, "Morals," Box 10, "Education in Florida" Series.

47. Quoted in "Educator 'Dismayed' by Results of Probe," 26 May 1961, "Morals," Box 10, "Education in Florida" Series.

48. Thomas D. Bailey, "Statement," 27 July 1961, "Reports 1953–1974," Box 11, "Education in Florida" Series.

49. Bailey, "Statement," 27 July 1961, pp. 2–3.

50. Bailey, "Statement," 27 July 1961, pp. 2–3.

51. News clipping, *St. Petersburg Times,* 22 July 1962, "Papers 1939–1974," M1968–16; "The 1961 Legislature and Education," p. 2, *Florida Education,* September 1961, File 5, Box 15, M86–011.

52. "Whitaker Bill on Revoking Teacher Licenses Passes," *Tampa Tribune,* 17 May 1961, "Morals," Box 10, "Education in Florida" Series; "The 1961 Legislature and Education," p. 4.

53. Testimony, n.d., p. 318, File 103, Box 7, S1486.

54. Testimony, n.d., pp. 313–24, File 103, Box 7, S1486.

55. Testimony, n.d., pp. 327–32, File 103, Box 7, S1486.

56. *Neal v. Bryant,* 149 So. 2d 529 (1962 Fla. LEXIS 3332; 97 A.L.R. 2d 819).

57. Bailey to Wilbur W. Whitehurst, 29 June 1960, File 13, Box 13, S1127.

58. Strickland to Whitehurst, 5 July 1960, File 11, Box 3, S1486; Bailey to Whitehurst, 29 June 1960, File 13, Box 13, S1127.

59. Whitehurst to Bailey, 22 June 1960, File 11, Box 3, S1486.

60. Floyd T. Christian to J. T. Kelley, 6 December 1960, File 13, Box 13, S1127.

61. Christian to Kelley, 6 December 1960, File 13, Box 13, S1127; Floyd T. Christian to Richard Barnes Kennan, 3 January 1961, File 13, Box 13, S1127; Ed Henderson to Robert Hatch, 9 September 1964, File 16, Box 6, M86–011.

62. J. T. Kelley to George R. Georgieff, 13 January 1961, File 13, Box 13, S1127.

63. Bailey to Bryant, Adams, Ervin, and Larson, March 1961, File 11, Box 13, S1127.

64. *Neal v. Bryant,* 149 So. 2d 529 (1962 Fla. LEXIS 3332; 97 A.L.R. 2d 819).

65. *Neal v. Bryant,* 149 So. 2d 529 (1962 Fla. LEXIS 3332; 97 A.L.R. 2d 819).

66. *Neal v. Bryant,* 149 So. 2d 529 (1962 Fla. LEXIS 3332; 97 A.L.R. 2d 819).

67. *Neal v. Bryant,* 149 So. 2d 529 (1962 Fla. LEXIS 3332; 97 A.L.R. 2d 819).

68. Kelley to Bailey, 8 November 1962, File 12, Box 13, S1127.

69. Kelley to Bailey, 15 March 1963, Box 13; Christian to Kelley, 21 March 1963, Box 13; Minutes of the BOE, 19 March 1963, p. 4, File 11, Box 13, S1127.

70. Kelley to John A. Freestone, 26 July 1963, and Kelley to H. Richard Shipp, 18 July 1963, File 12, Box 13, S1127.

71. "Report on Discussion at Meeting on Problems of Homosexuality in Florida," Tallahassee, 22 January 1962, pp. 6–7, File 11, Box 1, and "Agency Handed Homosexual Problem," *Pensacola Journal,* 1962, File 10, Box 16, S1486. (Note: Original date marked 3/6/62).

72. Legislative Investigations Committee, "Informal Report #1," 16 September 1963, pp. 1–4, File 16, Box 1, S1486.

73. John E. Evans to Thomas D. Bailey, 11 February 1964, 53, in "Report of the Florida Legislative Investigation Committee," February 1965.

74. Bailey to Evans, 25 February 1964, and Evans to Bailey, 27 February 1964, pp. 55–58, in "Report of the Florida Legislative Investigation Committee," February 1965.

75. See "Homosexuality and Citizenship in Florida," 1964, File 21, Box 1, and Investigation Committee records and news reports on the controversy surrounding its release, Boxes 2, 16, 19, S1486.

76. See Karen Graves, "Confronting a 'Climate of Raucous and Carnival Invasion': The AAUW Takes On the Johns Committee," *Florida Historical Quarterly* 85, no. 2 (Fall 2006): 154–76.

77. John E. Evans, "Remarks of John E. Evans Staff Director Florida Legislative Investigation Committee to the Annual Convention of the Florida Federation of Women's Clubs," 15 April 1964, 10, File 3, Box 25, Sessums Papers.

78. Evans, "Remarks of John E. Evans Staff Director Florida Legislative Investigation Committee," p. 10.

79. Evans, "Remarks of John E. Evans Staff Director Florida Legislative Investigation Committee," p. 11.

80. "Johns Committee Shut Up," *Miami Herald,* April 1964, File 13, Box 16, S1486.

81. John E. Evans, 18 April 1964, p. 1, File 18, Box 1, S1486.

82. John E. Evans, 18 April 1964, pp. 2–3, File 18, Box 1, S1486.

83. Robert Sherrill, "Teacher 'Morals' Case List Said to Be Nonexistent," *St. Petersburg Times,* 1 June 1964, File 4, Box 16, S1486.

84. Richard Mitchell, document included in letter from John Evans to Roland Monteiga, 4 June 1964, p. 1, File 4, Box 2, S1486.

85. Bailey quoted in Mitchell, document included in letter from John Evans to Roland Monteiga, p. 1.

86. Mitchell, document included in letter from John Evans to Roland Monteiga, pp. 1–3.

87. "Report of the Florida Legislative Investigation Committee," p. 10.

88. "Report of the Florida Legislative Investigation Committee," pp. 10–20.

89. "Report of the Florida Legislative Investigation Committee," pp. 8–9, 59.

90. Governor Burns to Mrs. George W. Mullins Jr., 18 March 1965, pp. 1–2, "General Board of Regents Correspondence Jan–Jun 1964," Box 13, J. Broward Culpepper Papers.

91. Minutes, Personnel Problems Committee, FEA, 7 January 1960, p. 2, File 1, Box 57, M86–011.

Chapter 5: A Profession at Risk

John E. Evans, press release, 18 April 1964, p. 3, File 18, Box 1, S1486.

1. See Eskridge, "No Promo Homo," 1327–1411, and Catherine A. Lugg, "A Shifting Rationale: U.S. Law, Public Schooling, and Queer Educators," paper presented at the Joint Meeting of the Canadian History of Education Association and the History of Education Society (USA), Ottawa, 27 October 2006.

2. Johnson, *The Lavender Scare,* 9.

3. See Blount, *Fit to Teach.*

4. "Homosexuality and Citizenship in Florida," 1964, preface, File 21, Box 1, S1486.

5. "Official Obscenity," 20 March 1964, WFTV News Editorial, File 29, Box 19, S1486. See Call, "Open Letter to the Florida Legislature's 'Johns Committee,'" 5–8.

6. "Homosexuality and Citizenship in Florida," 3.

7. "Homosexuality and Citizenship in Florida," 3.

8. Letter to Richard Mitchell, n.d., #11–297, File 5, Box 2, S1486.

9. Ministers, Business and Professional Men, and Parents to Charlie [Charley] Johns, 8 February 1963, File 13, Box 2, S1486.

10. "Homosexuality and Citizenship in Florida," 1.

11. "Homosexuality and Citizenship in Florida," 13.

12. Quoted in testimony, n.d., p. 349, File 103, Box 7, S1486.

13. Testimony, n.d., p. 349, File 103, Box 7, S1486.

14. Quoted in "Homosexuality and Citizenship in Florida," 6.

15. "Homosexuality and Citizenship in Florida," preface, 12–13.

16. "Homosexuality and Citizenship in Florida," 13.

17. "Homosexuality and Citizenship in Florida," 2.

18. *Neal v. Bryant,* 149 So. 2d 529 (1962 Fla. LEXIS 3332; 97 A.L.R. 2d 819).

19. "Homosexuality and Citizenship in Florida," 10.

20. *Fourth Annual Report of the Board of Education, Together with the Fourth Annual Report of the Secretary of the Board* (Boston: Dutton and Wentworth, State Printers, 1841), 59.

21. Harbeck, *Gay and Lesbian Educators,* 102–3.

22. Quoted in Thomas D. Bailey, "Proposed Teaching Guides on 'America's Moral and Spiritual Heritage,'" adapted from *Florida School Bulletin* (December 1955): 2, File 4, Box 9, S1127.

23. Howard K. Beale, *Are American Teachers Free?* Part 12: Report of the Commission on the Social Studies, American Historical Association (New York: Charles Scribner's Sons, 1936), 392.

24. Kate Rousmaniere, *City Teachers: Teaching and School Reform in Historical Perspective* (New York: Teachers College Press, 1997), 28–29.

25. Quoted in Harbeck, *Gay and Lesbian Educators,* 107–8. See also Rousmaniere, *City Teachers,* 38.

26. Beale, *Are American Teachers Free?* 374. See the chapter on "Conduct of Teachers," 374–409.

27. Beale, *Are American Teachers Free?* 381–82. Emphasis in the original.

28. Willard Waller, *The Sociology of Teaching* (New York: John Wiley and Sons, 1932), 45.

29. Blount, *Fit to Teach,* 16.

30. Rousmaniere, *City Teachers,* 37.

31. Jonna Perrillo, "Beyond 'Progressive' Reform: Bodies, Discipline, and the Construction of the Professional Teacher in Interwar America," *History of Education Quarterly* 44, no. 3 (Fall 2004): 363. See also pp. 337–43, 362; and Rousmaniere, *City Teachers,* 37–39, 74.

32. Waller, *The Sociology of Teaching,* 34.

33. Waller, *The Sociology of Teaching,* 40.

34. Margaret K. Nelson, "Female Schoolteachers as Community Builders," in *The Teacher's Voice: A Social History of Teaching in Twentieth-Century America,* ed. Richard J. Altenbaugh (London: Falmer Press, 1992), 78, 85–86.

35. Nelson, "Female Schoolteachers as Community Builders," 86–87.

36. Anonymous teacher, quoted in Frances R. Donovan, *The Schoolma'am* (New York: Arno Press, 1974 [originally published New York: Frederick A. Stokes, 1938]), 44.

37. Richard A. Quantz, "The Complex Visions of Female Teachers and the Failure of Unionization in the 1930s: An Oral History," in *The Teacher's Voice,* ed. Richard A. Altenbaugh, 154. Regarding the distinction between teaching and other professions on this score, see also Steven E. Tozer, Paul C. Violas, and Guy Senese, *School and*

Society: Historical and Contemporary Perspectives, 4th ed. (New York: McGraw-Hill, 2002), 67.

38. Beale, *Are American Teachers Free?* 403.

39. Beale, *Are American Teachers Free?* 403.

40. *The Teacher's Voice,* ed. Richard J. Altenbaugh, 63–64.

41. Emma Willard, *An Address to the Public, Particularly to the Members of the Legislature of New-York, Proposing a Plan for Improving Female Education,* pp. 47–48. 2nd ed. Middlebury, Vt., 1819. 60pp. Available from Thomson Gale, *Sabin Americana, 1500–1926* at http://0galenet.galegroup.com.dewey2.library.denison.edu:80/servlet/Sabin?af=RN&ae=CY101591934&srchtp=a&ste=14 (accessed 13 December 2007).

42. See Anne Firor Scott, "The Ever Widening Circle: The Diffusion of Feminist Values from the Troy Female Seminary, 1822–1872," *History of Education Quarterly* 19, no. 1 (Spring 1979): 3–25.

43. See, for example, Horace Mann's argument in *Sixth Annual Report of the Board of Education, Together with the Sixth Annual Report of the Secretary of the Board* (Boston: Dutton and Wentworth, State Printers, 1843), 28; David M. Donahue, "Rhode Island's Last Holdout: Tenure and Married Women Teachers at the Brink of the Women's Movement," *History of Education Quarterly* 42, no. 1 (Spring 2002): 52; Tozer, Violas, and Senese, *School and Society,* 62–69; Linda K. Kerber, *Women of the Republic: Intellect and Ideology in Revolutionary America* (New York: W. W. Norton, 1986 [previously published by the University of North Carolina Press, 1980]); Geraldine Jonçich Clifford, "'Daughters into Teachers': Educational and Demographic Influences on the Transformation of Teaching into 'Women's Work' in America," in *Women Who Taught: Perspectives on the History of Women and Teaching,* ed. Alison Prentice and Marjorie R. Theobald (Toronto: University of Toronto Press, 1991), 115–35.

44. Blount, *Fit to Teach,* 24.

45. Blount, *Fit to Teach,* 24–25.

46. Michael Sedlak and Steven Schlossman, "Who Will Teach? Historical Perspectives on the Changing Appeal of Teaching as a Profession," *Review of Research in Education* 14 (1987): 123.

47. Kathleen Weiler, "Women's History and the History of Women Teachers," *Journal of Education* 171, no. 3 (1989): 9, 16–18.

48. Quoted in Thomas Woody, *A History of Women's Education in the United States,* vol. 1 (New York: Science Press, 1929), 516.

49. Weiler, "Women's History and the History of Women Teachers," 19–20.

50. Kathleen Weiler, *Country Schoolwomen: Teaching in Rural California, 1850–1950* (Stanford, Calif.: Stanford University Press, 1998), 34. There are a few caveats to the widely accepted account of the nineteenth-century feminization of teaching in the United States. Weiler reminds us that, in fact, teaching has been a source of power for a good number of women, providing them some measure of respect, autonomy, and income. She adds, however, that this has not been true for all women, and what gains women did make in the profession came as a result of constant struggle. Further, as in the case of all ideologies, we do not know the extent to which women and men accepted

the premises and beliefs disseminated through dominant social structures. See p. 4 and Weiler, "Women's History and the History of Women Teachers," 18–19. For a helpful discussion on ideology, see Tozer, Violas, and Senese, *School and Society,* 9–10. In addition, Alison Prentice and Marjorie Theobald caution that the "so-called feminization of teaching in the nineteenth-century Western democracies is a misnomer," given the wider history of education that encompasses more than state-sponsored schooling. See Alison Prentice and Marjorie R. Theobald, "The Historiography of Women Teachers: A Retrospect," in *Women Who Taught,* 16. The point is well taken but since the larger analysis of this book is trained precisely on the state system of schooling in the United States, the feminization of teaching that occurred in that system remains relevant as another factor that has made the profession more susceptible to public control than professions where men have occupied most positions, traditionally.

51. Jurgen Herbst, *And Sadly Teach: Teacher Education and Professionalization in American Culture* (Madison: University of Wisconsin Press, 1989), 3.

52. Tozer, Violas, and Senese, *School and Society,* 66, 62–67.

53. Horace Mann, *Lecture on Education,* p. 25. Boston, 1840. 62pp. Available from Thomson Gale, *Sabin Americana, 1500–1926* at http://0-galenet.galegroup.com.dewey2 .library.denison.edu:80/servlet/Sabin?af=RN&ae=CY3800561648&srchtp=a&ste=14 (accessed 11 December 2007).

54. Margaret A. Haley, "Why Teachers Should Organize," in National Education Association, *Addresses and Proceedings* 43 (Washington, D.C.: 1904): 148.

55. Stephen Ewing, quoted in Weiler, *Country Schoolwomen,* 31.

56. See Linda M. Perkins, "The Impact of the 'Cult of True Womanhood' on the Education of Black Women," in *Black Women in United States History: From Colonial Times through the Nineteenth Century,* vol. 3, ed. Darlene Clark Hine (Brooklyn, N.Y.: Carlson, 1990), 1069.

57. Donahue, "Rhode Island's Last Holdout," 50, 54–55. Sheila L. Cavanagh notes that marriage bans continued until the 1950s in North America in "Female-Teacher Gender and Sexuality in Twentieth-Century Ontario, Canada," *History of Education Quarterly* 45, no. 2 (Summer 2005): 247.

58. Blount, *Fit to Teach,* 61, 79, 81. Also see Cavanagh, "Female-Teacher Gender and Sexuality," 247–48.

59. Weiler, "Women's History and the History of Women Teachers," 25–26.

60. Lawrence A. Cremin, *American Education: The Metropolitan Experience, 1876–1980* (New York: Harper and Row, 1988), 239.

61. Marjorie Murphy, *Blackboard Unions: The AFT and the NEA, 1900–1980* (Ithaca N.Y.: Cornell University Press, 1990), 1–2.

62. Quantz, "The Complex Vision of Female Teachers and the Failure of Unionization," 140–41.

63. Geraldine Jonçich Clifford, "Man/Woman/Teacher: Gender, Family, and Career in American Educational History," in *American Teachers: Histories of a Profession at Work,* ed. Donald Warren (New York: Macmillan, 1989), 316.

64. Clifford, "Man/Woman/Teacher," 316.

65. "Art. 1.—Second Annual Report of the Board of Education, Together with the Second Annual Report of the Secretary of the Board," *Boston Quarterly Review (1838–1842),* October 1, 1839, 411–12. Available at http://www.proquest.com/ (accessed December 11, 2007). The article is attributed to Orestes Brownson in Tozer, Violas, and Senese, *School and Society,* 76.

66. Francis Parker, quoted in Beale, *Are American Teachers Free?* 640.

67. Beale, *Are American Teachers Free?* 13, 634, 639.

68. Courtney Vaughn-Roberson, "Having a Purpose in Life: Western Women Teachers in the Twentieth Century," in *The Teacher's Voice,* ed. Richard J. Altenbaugh, 21.

69. Wayne J. Urban, "Teacher Activism," in *American Teachers: Histories of a Profession at Work,* ed. Donald Warren (New York: Macmillan, 1989), 190.

70. Rousmaniere, *City Teachers,* 19.

71. Joseph W. Newman, "Religious Discrimination, Political Revenge, and Teacher Tenure," in *The Teacher's Voice,* ed. Richard J. Altenbaugh, 91.

72. Rousmaniere, *City Teachers,* 20–23; Beale, *Are American Teachers Free?* 383. See also Beale, *Are American Teachers Free?* xiv.

73. Weiler, *Country Schoolwomen,* 216; Richard J. Altenbaugh, introduction to *The Teacher's Voice,* ed. Richard J. Altenbaugh, 4.

74. Patricia Carter, "Becoming the 'New Women': The Equal Rights Campaigns of New York City Schoolteachers, 1900–1920," in *The Teacher's Voice,* ed. Richard J. Altenbaugh, 58.

75. Vanessa Siddle Walker, "African American Teaching in the South: 1940–1960," *American Educational Research Journal* 38, no. 4 (Winter 2001): 761; Vanessa Siddle Walker, "Organized Resistance and Black Educators' Quest for School Equality, 1878–1938," *Teachers College Record* 107, no. 3 (March 2005): 355–56.

76. Siddle Walker, "Organized Resistance," 358. See also p. 372 and Siddle Walker, "African American Teaching in the South," 758–59.

77. Siddle Walker, "Organized Resistance," 369–70.

78. Siddle Walker, "Organized Resistance," 358–59.

79. Lillian Herstein, quoted in Beale, *Are American Teachers Free?* 654.

80. Beale, *Are American Teachers Free?* x, 640.

81. Harbeck, *Gay and Lesbian Educators,* 106–8.

82. Waller, *The Sociology of Teaching,* 28.

83. Rousmaniere, *City Teachers,* 10–11, 21–22; Murphy, *Blackboard Unions,* 2; Urban, "Teacher Activism," 197; Weiler, *Country Schoolwomen,* 28–29.

84. Rousmaniere, *City Teachers,* 10.

85. Marvin Lazerson, "If All the World Were Chicago: American Education in the Twentieth Century," *History of Education Quarterly* 24, no. 2 (Summer 1984): 174. On teacher demographics, see John L. Rury, "Who Became Teachers? The Social Characteristics of Teachers in American History," in *American Teachers,* ed. Donald Warren, 9–48. See also Murphy, *Blackboard Unions,* 4–5.

86. Blount, *Fit to Teach,* 81.

87. Blount, *Fit to Teach,* 35, 38–41.

88. Randy Shilts, *Conduct Unbecoming: Gays and Lesbians in the U.S. Military* (New York: St. Martin's Press, 1993), 11, 16–17; Bérubé, "Marching to a Different Drummer," 383–84.

89. Bérubé, "Marching to a Different Drummer," 392. See also chapter 8, "Fighting Another War," in Allan Bérubé, *Coming Out under Fire: The History of Gay Men and Women in World War Two* (New York: Free Press, 1990), 201–27.

90. Bérubé, "Marching to a Different Drummer," 388; D'Emilio, *Sexual Politics, Sexual Communities,* 44. See also Bérubé, *Coming Out under Fire*; Faderman, *Odd Girls and Twilight Lovers,* 118–30.

91. Johnson, *The Lavender Scare,* 7–8. See also, D'Emilio, *Sexual Politics, Sexual Communities,* 40–53.

92. Johnson, *The Lavender Scare,* 8.

93. D'Emilio, *Sexual Politics, Sexual Communities,* 41–44.

94. D'Emilio, *Sexual Politics, Sexual Communities,* 44.

95. Johnson, *The Lavender Scare,* 5.

96. See Eskridge, "Privacy Jurisprudence and the Apartheid of the Closet, 1946–1961."

97. Quoted in Bérubé, "Marching to a Different Drummer," 383.

98. D'Emilio, *Sexual Politics, Sexual Communities,* 43.

99. "How to Obtain and Hold Good Teachers in Florida's Schools: A Report from the Continuing Educational Council to the Honorable LeRoy Collins, Governor," 15 February 1957, p. 6, File 2, Box 56, M86–011.

100. Ed Henderson to Charley Johns, 1 December 1961, File 18, Box 2, S1486.

101. "How to Obtain and Hold Good Teachers," pp. 6–7.

102. Mormino, *Land of Sunshine, State of Dreams,* 12.

103. Mormino, *Land of Sunshine, State of Dreams,* 11–19, 45–46.

104. LeRoy Collins, "Message of Governor LeRoy Collins to the Joint Session of the Senate and House of Representatives of the State of Florida in the Chamber of the House of Representatives April 7, 1959," pp. 7–8, File 1, Box 8, S1127.

105. Minutes, FEA Ethics Committee, 14 March 1957, pp. 3–5, File 2, Box 56, M86–011.

106. Minutes, FEA Report and Resolutions Committee, 21 March 1959, p. ix, and Minutes, Steering Committee of Teacher Education and Professional Standards Committee, 9 October 1959, p. 3, File 3, Box 56, M86–011.

107. Aruel L. Morgan, Minutes, FEA Board of Directors, 31 May–1 June 1963, p. 1, File 3, Box 57, M86–011.

108. Richard J. Altenbaugh, "The History of Teaching: A Social History of Schooling," in *The Teacher's Voice,* ed. Richard J. Altenbaugh, 194.

109. Newman, "Religious Discrimination, Political Revenge, and Teacher Tenure," 90.

110. Beale, *Are American Teachers Free?* 13, 634.

111. Siddle Walker, "African American Teaching in the South," 769–70.

112. Henderson to Johns, 1 December 1961.

113. Minutes, FEA Personnel Problems Steering Committee, 6 November 1961, pp. 2–3, File 1, Box 16, M86–011.

114. Richard O. Mitchell to FEA president, 22 April 1964, pp. 1–2, File 6, Box 2, S1486.

115. Anita Bryant, *The Anita Bryant Story: The Survival of Our Nation's Families and the Threat of Militant Homosexuality* (Old Tappan, N.J.: Fleming H. Revell, 1977), 114. Bryant devotes an entire chapter to the question, "Homosexual Teachers: Are They Dangerous Role Models?"

116. Quoted in Blount, *Fit to Teach,* 133.

117. Blount, *Fit to Teach,* 134.

118. Elizabeth Birch, quoted in Mireya Navarro, "2 Decades on, Miami Endorses Gay Rights," *New York Times,* 2 December 1998, A1, LexisNexis Academic. Available at http://o–www.lexisnexis.com.dewey2.library.denison.edu:80/us/lnacademic/results/docview/docview.do?risb=21_T2772223135&format=GNBFI&sort=RELEVANCE&startDocNo=1&resultsUrlKey=29_T2772223143&cisb=22_T2772223142&treeMax=true&treeWidth=0&csi=6742&docNo=3 (accessed 2 January 2008).

119. "Florida Employment Information," *Lambda Legal.* Available at http://www.lambdalegal.org/our-work/states/florida.html (accessed 2 January 2008).

120. 2007 Florida Statutes, Title XLVIII K-20 Education Code, Chapter 1012 Personnel, Part III Public Schools; Personnel. Available at http://www.flsenate.gov/Statutes/index.cfm?App_mode=Display_Statute&URL=Ch1012/ch1012.htm (accessed 2 January 2008).

121. Lugg, "Thinking about Sodomy," 50.

Conclusion

"Homosexuality and Citizenship in Florida," 13, emphasis added; letter to the editor, *The Ladder* 8, no. 2 (November 1963): 26.

1. Robert J. Corber, "Queer Regionalism," *American Literary History* 11, no. 2 (Summer 1999): 400.

2. Corber, "Queer Regionalism," 400.

3. Eskridge, "No Promo Homo," 1335.

4. Eskridge, "No Promo Homo," 1335.

5. Education historians have been particularly negligent in addressing the abuses of the Cold War era. See Karen Graves, Timothy Glander, and Christine Shea, *Inexcusable Omissions: Clarence Karier and the Critical Tradition in History of Education Scholarship* (New York: Peter Lang, 2001), xiv. Robert Corber emphasizes the importance of recognizing the state as a major locus of disciplinary power during

the Cold War, particularly regarding contemporary queer political strategies. See Corber, "Queer Regionalism," 401.

6. Siddle Walker, "Organized Resistance," 358. Here, Siddle Walker is referencing Sterling Stuckey's work, *Slave Culture: Nationalist Theory and the Foundations of Black America.*

7. Siddle Walker, "Organized Resistance," 381. See also James D. Anderson, *The Education of Blacks in the South, 1860–1935* (Chapel Hill: University of North Carolina Press, 1988).

8. Eskridge, "No Promo Homo," 1332.

9. Bell, *Silent Covenants,* front piece.

10. D'Emilio, *Sexual Politics, Sexual Communities,* 4–5.

11. Harbeck, *Gay and Lesbian Educators,* 188. On teachers who fought against employment discrimination, see Harbeck, *Gay and Lesbian Educators,* 23–24, 209–71; Blount, *Fit to Teach,* 108–55.

12. Harbeck, *Gay and Lesbian Educators,* 187.

13. Harbeck, *Gay and Lesbian Educators,* 187–90.

14. "Report of the Florida Legislative Investigation Committee to the 1961 Session of the Legislature," 21.

15. Blount, *Fit to Teach,* 59–107. Even after the landmark *Lawrence v. Texas* U.S. Supreme Court decision (2003), thirteen states (including Florida) maintain laws criminalizing consensual sodomy; none have amended their public school codes to comport with the decision. As Catherine Lugg observes, "The legal status of queers and queer educators remains fragile." See Lugg, "Thinking about Sodomy," 36.

16. "Homosexuality and Citizenship in Florida," 13.

Index

academic freedom, 60–61, 72–82, 136
accountability of the Johns Committee, 67–68, 107–8
activism, civil rights, 4, 52–58, 68, 135–36, 146
African Americans: civil rights, 52–55, 135–36, 146; poll taxes and, 103; segregation of, x, xv, 2–4, 52–55, 99–100, 156–57n9; Tallahassee bus boycott and, 4, 52–53; targeted by the Johns Committee, 24–25, 93–95, 156–57n9; teachers, 24–25, 100, 132, 135–36; white racist groups and, 72
Alger, Horatio, 138
Allen, John, 58–60, 62–64, 73, 79
Altenbaugh, Richard, 128
American Association of University Professors (AAUP), xv; academic freedom and, 72–82; legal defense provided by, 82–83
American Association of University Women (AAUW), 50, 114; academic freedom and, xvi, 78–82; legal defense provided by, 82–83
American Civil Liberties Union (ACLU), 94–95
American Federation of Teachers, 133
anti-discrimination legislation, 143
antigay legislation, 18, 21–22, 26, 116–17, 124–25, 167–68n1
antigay rhetoric, 121–25
authority and power of the Johns Committee, 8–9, 15, 20–21, 46–48, 63–64, 166n181

Bailey, Lewis, 50, 169n25
Bailey, Thomas D., 38, 58, 89, 107, 114, 118, 140; on due process, 108, 118–19; influence and power of, 100–1; Johns Committee and, 108–9; Pork Choppers and, 98–99, 102–3; Remus J. Strickland and, 108, 110–11; segregation and, 99–100
Barker, James, 34
Beale, Howard, 126, 128, 134, 136, 141
Bell, Derrick, 9
Bernstein, Mary, 97
Bertwell, Dan, 93
Bérubé, Allan, 138
Birch, Elizabeth, 143
Black Struggle, Red Scare, 2
Blackwell, Gordon, 60
Blount, Jackie, xiv–xv, 19, 127; on the gay civil rights movement, 143; on moral conduct expectations of teachers, 130, 132, 137–38; on stereotyping of teachers, 23
Board of Education (BOE), Florida, 14, 85, 118; authority and powers of, 102–3, 106, 110–13; cooperation with the Johns Committee, 108–9; revocations of teaching certificates by, 8–9, 90, 112–13
Boyd, Nan, 16, 22, 96
The Boys of Boise, 18–19
Brennan, William, 96–97
Briggs Initiative, xiv
Brooklyn Teachers Association, 135
Brownson, Orestes, 134

Brown v. Board of Education, x, 1, 9, 99
Bryant, Anita, xiv, 142–43
Bryant, C. Farris, 61, 79, 81, 90, 114
Burns, Haydon, 117

Cahill, Leo, 88
Caldwell, Millard F., 61
Call, Hall, 91, 122
Canadian Immigration Act, 17
Carleton, William, 73, 93, 166n181
Carter, Patricia, 135
Chesley, Mabel, 79
Christian, Floyd, 89, 108, 111, 113, 169n25
civil liberties, 31–34, 166n181; gay rights
    movement and, 51–52, 146
civil rights activists, 4, 52–58, 68, 135–36,
    146. *See also* NAACP
Clifford, Geraldine, 133–34
Cold War, the. *See* communism and the
    Cold War
The Cold War and Its Origins, 60
*College Education as Personal Develop-
    ment,* 64
Collins, LeRoy, 1–2, 5, 61, 92, 140, 166n181,
    169n25
Common School movement, 129, 131, 134
communism and the Cold War, xii, 95,
    120–21, 135, 145, 178–79n5; federal em-
    ployment of homosexuals and, 16–17, 139;
    gender and, 64–65; homosexuality linked
    to, 9, 16–19, 48, 51, 95, 137–40; Johns
    Committee and, 9, 16–19, 48, 51; media
    coverage on, 57–58; NAACP linked to, 55;
    oppressive state power and investigations
    of, 145–46; teacher conservatism and, 137
conservatism in teaching, 134–37, 141–42
Corber, Robert J., 95, 100, 145
criminal justice system treatment of homo-
    sexuals, 11–12, 147
criticisms of the Johns Committee, 10, 50,
    75–82, 92–94, 108
Culpepper, J. Broward, 102
Cutler, Ed, 73

Daughters of Bilitis, 22, 47, 96
Defense Department, U. S., 17
definitions of homosexuality, 11–12, 49,
    66–67, 122; Johns Committee, 25–29,
    43–45
D'Emilio, John, 16, 96–97, 138–39, 146
denials of homosexuality by teachers,
    26–29, 37, 39–41

Department of Education (DOE), Florida,
    xvi, 14–15, 31, 89–90, 101, 124
desegregation. *See* segregation
Diamond, Sigmund, 48–49
Dietrich, Sigismond, 13
discrimination against gay and lesbian
    teachers, vii–xvii, 120, 142–43. *See also*
    homophobia; investigations and purges,
    teacher
Dudziak, Mary, 9
due process, 63–64, 108, 110, 118–19

Education Association (FEA), Florida, xvi,
    83–88, 101, 117–19, 141
Egerton, John, xii, 75, 77, 79, 82
Eisenhower, Dwight D., 17, 139
*Employment of Homosexuals and Other Sex
    Perverts in Government,* 139
Eskridge, William N., Jr., 18, 145
Evans, John, 114–16, 120–21
evidence used against teachers, 30–31,
    45–46; hearsay, 36–37, 65–66
Ewing, Stephen, 132

Farnell, Crockett, 5, 152n17
Federal Bureau of Investigation, 17, 19
federal government employment of homo-
    sexuals, 16–17, 139–40
feminization of teaching, 120–21, 129–34,
    174–75n50
Fenn, Henry, 71
Fisher, Margaret, 64–67, 72–73, 78, 80–81, 93
*Fit to Teach: Same-Sex Desire, Gender, and
    School Work,* xiv, 127
Fleming, D. F., 60
Florida: Board of Education (BOE), 8–9, 14,
    85, 90, 102–3, 106–13, 118; Department of
    Education (DOE), xvi, 14–15, 31, 89–90,
    101, 124; Education Association (FEA),
    xvi, 83–88, 101, 117–19, 141; geography and
    demographics, 13–14; Interim Legislative
    Committee on Education (ILCE), 103–5;
    legislation in, 18, 21–22, 26, 116–17, 124–25,
    167–68n1; legislature and investigations,
    105–10; population growth, 140–41; Pork
    Choppers of, 2–3, 14, 98–99, 102–3, 118;
    Supreme Court, 93–95, 118–19, 124–25;
    teacher shortages in, 140–41
Florida Agricultural and Mechanical Uni-
    versity (FAMU), 4, 52–54, 70
Florida Education, 85
Florida Federation of Women's Clubs, 114–15

Florida Legislative Investigation Committee, the, 39, 140, 145; antigay rhetoric used by, 121–25; establishment of, 1; investigations and interrogations of teachers by, vii–xiii, xv, xvi; legislation efforts of, 116–17; teachers targeted by, 22
Florida State University, 4, 43
Florida Times-Union, 102
Fourth Annual Report, 125
Foutz, Lucille, 78–79
Freedman, Estelle, 30, 49
Ft. Lauderdale Daily News, 107

Gay and Lesbian Educators: Personal Freedoms, Public Constraints, xiv
gay rights movement, 51–52, 146
gays and lesbians. *See* homosexuals
gender: feminization of teaching and, 120–21, 129–34, 174–75n50; purge of teachers and, 22–23, 64–65
Georgieff, George, 111–12
Gerassi, John, 18–19
Gerstein, Richard E., 10
Gibson, Theodore, 55–57, 70
Gibson v. Florida Legislative Investigation Committee, 9, 93–95
Godby, Amos, 83
Gore, George, 52–53, 61
government employment of homosexuals, 16–17, 139–40
Graves, Grattan, 56
Grebstein, Sheldon, 60

Haley, Margaret, 131–33
Harbeck, Karen, xiv–xv, 126, 136, 146–47
Harper's Magazine, 72
Hawes, Mark, 3, 20, 31, 69, 114; on due process, 63–64, 110; on medical explanations of homosexuality, 123–24; treatment of witnesses by, 34–36
hearsay information, 36–37, 65–66
Henderson, Ed, 85–88, 103, 140, 169n25
Herbst, Jurgen, 131
Herrell, Cliff, 31, 54, 57, 69, 108
Herstein, Lillian, 136
Hillsborough County School System, 4
Hohnadel, Betty, 78–79
homophile organizations and publications, 96–97, 143, 148
homophobia, xvi–xvii, 43, 98, 113–14, 142–43, 147–48; antigay rhetoric and, 121–25; the Cold War and, xii, 9; legisla-

tion and, 18, 26; linked to communism, xii, 9, 16–19, 48, 51, 95, 137–40; linked to juvenile delinquency, 18–19; "purple pamphlet" and, 122–24; racism and, 24–25; women's clubs and, 114–15
homosexuals: antigay rhetoric aimed at, 121–25; attempts to define, 11–12, 25–29, 43–45, 49, 66–67, 122; criminal justice system treatment of, 11–12, 147; federal government employment of, 16–17, 139–40; gay rights movement and, 51–52, 146; juvenile delinquency linked to, 18–19; laws against, 18, 21–22, 26, 116–17, 124–25, 167–68n1; linked to communism, 9, 16–19, 48, 51, 95, 137–40; the media and, 5–7, 91–92, 95–96; medical research and opinions on, 123–24; in the military, 17, 43; political involvement, 96–97; politicians campaigns' against, 5–6; stereotyping of, 23, 26, 29–31; surveillance of, 33; terminology used in referring to, 149–50n17; violence against, 4–5, 5. *See also* teachers, homosexual
Hooper, Dave, vii–viii, x
Hoover, J. Edgar, 19
Human Rights Campaign, 143

Ingram, Hugh B., Jr., 85–86
Interim Legislative Committee on Education (ILCE), 103–5
investigations and purges, teacher: academic freedom and, 72–82; authority and power of, 8–9, 15, 20–21, 46–48; criminal justice system and, 11–12, 147; definitions of homosexuality and, 11–12, 25–29, 43–45, 49; due process in, 63–64, 108, 110, 118–19; evidence used in, 30–31, 36–37; Florida Education Association (FEA) and, xvi, 83–88, 169n25; gender and, 22–23, 64–65; hearsay information in, 36–37, 65–66; Interim Legislative Committee on Education (ILCE) and, 103–5; interrogations in, vii–xi, 7–8, 10–11, 20–21, 26–29, 111–13; oppressive state power and, 145–46; political influences on, 89–90, 103–5; polygraph examinations used in, 36–37, 45–46; profiles of teachers targeted in, 21–31; settings for, 24, 27, 32; surveillance used in, 33; tactics used in, 31–39; teachers' reactions to, 39–46; threats toward teachers in, 46–49; transcripts of, 26–29, 40–46, 65–67; witnesses legal rights in, 31–34; witness treatment by prosecutors

in, 34–36, 47–49, 64–67. *See also* Johns
Committee, the; teachers, homosexual
Irvin, Richard, 71

Jenkins, L. J., 36, 83
Jim Crow laws, 3
John Birch Society, 72
Johns, Charley: Florida Education Association and, 88; Johns Committee and,
1–2, 4, 10, 21, 36, 60, 71, 76, 101; Margaret Fisher and, 65; media coverage of, 78;
NAACP and, 56, 58; Palm Beach Ministers Conference and, 123; University of
South Florida and, 58, 60, 68
Johns Committee, the: academic freedom
and, 60–61, 72–82; authority and powers of, 8–9, 15, 20–21, 46–48, 63–64, 118,
166n181; civil rights activists and, 52–58,
68; communism and, 9, 16–19, 48, 51; court
rulings affecting, 93–95, 118–19; Florida
Education Association (FEA) collabora-
tion with, 83–88; homophobic agenda
promotion by, 113–14; investigation of University of South Florida, 58–67; legislation
efforts, 116–17; media coverage of, 57–58,
75–82, 90–92; members, 3–4; NAACP
and, 6–7, 9–10, 50–58, 68–71, 93–95, 106;
origins of, 1–3, 92; Pork Choppers and,
2–3; public accountability of, 67–68, 107–8;
public criticism of, 10, 50, 75–82, 92–94,
108; reports to the Florida legislature,
105–10; segregation and, 1–4; tactics used
by, 31–39; teachers' reactions to, 39–46;
Thomas Bailey and, 108–9. *See also* investigations and purges, teacher
Johnson, Beth, 78
Johnson, David, xii, 17, 120, 138
Johnson, Dewey, 1
Johnson, James Weldon, 70
Jones, Richard T., 11

Karier, Clarence, 49
Kelley, J. T., 84–85, 89–90, 104, 109–10,
112–13, 116
Kerber, Linda, 129
Kerns, W. H., 81
Kimmel, David, 17
Kinsey, Alfred, 25, 45, 65
Klein, Kevin, 13–14
Knowles, Robert E., 81–82
Ku Klux Klan, 72

The Ladder, 91
*The Lavender Scare: The Cold War Persecu-
tion of Gays and Lesbians in the Federal
Government,* 17
Lawrence v. Texas, 22, 143, 148
Lazerson, Marvin, 137
legal defense of teachers, 68–71, 82–83,
93–95, 111
legal rights: academic freedom and, 60–61,
72–82; due process, 63–64, 108, 110,
118–19; of witnesses, 31–34, 166n181
legislation: anti-discrimination, 143; antigay,
18, 21–22, 26, 116–17, 124–25, 167–68n1;
Canadian immigration, 17; the Johns
Committee and, 10, 92; Supreme Court
rulings on, 21–22, 68, 93–95, 99, 118–19,
124–25, 143
legislature, Florida, 105–10
lesbians and gays. *See* homosexuals
Lesbian Tide, 143
Lorde, Audre, 51, 97
Love, James, 71
Lugg, Catherine, 22, 143
Lyon, Phyllis, 22

Mann, Horace, 125–27, 129, 131
Manning, E. D., Jr., 89
Martin, Del, 47
Mattachine Review, 90, 122
Mattachine Society, xvi, 96
McCarthy, Joseph, 16, 101
McCarty, Dan, 5
McFatter, W. T., 85
McIntire, Dal, 4–5
media coverage: of academic freedom,
75–82; homophile, 5–7, 91–92, 95–96,
122, 143; of investigations into homo-
sexuality, 81–82, 90–92; of the NAACP,
57–58, 71
Miami Herald, 115–16
Miami Times, 57–58
Michigan Daily, 91
military, homosexuals in the, 17, 43
Mitchell, Pearl, 50
Mitchell, Richard, 116, 142
moral conduct of teachers, 125–28, 132, 135
Morgan, Edward P., 78, 81
Morgan, Fletcher, 4, 6
Morgan, Thomas N., 85
Mormino, Gary, 140
Murphy, Marjorie, 133

NAACP, x, xv; investigations of, 2–4, 6–7, 31, 50–51, 106; legal defense efforts, 68–71, 82, 93–95; linked to the Communist Party, 55; media coverage of, 57–58, 71; membership records of, 9–10, 56–57; Supreme Court victory over the Johns Committee, 93–95; University of South Florida and, 52–58
National Education Association (NEA), xvi, 111, 131–33
Neal v. Bryant, 8, 15, 91, 101, 118, 125
Nelson, Margaret, 127–28
Newman, Joseph, 135
Noble, Jean, 64–65

Odum, Ralph, 85
One, 5–7, 91–92, 96
O'Neill, William, 39, 89, 107

Palm Beach Ministers Conference, 123
Parker, Francis, 134
Paul, Helen, 78
Perrillo, Jonna, 127
Perry, Ruth Willis, 50, 55–57, 69–70, 92
Peter, Emmett B., 77–78
Peurifoy, John, 16
Plant City Conservative Club, 76
Podhoretz, Norman, 60
politics: Cold War, 138–40; demographics of Florida, 13–14; homophile movement, 96–97, 148; influence over investigations of teachers, 61, 79, 81, 89–90, 103–5; Pork Chop, 2–3, 14, 98–99, 102–3, 118
poll taxes, 103
polygraph examinations, 36–37, 45–46
Pork Choppers, 2–3, 14, 98–99, 102–3, 118
Poucher, Judith, 6
Preskill, Stephen, 16
professional teachers organizations, 133–34
public criticisms of the Johns Committee, 10, 50, 92–94
public support for teachers, xv–xvi, 47–48, 82–83, 90
purges, teacher. *See* investigations and purges, teacher
"purple pamphlet," 122–24

Quantz, Richard, 128, 133

racism: African American teachers and, 24–25, 100, 132; organizations promoting, 72; purge of teachers and, 24–25, 72, 156–57n9
Rawls, John, 1, 104–5
Reitz, Wayne, 71
revocations of teaching certificates, 8–9, 90, 112–13, 147
rhetoric, antigay, 121–25
Riordan, Julia, 141
Robinson, Daniel, 17
Rousmaniere, Kate, 126, 135
Ryals, Howell, 5

Saunders, Robert, 53
Schlesinger, Arthur, Jr., 95
Schlossman, Steven, 130
Scott, Carol, 79, 95
Sears, James, 10
Sedlak, Michael, 130
segregation, x, xv, 2–4, 52–55, 99–100, 156–57n9. *See also* African Americans
Senese, Guy, 131
Sessums, Terrell, 76–77, 79
settings for interrogations of teachers, 24, 27, 32
Sexual Politics, Sexual Communities: The Making of a Homosexual Minority in the United States, 1940–1970, 96
Sherrill, Robert, 116
Siddle Walker, Vanessa, 135–36, 142, 146
Smith, Jane, 75–77
societal expectations of teachers, 125–28, 135
sodomy laws, 21–22, 68, 167–68n1
Southern Association of Colleges and Schools (SACS), 80
Southwest Florida Tuberculosis Hospital, 4
Spring, Joel, 133
stereotyping of homosexuals, 23, 26, 29–31
Stetson University v. Hunt, 58
Stevens, Jack, 85
Stewart, Herb, 78
Stone, M. L., 104
St. Petersburg Independent, 108
St. Petersburg Police Department, vii–viii
St. Petersburg Times, 75, 116
Strickland, Remus J., vii–xi, 10–12, 20, 88, 114; Florida Education Association (FEA) and, 84, 87; hearsay and polygraph information used by, 36–37; interrogation techniques of, 26–29, 111–13; media coverage of, 78; teachers advised of legal rights by, 31–33; teachers' reactions to, 39–46;

Thomas Bailey and, 108, 110–11; University South Florida and, 58–59, 68. *See also* Johns Committee, the
Strozier, Robert M., 61
student protests, 59–60
support for teachers, xv–xvi, 47–48, 82–83, 90, 142
Supreme Court: Florida, 93–95, 118–19, 124–25; U. S., 21–22, 68, 99, 143
surveillance of teachers, 33
Swann v. Adams, 3

Tallahassee bus boycott, 4, 52–53
Tallahassee Democrat, 75
Tampa Tribune: on academic freedom, 77; on Charley Johns, 60; on the Johns Committee, 3, 8, 81–82, 108; on removal of homosexuals from Tampa, 5
Taylor, Frederick, 131
teachers, African American, 24–25, 100, 132, 135–36
teachers, homosexual: advised of their legal rights, 31–34; criminal justice system and, 11–12, 147; demographics of, 22–23; denials by, 26–29, 37, 39–41; discrimination against, vii–xvii, 120, 142–43, 148; feminization of teaching and, 120–21, 129–34, 174–75n50; Johns Committee reports on, 105–10; legal defense of, 68–71, 82–83, 93–95, 111; new teacher screening and, 105, 141; oppression of, xii; race and, 24–25, 156–57n9; reactions to investigations, 39–46; research on, xiii–xv; resignations by, 46; resistant to testifying, 41–42, 45–46, 48; revocations of teaching certificates of suspected, 8–9, 90, 112–13, 147; support for, xv–xvi, 47–48, 82–83, 90, 142; surveillance of, 33; threats toward, 46–49; at University of South Florida, 60–65. *See also* homosexuals; investigations and purges, teacher
teaching: academic freedom in, 60–61, 72–82, 136; Common School movement and, 129, 131, 134; conservatism in, 134–37, 141–42; feminization of, 120–21, 129–34, 174–75n50; mission of, 125–26; moral conduct expectations in, 125–28, 132,

135; racism in, 24–25, 100, 132, 156–57n9; shortages, 140–41; unionization and professionalization of, 133–34
Thomas, Wayne, Jr., 76
threats toward teachers, 46–49
Tozer, Steven, 131
transcripts of interrogations, 26–29, 40–46, 65–67
Truman, Harry S., 16–17, 138
Turner, Fred, 58
Turner, Robert B., Jr., 88
Tyack, David, 133

unions, teacher, 133–34
University of Florida, 4, 7, 21, 93
University of Florida Law Review, 11
University of South Florida (USF), vii, xv, 8, 10, 31–32, 50–51; academic freedom at, 60–61, 72–82; administrators, 60–62; civil rights activists at, 58, 68; Johns Committee investigation of, 58–67; NAACP and, 58; parents of students at, 65–67, 75–76; politics and, 60–61; professors targeted at, 60–65; student protests and students investigated at, 59–60
Urban, Wayne, 133–35
U. S. Supreme Court, 21–22, 68, 99, 143

Van Waters, Miriam, 30
Vaughn-Roberson, Courtney, 134
Violas, Paul, 131
violence against homosexuals, 4–5

Walker, Walton O., 36
Waller, Willard, 127, 137
Weiler, Kathleen, 130
White Citizen Councils, 72
Whitman, Walt, 138
Willard, Emma, 129
Women's Republican Club of St. Petersburg, 76
Woods, Jeff, 2
Woodward, C. Vann, 72
Woody, Thomas, 130

Zimmerman, Gill, 95

KAREN L. GRAVES is an associate professor of education at Denison University. She is the author of *Girls' Schooling during the Progressive Era: From Female Scholar to Domesticated Citizen* and coeditor of *Inexcusable Omissions: Clarence Karier and the Critical Tradition in History of Education Scholarship.*

The University of Illinois Press
is a founding member of the
Association of American University Presses.

Composed in 10.5/13 Adobe Minion Pro
with Frutiger LT Std display
by Celia Shapland
at the University of Illinois Press
Manufactured by Sheridan Books, Inc.

University of Illinois Press
1325 South Oak Street
Champaign, IL 61820-6903
www.press.uillinois.edu